Weathering Change

Weathering Change

Gays and Lesbians, Christian Conservatives, and Everyday Hostilities

Thomas J. Linneman

NEW YORK UNIVERSITY PRESS
New York and London

NEW YORK UNIVERSITY PRESS
New York and London

Library of Congress Cataloging-in-Publication Data
Weathering change : gays and lesbians, Christian conservatives, and everyday hostilities /
Thomas J. Linneman.
p.   cm.
Includes bibliographical references and index.
ISBN 0-8147-5187-3 (cloth : alk. paper) — ISBN 0-8147-5188-1 (pbk. : alk. paper)
1. Public opinion—Washington (State)—Seattle. 2. Public opinion—Washington
(State)—Spokane. 3. Seattle (Wash.)—Politics and government—Public opinion.
4. Spokane (Wash.)—Politics and government—Public opinion. 5. Gays—Washington
(State)—Seattle—Attitudes. 6. Gays—Washington (State)—Spokane—Attitudes.
7. Christian conservatism—Washington (State)—Seattle. 8. Christian conservatism—
Washington (State)—Spokane.   I. Title.
HN79.W23P85 2003
305.6—dc21   2003002211

New York University Press books are printed on acid-free paper,
and their binding materials are chosen for strength and durability.

Manufactured in the United States of America
10 9 8 7 6 5 4 3 2 1

To my mother and in memory of my father

Contents

Acknowledgments

"It takes a village." While the original incarnation of this phrase concerned babies, I believe it is also true of books. Throughout the process that brought about this book, I have relied on dozens of people for practical, intellectual, and emotional support. One person—Judith Howard—provided all three of these in abundance. As my primary advisor, she provided endless amounts of thoughtful and useful advice, and calmed my fears more than once.

With regard to practical support, this project was made much more feasible because it was assisted by a fellowship from the Sexuality Research Fellowship Program of the Social Science Research Council, with funds provided by the Ford Foundation. I also thank the College of William and Mary, whose Summer Grant program provided support during critical stages of the book's development.

Tracking down the national data for the opinion analyses was made significantly easier by the staff of the Center for Social Science Computation and Research at the University of Washington and Ron Rapoport at the College of William and Mary. I thank the *Seattle Times* and Elway Research for allowing me access to one of their Front Porch Forum data sets. With the content analysis of editorial pieces, two librarians were quite helpful: Alvin Fritz helped with the preliminary analysis, while Glenda Pearson exemplified hospitality while her microform room was invaded for a month during the second phase of the content analysis. I also thank the students of Sociology 499, who went above and beyond the call of duty to complete the data collection in the allotted time. I appreciate their hard work.

I thank my interview subjects for their willingness to speak openly about a large number of complex issues, and to help me to find further interview contacts. Several people were crucial in the latter endeavor. I would like to thank them personally, but confidentiality does not permit me to do so. After I conducted the interviews, much work remained. I assembled an army of transcribers: fellow graduate students, friends, friends of friends, even a sister-in-law. One person in particular is worthy of special note. Charis Kubrin's transcriptions were speedy and virtually error free. She brought to the project necessary energy at just the right time. I also thank Kelley Hall, who assisted in checking the reliability of the coding mechanism, a frustrating task if ever there was one. Finally, Primrose at Open Market technical support helped me to iron out some problems with the FolioViews qualitative analysis program.

During the early stages of writing, I received advice from Sharon Reitman, Paul Burstein, Julie Brines, Marieka Klawitter, and Susan Pitchford. After the initial drafts, Peter Nardi, Mitchell Stevens, and Laura Pierce all provided very different reads on what remained to be done. During the later stages of writing, my primary source of intellectual support came from the Sociology Writing Group at the College of William and Mary. Over many a latte, they pushed me to clarify my ideas and they often strongly affected my thinking. While the membership of this group was in continual flux, three people have been there for the duration: Jennifer Bickham Mendez, Gul Ozyegin, and Michael Lewis. Other participants also offered their ideas at various points: Monica Griffin, Dee Royster, Timmons Roberts, Sal Saporito, Dan Krier, Satoshi Ito, and David Aday. Kathleen Slevin, my department chair, also provided support at key times. She also served as a model for how to keep the teaching, service, and scholarship plates spinning on their respective sticks.

While all the practical and intellectual support was necessary, it was the emotional support—mainly in the form of cheerleading and taskmastering—that got me through the stressful times. Logging in the most hours here were my brother, Scott Linneman, and my sister-in-law, Rebecca Craven (who also served as a sounding board for many questionable phrases). Also providing important support were LaVonne Linneman, Tim Breidigan, Rebecca Chatfield, Jocelyn Hollander, Amy Singer, and Virginia Rutter.

Finally, I would like to thank everyone at New York University Press for his or her hard work on the book, especially Stephen Magro and Despina Gimbel, whose calm replies to my anxious queries were exactly what I needed to hear.

1

Experiencing Political Climates

There was a student last March who, someone got into his locker, didn't even break into it, it must have been a friend with a combination, and wrote "Die Fags" and put swastikas and stuff. And so I testified in front of the school board—my dad was on it as well, and still is—and the general reaction: all they did was give the kid a new locker and that was about it. And so I tried to call their bluff and asked them to include [sexual] orientation in their harassment policy, but the districts aren't willing to do that. Even though most of the administrators here are at least sympathetic if not supportive on some level, they still realize that it would probably cost them a bond or a school levy, and so they're not willing to go there yet. It's still OK to use words like "fag" in the hall, but not other words, and that's clear.

If you go down to the part of the country where I was raised in Alabama, Mississippi, Florida, you will have 103,000 people in a football stadium, and they will have a pastor open the whole thing with a prayer. To acknowledge God, to acknowledge his sovereignty over everybody, and it will be in Jesus' name. Here, they would never dream of doing anything like that. Never dream of it. Never be permitted, in fact. For example, whereas politicians are free to stand at the stadium with their signs up at certain times of the year, a few years back when we sent some Christians over there to hold some signs up with some scripture and to hand out tracts, they were hustled off by the security.

These quotations come from two very different residents of Washington State. The first is a gay activist in Spokane; the second a Christian conservative pastor near Seattle. Though they make vastly different claims, their stories are similar in that they starkly characterize the political climates of their respective local environments. Spokane and Seattle—two cities on opposite sides of the state—have contrasting political landscapes: Seattle is well known across the state for its liberal climate, Spokane is markedly more conservative. In this book, I demonstrate how these differing political climates manifest themselves in the lives of Christian conservatives, gay men, and lesbians in both cities.

Every significant effort for social change begins with an assessment of current conditions and the potential for change. This assessment of obstacles, receptivity, and hostility in the social and political environment is one of the most crucial factors in the decisions about when to act, where to act, and how to act. Yet few scholars of social movements have focused attention on how competing activist groups assess the specific climates within which they hope to effect social change. We usually consider social change to be a slow-moving, societal-level phenomenon. However, change can occur within far more localized contexts: states, cities, football stadiums, school hallways, workplaces, newspaper pages, and people's daily interactions. I show that ordinary people are quite adept at perceiving these political climates and changes within these climates, and argue that these perceptions have important consequences.

To illustrate this phenomenon, I concentrate on people from two groups who currently are experiencing a great deal of change: gay men and lesbians on the one hand, and Christian conservatives on the other. How do people in these two groups perceive the political and social climates around them? How do they know if their environment is hostile or hospitable, or becoming more hostile or more hospitable? In the following chapters, I offer many examples of people formulating perceptions of political climates using a wide array of information. Members of these groups carefully analyze how the media treat their group and other groups. Some demonstrate creative ways of assessing how the general public feels about their group. Many infuse local and national government actions with much symbolic meaning. They assess the health of their own minority communities in a variety of ways. And they sometimes focus very specifically on the actions of the other group (Christian conservatives on gays, gays on Christian conservatives).

Even as the two groups share a number of foci, they differ in important ways as well. While the members of both groups concentrate on each of these elements of the political climate, Christian conservatives often pay attention to different aspects of it than gay men and lesbians. I compare and contrast how these two groups perceive their political and social environments. By examining how individuals from these groups regard the hostility from the various elements of the political and social climate, I offer comparisons that show where these groups have common ground.

Such an exploration should be of interest to a number of audiences. First, of course, are Christian conservatives and gay men and lesbians. Some of my claims may simultaneously provoke nods of agreement from some and shaking heads of disbelief from others. Indeed, some may even find the overall comparison objectionable. However, I believe that members of both groups will learn much about their own group as well as something about the "opposing" group from this book. Scholars who study social change and social movements may discover insights into how social change is experienced by both activists and nonactivists. Finally, this book is for anyone interested in learning more about how social change actually happens in American society, and about two groups who are at critical junctures in their respective histories.

Understanding Political Climates

Politicians, activists, and journalists utter the phrase "political climate" on a regular basis, yet political scientists and sociologists hardly ever use the term except in the most cursory way. A search for the term in major newspapers yields these and hundreds of other headlines:

"Political Climate Warms to Initiatives on Quality of Life"
"'99 Political Climate Threatens Proposals"
"Republicans Aim for Goal of Senate Control, Political Climate Favors GOP, Making 5-Seat Gain Possible"
"Packwood, Sensing Change of Climate, Weighs a Race"

Using such reports, it is possible to piece together a popular definition of political climate. One thing is clear: political climate is a powerful phenomenon. It has the potential to threaten policy outcomes, to make other outcomes possible, and to determine whether or not a politician will even run for office. A second observation concerns the levels at which a political climate operates. Since its implications concern both large-scale political structures and individuals, political climate is a phenomenon that is active at both the macro and micro levels of analysis. A third characteristic involves its ability to warm up or cool off, to change over time. The climate can become more hostile toward some elements while being more hospitable toward others, and it can do so very quickly as a result of a single current event. A final, crucial piece of the puzzle lies in the final headline: political climate is something that can be sensed, either by political bodies or individuals. This points to the subjective quality of climate: what one person senses, another may not. Because it is a perceptual phenomenon, climate can sometimes be manipulated by those who have a stake in it. While these are important clues, it remains difficult to decipher what political climate actually *is*. The term seems to have been institutionalized in mainstream discourse to the point that it requires no introduction, making it difficult to develop an explicit definition based on usage in popular media. However, combining these characteristics results in the following initial definition: political climate is a powerful, multilevel, dynamic, socially constructed phenomenon similar to a mood or an attitude.

My research goal is to understand how individuals perceive their political and social environments. With this goal in mind, I conceptualize political climate somewhat differently from popular discourse, though the underlying idea remains similar to the concept described above. My definition is as follows: *Political climate is a socially constructed manifestation of hostility or hospitableness toward different individuals or groups in society on a variety of levels, ranging from the interpersonal to the global.*

I conceptualize political climate as a phenomenon that has no objective existence. Its effects occur only via the perceptions of individuals or groups. While most political climates definitely lean one way or another, toward the hostile or the hospitable, often the climates are quite mixed and open to interpretation. People in differing social situations, working with different backgrounds of information, can interpret objective information in completely different ways. The individual, in my conceptualization, is an active perceiver of the climate, bringing it into existence. This is not to say that her perceptions are completely her own. On the contrary, her perceptions of the climate are socially constructed: she is influenced by other perceivers and several other factors I discuss below.

People can perceive climates on a wide variety of levels. Just as weather climates are often highly localized, political "microclimates" also exist (Gardner 1995). In addition to the national level (the most typical popular treatment of climate), I argue that climate can also be perceived at the state level (a state's climate can be hostile), the city level (a city within that state can have a hospitable climate), and the local level (something could lead an individual or group to believe that a certain part of town has a hostile or hospitable climate). All of these combinations raise a plethora of possibilities, as perceptions at one level surely affect perceptions at another level.

The Elements of Climate

One's overall view of the political climate is made up of assessments of a number of elements: media representations, the opinions of the general public, practices of government entities, critical events, and the actions of social movement organizations (both one's own and one's opposition). While particular individuals may deem some of these factors more important than others, most people are savvy enough to understand how each of these elements affects the overall level of hostility their group faces. Here I briefly discuss each of these elements.

The media play an important role in people's assessments of the levels of hostility toward their groups. In his research on working-class conversations about politics, William Gamson (1992a) found that his subjects would employ experiential knowledge, popular wisdom, and media discourse to make their points. A particular individual may not have any experiential knowledge about a given topic, but he or she is still able to understand the topic and be affected by it due to the treatment of the topic by popular wisdom or by media discourse. Large-scale, climate-altering events are most likely to be experienced only through media discourse (Mutz 1998). People know of an event, yet have experienced only the mediated version of it. People who lack experiential knowledge may be more likely to employ mediated knowledge in their talk of climates. It is important to note that those who lack both experiential and mediated knowledge may still have strong opinions about the political climate, however uninformed those opinions may be. The media play a particularly important role in broadcasting the actions of social-movement organizations. Given that many movement goals involve changing the public's perceptions about some element of society, a movement action that fails to garner media attention is often considered a failure. The media have been instrumental in popularizing—and depopularizing—social movements (Priest 2001; Gitlin 1980). To get the media's attention, social movement activists will often go to extreme lengths, often negatively affecting their cause:

> Public officials and heads of large established organizations receive automatic standing from the mass media by virtue of their roles. This is not so for movement actors, who must often struggle to establish it and may require extrainstitutional collective action to do so. Members of the club enter the media through the front door, but challengers must find their way in through a window, often using some gimmick or disorderly act to do so, which may impair their effectiveness once inside. "Those who dress up in costume to be admitted to the media's party," Gamson and Wolfsheld point out (1992), "will not be allowed to change before being photographed." (Gamson and Meyer 1996, 288)

This leads to a paradox: gaining media attention could ultimately create a more hostile climate for the movement's cause. It is not merely the ability of a movement to capture media attention that matters; the type of attention is just as important. I will illustrate these claims in the coming chapters in the context of the media attention given Christian conservatives and gay men and lesbians. Both groups see media attention as critical to their success.

Research within the field of public opinion has generated the concept of opinion climates. In her work, Noelle-Neumann (1993) sought evidence for what she called a "spiral of silence." In a spiral of silence, one direction of public opinion becomes dominant, causing those who hold the opposite opinion to silence themselves for fear of being isolated or exposed as deviant. As more and more people silence their opinions, they feed this spiral until it seems that there is only one possible opinion on a subject. In a typical Noelle-Neumann experiment, the researcher would put the subject in a hypothetical situation in which the subject was sharing a train cabin with one or more persons who held the opposite opinion on certain issues (e.g., corporal punishment, the effects of smoking). When the subject's opinion on the issue was outnumbered two-to-one, he would be significantly less willing to talk about the issue. While her research offers evidence that people do think about climates before they act, the contrived nature of the hypothetical situations does not allow us to study the subjective and socially constructed nature of climate perception.

Unfortunately, little research has examined the processes through which people perceive public opinion. Jelen (1992) suggests that those with deviant opinions may be more likely than others to recognize that their opinions are deviant, and thus may communicate these opinions infrequently. Glynn (1989) offers evidence that people have a tendency to misperceive the opinion climates around them, overestimating either the conservativeness of a climate (if the respondent is liberal) or the liberalness of a climate (if the respondent is conservative). Lang and Lang (1993) propose that in uncertain climates, people rely on others' opinions more often, becoming more susceptible to the power of rumor. Kuran (1995) theorizes that people, under pressure, may not only silence their opinions, but falsify them, making the perceived opinion climate appear more uncertain, or even very different from the actual opinions of members of the public. However, our understanding of the cognitive processes involved in perceiving public opinion is elementary at best. This book uncovers the ways both Christian conservatives and gay men and lesbians perceive public support or disdain, even in the absence of conventional, poll-oriented evidence.

The claim that government actions toward particular groups affect the climate perceived by these groups is similar in some ways to the discussion of political opportunity structure, a concept popular in research on social movements. First introduced in the 1970s (Eisinger 1973; Jenkins and Perrow 1977) and later fully developed by McAdam (1982), political opportunity structure concerns the viability of social change in different political contexts:

> while excluded groups do possess the latent capacity to exert significant political leverage at any time, the force of environmental constraints is usually sufficient to inhibit mass action. But this force is not constant over time. The calculations on which existing political arrangements are based may, for a variety of reasons, change over time, thus affording certain segments of the population greater leverage with which to advance their interests. (McAdam 1982, 39)

Social movement researchers have shown that these political opportunities can vary over geographic space (Miller 2000; Kitschelt 1986) and time (Jenkins and Perrow 1977; Almeida and Stearns 1998). But in order for an aggrieved population to take advantage of an open political opportunity structure, they have to experience "cognitive liberation" (McAdam 1982): they must see change as possible. James Jasper emphasizes the lack of attention given to the subjective nature of the possibility for change:

Cognitive liberation depends on cultural processes, some of which may be independent of strategies and political structures. For people to think that repression has eased, they need to interpret the pieces of information they receive, which may or may not be accurate. As crowd theorists saw, rumors can be as effective in shifting perceptions as sound information—because they are often taken to be sound. Process theorists have had little to say about this interpretive filter, giving the impression that potential protestors respond straightforwardly to objective conditions and probabilities of success. (Jasper 1997, 37)

With regard to political opportunity structure, then, researchers have paid little attention to the microlevel: how different individuals *perceive* the political opportunity structure and the ways in which they are affected by it. By analyzing how people perceive an open opportunity structure—or, in my terms, a hospitable political climate—I advance this discussion.

Another way I expand the concept of political climate is to address the importance of critical events in shaping it. A major way people assess political climates is by keeping track of events that could affect the climate. Such events are used by individuals as physical manifestations of the political climate: "Look, there it is, *that's* what I mean when I say my environment is hostile." These events can occur to the climate perceiver himself, or they could be passed on to him by other people or by the media. Gary Alan Fine (1995) calls for the examination of narrative in social movement research: whether they are "horror stories" or "success stories," people use narrative to spread information about such events. Fine claims that such stories are often overlooked by researchers. Ken Plummer (1995) points out that we now tell stories (i.e., coming-out stories, recovery stories) that we wouldn't have dared to tell even a generation ago, and studying the nature of such stories could help to understand social change. This element of climate also has connections to concepts in the literature on social problems: typifying examples, which represent a certain class of social problem (Lowney and Best 1995), and landmark narratives, which are definitive stories with especially resonant narrative themes (Lee and Ermann 1999; Nichols 1997). Through the telling of stories, we let others experience events vicariously, and in doing so we let them experience the political climate we have known firsthand. Through such stories about a wide-ranging set of events, from the personal to the media oriented, people partially develop an understanding of the political climates around them.

In characterizing the climate, people also take into account social movement activity. Such activity has multiple effects on political climate. First, it can assist in the goal of getting an issue on the table, bringing the grievances of a particular group to the attention of the media, the public, and the lawmakers. Once the issue is on the table, movement activity can improve the political climate for a particular group. Finally, movement activity can impel countermovement activity, which can create a negative effect on the political climate a group perceives.

In order for the political climate to change, the opportunity for change must first be created. A particular issue must *become* an issue within the arena of public discourse (Klandermans 1992; Jenson 1987). That is, the issue must become important for a large proportion of the public, or at least a critical mass. If this goal is not achieved, then the likelihood of change in climate is negligible. There is limited space within the public arena, therefore social problems and the social movements connected to them must compete for attention (Hilgartner and Bosk 1988). Social movement activity is often focused on pushing the movement cause into the arena of public discourse. This is especially crucial for those social movements for which a major goal is to change public attitudes about an issue (Scott 1990; Melucci 1985). A precursor to changing one's mind about an issue is one's willingness to think about the issue. People may have opinions, but these opinions may be latent and not in the forefront of consciousness. Movements, in accomplishing this goal of getting people to think about an issue, do not necessarily change climates as much as create the possibility for change.

Social movements also may change the climate simply through their presence, manifested in the form of marches or campaigns, bumper stickers or buttons (Noelle-Neumann 1993). Movements often increase their presence by creating "alliance systems" (Tarrow 1994): connections to those organizations or political figures who have pledged their support to the movement's cause. These alliances help the movement to gain legitimacy, and in doing so potentially create the impression that the climate surrounding the movement's adherents is improving. In addition, by gaining prominence, the movement helps people to develop a practical consciousness: recognizing connections between events in their own lives and events happening on a grander scale (Mutz 1994; Gamson 1992b; Giddens 1984).

Finally, it is important to realize that the growing presence of a movement, which may improve the political climate, often brings with it the growing presence of a countermovement, which may impair the political climate (Meyer and Staggenborg 1996; Tarrow 1994; Mottl 1980). This tug-of-war can often have a polarizing effect on the population:

> [A]ction mobilization can backfire and produce a reverse effect because it generally polarizes a population—cognitively and socially. . . . Opponents and countermovement organizations are often extremely skilled in creating caricatures of the movement and sowing doubt in the hearts of half-hearted sympathizers. Often a movement organization bears within itself the ammunition for a countercampaign. In other words, action mobilization forces a shift in public discourse: In the media and in informal conversations among citizens, public discourse becomes increasingly focused on campaign issues. As a result, individual citizens and societal actors are forced to take sides. (Oegema and Klandermans 1994, 706)

Thus, while bringing the issue to the forefront, movements also raise the ire of their opponents, forcing them to further mobilize and vie for the attention of the public at large. People who were formerly standing on neutral ground (whether they knew it or not) are suddenly forced to take sides, since neutrality is often perceived by both sides of the conflict as collaboration with the enemy (Kuran 1995). The public's heightened awareness makes the strategies used by movement organizers ever more important, since the use of the wrong tactic could turn the public against the movement (Burstein 1985; Schuman 1972). In contrast to other areas of research on social movements, few have studied the movement-countermovement dialectic (Einwohner 1997; Mottl 1980). I contribute to this area by showing how political climates play a role in the interactions between two oppositional movements.

I explore all of these elements by combining these initial ideas with the wide variety of observations made by real people in the two cities. By examining, for example, the particular ways the Spokane general public is perceived to be more hostile than the Seattle public toward gays and lesbians, I expand our understanding of what aspects of opinion climates really matter to the level of hostility experienced by marginalized groups. Also, by analyzing the extent to which each group discusses each element (and the passion with which they discuss them), I further contrast the ways Christian conservatives and gay men and lesbians understand their political and social environments.

A Brief Look at the Two Groups

For the benefit of those who may be unfamiliar with the two groups in the study, here I provide brief backgrounds of the groups and the movements that act on their behalf. In addition, I postulate comparisons and contrasts between the two groups that will arise throughout the book. Some of the comparisons I make in this section will be upheld by the data, while others will be repudiated.

The Gay and Lesbian Rights Movement

In the second half of the twentieth century, the United States has witnessed a proliferation of social movements, to the point where movement organizing has become a commonplace method of attempting social change (Tarrow 1994). Of all the social movements that have emerged during this period, the gay and lesbian rights movement has been one of the most effective in moving its goals into the spotlight of public discourse, on both local and national levels. Below is a brief history of the gay movement that summarizes its goals, tactics, and accomplishments.[1]

Sexual orientation is a relatively recent conceptual development. Although today a sizable number of people identify as gay or lesbian, such identities have been around only one hundred years (Katz 2001, 1995). Prior to this time, although same-sex sexual behavior existed, the application of a distinct label for people who engaged in such behavior was uncommon. The move from "a love with no name" to "the love that dare not speak its name" occurred around the turn of the century, as psychologists pathologized such behavior and those engaging in it (Katz 1995). Doctors defined those with same-sex desires as mentally ill, and the American Psychiatric Association officially considered homosexuality a sociopathic personality disturbance (Bayer 1987). Although historians have argued that some urban enclaves temporarily accepted homosexuality (Chauncey 1994), the behavior and identity remained primarily stigmatized for the first half of the twentieth century.

The seeds for a social movement were planted in the 1940s and 1950s. While serving in World War II, many gays and lesbians for the first time found themselves living among others like themselves (Berube 1990), allowing for the formation of a social identity based on sexual desire. After the war, many of these people chose to settle in urban areas, such as New

York City and San Francisco, rather than return to lives of isolation in smaller towns. Increasingly high concentrations of gay men and lesbians produced thriving social scenes and the environments necessary to generate the first gay and lesbian political organizations in the 1950s, such as the Mattachine Society and the Daughters of Bilitis (D'Emilio 1998). Members of these groups began envisioning a world in which their identities and behaviors were no longer stigmatized by society.

Although such groups continued to grow during the 1960s, many mark June 27, 1969, as the official starting date of the modern gay and lesbian rights movement in the United States. Late that night, New York City police officers raided the Stonewall Inn, a gay bar in Greenwich Village, inciting a riot among gay men, lesbians, and drag queens that lasted for several days (D'Emilio 1998; Duberman 1993). Out of the riot grew the gay liberation movement of the 1970s, during which gay men and lesbians used many of the social movement tactics that had proven effective during the civil rights and student movements of the 1960s. Street protests became popular, and gay pride parades became annual institutions in major cities during the 1970s. With the first protests came the first policy-oriented accomplishments of the movement. In 1973, activists were successful in lobbying the American Psychiatric Association to remove homosexuality from its list of mental disorders (Bayer 1987). The 1970s also brought the passage of numerous local ordinances that prevented job and housing discrimination against people based on their sexual orientation (Adam 1995). Such ordinances were the impetus for the growth of a countermovement against gay and lesbian rights, and often these ordinances were quickly overturned (Button, Rienzo, and Wald 1997).

In the 1980s, the attention of gay men and lesbians turned to the AIDS epidemic, which decimated a large percentage of the gay male community. While horrible in its physical effects, AIDS brought homosexuality into the public's consciousness (Bayer 1991), as Americans could not ignore that some of their celebrities and sons were dying. In addition, it politicized many gay men and lesbians, who were shocked at the heel-dragging of both the American government and the medical establishment (Gould 2001; Epstein 1996). This increased mobilization was often quite radical and performative (Gamson 1989). With the advent of organizations such as ACT-UP (Aids Coalition to Unleash Power) and Queer Nation, the tactics sometimes took the form of die-ins in city streets or kiss-ins in suburban shopping malls.

The issues tackled by the gay and lesbian rights movement in the 1990s became increasingly varied, yet remained policy oriented. While AIDS and job discrimination were still key issues, the movement placed importance on several other goals: permitting openly gay people to serve in the military, allowing gay men and lesbians to marry (or at least receive the financial and legal benefits of marriage), permitting gay men and lesbians to adopt children, focusing attention on the issues faced by gay and lesbian youth in schools, and responding to the continued prevalence of violence aimed at gay men and lesbians. Several large national organizations—the National Gay and Lesbian Task Force, Human Rights Campaign, Gay and Lesbian Alliance Against Defamation, just to name a few—have developed structures and techniques for effecting institutional change.

While movement vanguards emphasize these policy-oriented movement goals, many in the gay community continue to stress the effectiveness of identity politics: if the general public simply realized how many gay men and lesbians there are, and that they permeate every stratum of society, the ultimate goal of depathologizing homosexuality might be achieved. Thus, in concert with ideas coming out of the "new social movements" literature, some emphasis is placed on effecting changes in the attitudes and beliefs of the general public (Johnston, Larana, and Gusfield 1994).

Signs of progress for the gay and lesbian rights movement are many, but homosexuality remains stigmatized in many institutions in American society. While some urban centers allow gay men and lesbians to live openly, many geographical locations remain quite hostile environments (Sharp 1999; Vaid 1995). News media increasingly cover issues pertinent to the movement, often providing signs of progress and decline simultaneously, making the reading of the political climate a difficult endeavor. However, few would contest the claim that the gay and lesbian rights movement has been successful in moving its issues into mainstream discourse.

The Christian Conservative Movement

Often sharing the spotlight with the gay and lesbian rights movement, the Christian conservative movement is also a major social movement in the United States at the dawn of the twenty-first century. I outline here a brief history of the Christian conservative movement, describing its adherents' goals and their attempts to achieve these goals.

Any discussion of the Christian conservative movement necessitates a brief foray into the philosophies of conservative Christianity. Defining the term is perhaps as complex as defining sexual desire.[2] Myriad belief systems that variously combine orthodoxy, fundamentalism, evangelicalism, and denominationalism lead one into a definitional quandary. For example, in the literature on conservative Christianity, some scholars equate fundamentalists with evangelicals, while others take great pains to separate the two (Harding 2000; Diamond 1998; Woodberry and Smith 1998; Smith 1998; Cox 1995). The two major similarities between the various strains of conservative Christianity are belief in the Bible as the only true religious authority and the realization that one can achieve eternal salvation only through a personal relationship with Jesus Christ (Crapanzano 2000; Hunter 1987). The major distinction between fundamentalism and evangelicalism is described as follows by sociologist Christian Smith:

> While archetypal fundamentalists are about the business of creating "total worlds" (Peshkin 1986; Ammerman 1987), archetypal evangelicals are about the business of creating "seeker friendly" churches, which are often anything but strict, yet can be very strong (Perrin and Mauss 1993). The difference is strategic: evangelicalism's core task of evangelizing and influencing the secular world encourages the movement to curb absolutism, conformity, and fanaticism, in a way that fundamentalism's core tasks of defending the theological fundamentals against liberalism and remaining pure from the world do not. For to influence the world, one must sustain ongoing interaction with it and not build rigid walls behind which simply to remain separate and preserve orthodoxy. (Smith 1998, 85)

Both groups see American society and culture as essentially and increasingly flawed. Evangelicals seek to repair this world, while fundamentalists, primarily concerned with their own salvation, seek to avoid the evils of this world. Given their predisposition, it is evangelicals who are more likely to be involved in the political sphere. However, both evangelicals and fundamentalists are concerned with the political climate around them. Evangelicals need to know what to change, fundamentalists need to know what to avoid. Since I am concerned with perceptions of political climates and environments, I use a rather broad definition of Christian conservatism based on the biblically based worldview these groups share, for it is this worldview that most affects their perceptions of the political climate.

Christian conservative social and political activism has arrived in various waves throughout the twentieth century. The first wave, starting at the beginning of the century and ending in the 1920s, focused on anti-Catholicism, Prohibition, and antievolutionism (Hunter 1987). The anti-Catholic sentiment stemmed mainly from concern over the number of Catholic immigrants from Europe and was not exclusively a Christian conservative cause. Christian conservatives became involved with the temperance movement because they viewed drinking as a worldly evil and a sign of moral decline. While this issue, too, was initially supported by others, by the end of Prohibition only Christian conservatives remained strident in their support. Christian conservative antievolutionism was a result of the increased teaching of evolution in the public schools, combined with the decreasing coverage of creationism. This campaign culminated in the famous Scopes trial, during which popular opinion shifted sharply against Christian conservatives, excommunicating them from the public arena for a period of time (Harding 2000).

The second wave, at the middle of the century, concerned anticommunism. While not all conservative Christian churches participated in this wave, those churches that participated did so fervently. Such churches were discredited as part of the fallout from the political demise of Joseph McCarthy, making Christian conservatives once again politically ineffective for some time to come (Hunter 1987).

The third wave, beginning in late 1970s and continuing today, concentrates on the moral decline Christian conservatives see in a world with which they must interact (Ammerman 1987), as evidenced by such issues as abortion, women's roles, school prayer, and homosexuality.[3] Most Christian conservative discontent was a result of political decisions: the 1973 *Roe v. Wade* decision legalizing abortion, the Equal Rights Amendment, the 1962 and 1963 Supreme Court decisions regarding school prayer, and the various gay rights ordinances described above. Because much of the social change surrounding these issues originated from the political sphere, Christian conservatives believed they had no choice but to organize politically. By 1980, several key organizations were in place, including the Moral Majority and the Religious Roundtable. These organizations were successful in mobilizing previously inactive Christian conservatives, forming a formidable political bloc.

While these specific organizations did not prove to have much staying power, they did have the ability to quickly move their constituencies into new organizations and causes. In 1988, Pat Robertson, founder of the

Christian Broadcasting Network and "The 700 Club," made a bid to be the Republican nominee for president. While ultimately unsuccessful in achieving the nomination, Robertson garnered unprecedented attention from the media and political establishments. The following year Robertson, using the mailing lists from his unsuccessful campaign, formed the Christian Coalition (Martin 1996). Under the guidance of a young political strategist named Ralph Reed, the Christian Coalition grew to a membership of 1.7 million in 1996 (Watson 1999). Although Reed has since left the Coalition, it remains a formidable political power, if not on the national level, then on the local and state levels. Christian conservatives once again played key roles in the Republican nomination process in 2000.

In his recent study of American evangelicalism, Smith (1998) argues that Christian conservatives' philosophy remains quite individualistic: the solution to society's problems is to change the hearts and behaviors of individuals. However, when the political system puts into place devices that prevent Christians from changing individual hearts, they sometimes see no choice but to become politically involved. For example, if a school district prevents Christian children from evangelizing on the playground, this may serve to mobilize Christians to action. Smith describes Christian conservatives as "embattled and thriving": embattled because American society presents them and their children with new temptations and restrictions at every turn, thriving because the Christian conservative population is growing, drawing people from mainline denominations (Smith 1998). This juxtaposition—a growing group of adherents with growing grievances—makes for a powerful social movement worthy of much attention.

Differences and Similarities between the Two Groups

These groups form an excellent combination for a study of the effects of political climates because they have nearly opposite stakes in the general climate's movement in liberal or conservative directions. Given the nature of its goals, the gay and lesbian rights movement seldom benefits from a general climate change toward the conservative. Its goals are steeped in a tenet of modern American liberalism: the extension of rights to new groups in society (Garner 1996). The Christian conservative movement, on the other hand, seldom benefits from a general climate change toward the liberal. A major theme of its goals is restoration of American society to values and norms of previous eras (Watson 1999).

While these two movements often find themselves in strict opposition to each other, it is important to note that they are not oppositional movements to each other *exclusively*. The Christian conservative movement has contributed to several movements that were formed to oppose the achievements of other movements: movements against homosexuality, against abortion, against evolution, against feminism (Martin 1996). However, the Christian conservative movement does serve as the major source of opposition to the gay and lesbian rights movement. Those who study or are involved in the gay rights movement see the Christian conservative movement as a major, if not the major, source of opposition to its goals (Herman 1997; Bull and Gallagher 1996; Vaid 1995). The multiple-issue nature of the Christian conservative movement needs to be kept in mind because critical events or media coverage involving any of the issues mentioned above could potentially affect the political climate perceived by its adherents. The role homosexuality plays in affecting the political climate perceived by Christian conservatives at this point in history will be a major subject of analysis throughout the book.

While these two movements serve as opposites in several respects, they also have striking similarities. Both groups often view themselves as embattled minority groups that face hostility from the general culture, such as policies directed against their group, caricatures of their group in the media, and public opinion that disfavors their group. For either group's major goals to be accomplished, fundamental changes in the general culture would be required. The political and social climates experienced by each group depend on the specific geographical location in question.

On the micro level, there are other similarities. Membership in each of these groups can be invisible: members of both groups have the ability to choose when to disclose their identities as members of the group (unlike, for example, membership in most racial or gender categories). In addition, people from both groups can still be fully identified as "members" even if they choose to be inactive in their respective social movement. For example, one can be a fully identified member of a Christian conservative community without being a member of Christian conservative political organizations, just as one can be a fully identified gay man or lesbian without joining gay and lesbian political organizations. In certain situations and locations, members of each group who choose to make their identities known may find that this identity is perceived by others as a "master status" (Becker 1963). Regardless of other characteristics of the individual's identity, it is the person's status as a member of this group that becomes the defining characteristic of her identity: people with whom she interacts can think of little else, and all her actions are interpreted through this filter. All of these similarities allow me to develop a single study of political climate perceptions and activism that is essentially parallel for both groups.

However, one may also argue that the two groups are not comparable in key ways. For example, in terms of sheer numbers, amount of power, and pervasiveness of cultural symbols, Christian conservatives seem to be far ahead. It is the perceptions of hostility, though, that concern me here. And Christian conservatives, as I will show, *perceive* a great deal of hostility. Even if they may be incorrect, these perceptions have consequences. This makes a comparative study of climate perceptions, and the subsequent revelation of important contrasts, even more important.

Some may wonder of another possibility: the intersections of these two groups within individuals. In fact, this concern regularly arises whenever I speak on these topics. Certainly, there are individuals who do maintain both a gay identity and a Christian conservative identity. While such individuals are definitely worthy of sociological study, they are not the subject of my work here. What I *will* engage in later in the book is a discussion of the prevalence of Christianity (more broadly defined) among gay men and lesbians and how this prevalence is interpreted by members of both groups in the study.

Washington State as a Research Site

To explore the differences in perceptions of political climates, I had to find two locations with significant populations of each of the two groups, as well as an array of organizations designed to serve each group. It would have been possible, for example, to conduct the study in a megalopolis with an extremely large gay and lesbian population and a small town where few gay and lesbian people live, but the contrasts between both the size of the gay and lesbian population and the numbers of gay organizations in the cities would have made the construction of a single method to study individuals in both areas very difficult. Therefore, while the sizes of the gay and Christian conservative communities could differ in each city, significant populations had to exist in both locations.

Another requirement: the two locations of the study had to have considerably different reputations with regard to political climate. I needed one location that had a long history of supporting liberal and progressive causes, and another with a history of supporting more conservative causes. Critical here was the relative difference between the two locations: the climate of one had to be considerably more conservative than that of the other. Also, because the focus of this book is on social change, it was necessary to identify locations whose climates toward these two groups are not static.

A final requirement was to find two locations within the same state. This was important because the movement adherents in each location should have at least some political knowledge in common. If I had studied these groups in cities from different states, an anomalous state-level event could potentially affect the climate in the city from that state, thus disrupting the study. Also by conducting the study in one state, I was able to see how people from cities with different climates think about the state-level climate they share in common.

Two cities that fulfill these requirements are Seattle and Spokane. Each city serves as the urban center for its respective side of the state. Seattle is the largest city in Washington State west of the Cascade mountain range. Spokane is the largest city in Washington State east of the Cascades. Both cities have significant numbers of both gay men and lesbians and Christian conservatives, as well as a large number of organizations designed to serve each group. Seattle, for the most part, is known as a liberal and progressive city. There are obvious exceptions to this, but if one had to provide an overall characterization of the political climate, one would have to conclude that, relative to other geographical locations, Seattle is liberal. Spokane is known statewide for its conservative nature. It may not be the most conservative city in the nation, but relative to Seattle, it is the most conservative large city in the state.

Washington State overall has a volatile political climate that in recent years has surprised both groups, positively and negatively. In 1993, Christian conservative groups began collecting signatures for two statewide ballot initiatives that would limit gay and lesbian rights, but they failed to collect enough signatures in time. A Christian conservative political candidate garnered enough support to become the Republican nominee for governor in 1996. She subsequently lost decisively (60 percent to 40 percent). Gay rights activists collected enough voters' signatures to place an antidiscrimination initiative on the statewide ballot in 1997, but the initiative was rejected by the same margin (60 percent to 40 percent), barely winning in liberal Seattle. In general, due to the presence of Seattle,

Washington State is perceived as liberal in contrast to other parts of the country. However, this liberalness is not constant throughout the state, with the eastern side of the state being considerably more conservative than the western. While the Cascade mountain range creates a meteorological border (with rainforest conditions on one side, desertlike conditions on the other), many residents of Washington State also use it as a symbolic political border dividing the two sides.

While the two cities fit the requirements of the project, differences between them are significant. Driving into Seattle on Interstate 90 (the major highway that connects Seattle and Spokane), you encounter a quickly growing cityscape. Between 1986 and 1996, the population of King County (in which Seattle is located) grew by 18 percent to just over 1.6 million people. Many of these people live in one of Seattle's distinct neighborhoods. There is a high level of neighborhood pride, with each having its own festivals and landmarks (the most famous of which is the Seattle Center's Space Needle, a remnant of the 1962 World's Fair). Getting around Seattle can be difficult: the growing traffic often gets jammed on one of the city's many bridges. Seattle's employment base is primarily white collar and service oriented, and the county has a median household income of $53,157. Using the median rather than the mean is appropriate here, as the mean is skewed by a large number of Seattlites who struck it rich during the technology boom of the 1990s. Evidence of the economic boom abounds: upscale stores, condos, eateries, and cafes are everywhere. Some of the area's major employers are Boeing, Microsoft, Group Health, U.S. West Communications, Alaska Airlines, Nordstrom Apparel, and the University of Washington. As the nineties came to a close, several of these industries experienced some decline, but overall the economy in Seattle remains robust. However, due to its temperate climate (notwithstanding the rain) and liberal reputation, Seattle also has a significant homeless population.

Travel east on I-90 for four or five hours and you will find yourself in Spokane. In contrast to Seattle, the cityscape is smaller and has an older feel to it. The city is divided geographically by both the interstate and the Spokane River. Along the river is the city's pride and joy: Riverfront Park. Set right in the center of town, it was home to the 1974 World's Fair. Spokane's downtown retail district is struggling, with many stores moving to malls at the northern end of the city. While trendy places to see and be seen in are available, they are not nearly as numerous as in Seattle.

Spokane County has grown in population, though not at the same rate as the west side of the state: it experienced a 16 percent increase from 1986 to 1996, to a population of 407,000. However, Spokane *does* serve as the urban hub for a large geographical area. To find a similarly large city to the east of Spokane, one must travel all the way to Minneapolis, Minnesota. With a more blue-collar economy, Spokane County's 1996 median household income was $37,308. Some major employers are Sacred Heart Hospital, Kaiser Aluminum, Empire Health, Burlington Northern, Hewlett-Packard, and Fairchild Air Force Base. The nearest large university is Washington State University in Pullman, which is about thirty minutes away. Spokane has somewhat of a psychological complex when it comes to comparisons to Seattle. While I was doing my research there, the *Spokane Spokesman-Review,* the major newspaper, ran a long series of articles entitled "The Great Divide," in which it examined the economic, political, and cultural differences between the two cities. A major theme of the series was the mixture of envy and antagonism that some Spokanites feel toward their counterparts across the state (Mapes, Turner, and Jones 1997).

Regarding the history of the two groups in the cities, the major difference concerns the gay and lesbian rights movement, which had an earlier start in Seattle than in Spokane. For example, Seattle had a gay cabaret as early as the 1940s (Paulson and Simpson 1996), and in 1978 became the first major American city to prevent the overturning of gay rights ordinances by a popular vote (Honig and Brenner 1987). Another telling sign of organization is community newspapers. While the cities' Christian newspapers and Spokane's gay newspaper are monthly, Seattle's gay and lesbian paper is weekly.[4] Furthermore, the Christian communities do not have community telephone directories, but the gay communities do; however, Spokane's is under fifty pages, while Seattle's is over two hundred.

And now for the million-dollar question that any geographically focused study must face: Why should one care about Seattle and Spokane? In other words, can the lessons in this book possibly apply to other regions of the United States? Part of my argument is very place specific: people use stories from their environments to characterize the climates within these environments. But it is the process of storytelling, of how they tell the stories, that interests me. True, Christian conservatives from the Bible Belt, or lesbians from Greenwich Village, would likely gauge their own climates based on different events than those described by Washington State residents. But the process of climate description is likely quite similar.

The Project

A number of empirical questions guided my project. Given that Seattle is liberal and Spokane is conservative, how does this liberalness or conservativeness, or changing levels thereof, manifest itself in the lives of both gay men and lesbians and Christian conservatives? For example, does the liberalness of Seattle translate into a hospitable climate for gay men and lesbians there? Does the conservativeness of Spokane translate into a hospitable climate for Christian conservatives there? Of course, I also investigate the reverse of these questions: Does the liberalness of Seattle and the conservativeness of Spokane translate into hostility toward Christian conservatives in Seattle and toward gay men and lesbians in Spokane, respectively? Another question I address is how members of these two groups attempt to effect changes in these climates. For example, how are Spokane's gay men and lesbians attempting to improve the hostile climate toward them, and in what ways does the hostile climate hinder them from doing so?

Like many researchers who attempt to connect individuals and larger contexts, I decided on an approach that used multiple sociological methods. One could easily drown in the methodological details that comprised these multiple parts, so I have relegated these details to an appendix in the back of the book. Here I provide only a thumbnail sketch of the study. I attempted to assess the climates of the cities from both objective and subjective perspectives. Objectively, I employed survey data and content analysis of media. To assess subjective perceptions of climates (the heart of the study), I conducted in-depth interviews.

Since I argued above that the opinions of the public play a role in people's perceptions of political climates, I first analyzed both national and local data sets of opinions regarding issues pertinent to both Christian conservatives and gay men and lesbians. The national data sets I used were the General Social Survey and the American National Election Studies. To analyze Washington State residents in greater depth, and to contrast Seattle to Spokane, I used the 1996 Front Porch Survey of Washington State residents. Through these analyses, I am able to paint a clear picture of the national, state, and local opinion climates in the two cities.

To assess the treatment of pertinent issues in the media, I conducted a content analysis of letters to the editor, editorials, and editorial cartoons in the largest-circulation newspaper in each city. My research assistants and I coded any piece about an issue of concern to Christian conservatives and/or gay men and lesbians. We coded each piece for whether it was hostile or hospitable to Christian conservative views and/or gay and lesbian views. We examined every newspaper from the years 1982 to 1997, yielding a total of 6,930 editorial pieces. Because this analysis was done for a number of years, it provides an objective assessment of changes over time in the political climate toward the groups, as it is expressed in an important component of the mainstream media.

I deal with the results from these two components in significant depth. However, they were designed to provide the backdrop for the main component of the project: eighty-four in-depth interviews with Christian conservatives, gay men, and lesbians in the two cities. I interviewed roughly equal numbers of each of these four groups. Within each group, I located both a wide variety of community leaders and activists as well as members of each group who were relatively uninvolved in their communities. I attempted to make the sample of respondents as diverse as possible with respect to several demographics, such as gender, race, and age. However, even though I fully appreciate the potential of studying the intersection of identities (Howard 2000), I concentrate on the overall comparison between the two groups and not the differences within each group.

In interviews, I asked the respondents a series of questions that required them to assess the level of hostility toward their groups on local, state, and national levels. I also guided the respondents through a series of hypothetical scenarios designed to clarify which events are most important to people as they assess the climate around them, and how they might react to such events. Finally, I asked them a series of questions about what they do to effect change in these climates, both via social movement organizations and in the course of their daily lives. Since the ways questions are asked can influence the responses, I suggest that the reader peruse the full interview schedule in the methodological appendix.

While I view my analysis as balanced, and while others have agreed with this assessment (one reader called it "audaciously fair"), it is important that I briefly describe my identities and my background. While all social research has subjective components, those engaging in qualitative research need to be especially cognizant of the ways their own identities influence how they conduct interviews and how they analyze the resulting data. I brought to the project two primary identities: I am a gay man from a conservative upbringing.

Though I currently hold one identity (gay) but not the other (Christian conservative), my background provided me an uncommon familiarity with conservative thinking. Raised in a small, Midwestern, blue-collar community, I attended Catholic grade school and Catholic high school. The latter included a semester-long course entitled "Christian Sexual Morality," during which I learned the conservative Catholic stands on a variety of topics. Though I did not share the philosophies of the Christian conservative respondents I interviewed, I was able to relate to them in their language, understand their references to the Bible, and follow their lines of reasoning. Most responded quite well to the interview process. For example, a Seattle respondent said in an e-mail message after his interview: "Thanks for the opportunity to do the interview. It made me process a lot of my beliefs. Your questions show that you have a deep sensitivity to the complexities within society and the challenges that Christians face relating to those complexities."

Conducting the interviews with Christian conservatives, concealing my gay identity along the way, was not without its stressful or surreal moments. I knew that maintaining neutrality during the interviews was paramount. Partly, I called upon my nonargumentative nature to accomplish this. More importantly, though, the lion's share of the respondents' comments made perfect sense to me when placed in the context of their lives, and the rapport the respondents and I built was genuine. Because I am gay, some may assume that I am unable to analyze the ideas of Christian conservatives without bias. But I'd argue my genuine desire to understand their points of view and my training as a sociological researcher helped me to tap into their unmitigated thoughts and to treat their ideas fairly.

After scrutinizing the data, I believe I have developed a solid understanding of the processes through which people make sense of the overwhelming amount of information they face with regard to the political climates that surround them. I also believe that in doing so, I have made a contribution to our understanding of contemporary social change. I have structured the book's chapters around the elements of climate I discussed above, with each element getting its own chapter. In chapter 2, I discuss the role of the media. In chapter 3, I address the importance of the general public in affecting the climates. Chapter 4 examines the roles of various political actors. In chapter 5, I turn to the role of identity in the gay and lesbian and Christian conservative communities and the organizations in those communities. Chapter 6 addresses the intersections between the two movements by examining how the members of each group think about the other group. Chapter 7 turns to the conscious efforts by individuals to improve the climates for their groups. Chapter 8 ties together all of the book's contributions and offers suggestions for the future, both in terms of studying these two groups and with regard to the general study of social change.

2

Watching the Media

Our relationship to the mass media can be characterized as an example of a fishbowl effect: they so pervade our everyday lives that we seldom recognize their influence on the ways we perceive the political and social worlds around us. Christian conservatives and gay men and lesbians, however, have a clear understanding of the impact of the media. For these groups, the media play an extremely important role, for it is primarily through these media that other members of the general public gain information about their actions. In this chapter, I offer numerous examples of the ways Christian conservatives and gays think about these portrayals.

A number of social scientists recently have turned their attention to how the media portray social movements. Taking Gitlin's classic study of Students for a Democratic Society as their inspiration (Gitlin 1980), these studies use content analysis of media coverage to examine which events get covered by the media (Oliver and Myers 1999; Danielian and Page 1994) and the frames that reporters use to cover such events (Smith et al. 2001). The media (in these studies, television and newspapers) are prone to covering dramatic events, giving movements a deviant reputation that can negatively affect their ability to change the attitudes of the public and political officials (Everett 1992; Page and Shapiro 1992). By exposing biases, such objective studies are important steps in understanding the relationship between media and movements.

However, a long-standing mantra in media studies is that audiences don't just passively take in the media, they actively process it:

> Texts in general and media imagery in particular can be read in different ways—to use the jargon, they are polysemic. Texts may have a preferred meaning and point of view which the reader is invited to accept. But many readers decline the invitation, either entering into some negotiation with the dominant meaning or rejecting it outright with an oppositional reading. (Gamson et al. 1992, 388)

Readers bring to their TV sets, newspapers, and computer screens a set of experiences and assumptions that influence their interpretations of media content. This may be especially true for those readers from groups that have been historically marginalized and whose reputations are in flux. These subjective readings can have serious consequences. If a group perceives unfair treatment, this may affect their future interactions with media professionals.

In this chapter, I illustrate how the two groups perceive the treatment they receive from their local media. First, I present results from the content analysis of editorial pieces in the two cities' newspapers. In these results, differences between Seattle and Spokane are readily apparent. Then, I turn to the in-depth interviews, in which the respondents' subjective perceptions of the media's treatment vary considerably from these objective findings.

Treatment of the Two Groups in the Editorial Pages

Though I read the front page first, and I like the comics, the editorial pages are my favorite part of the newspaper, for it is in these pages that a significant daily dialogue takes place. While the rest of the paper is ostensibly objective, in the editorial pages a wide variety of voices engage in a daily stream of subjective discussion. Many have a say: the paper's staff, the cartoonists, a few national pundits, and, perhaps most importantly, average citizens who feel they have something to contribute to a dialogue on any number of topics. Through the editorial pages, we get a glimpse of democracy in action, of the people having a voice. And it often does feel like a dialogue, a public working things through: people state their opinions, and within a day or two, someone else responds to that opinion. Resolution to these arguments is infrequent, but the dialogue serves as an end to itself, and as an indicator of civic life (Perrin 2002).

Of course, not everyone's voice is heard. As with any source of media, the editorial pages are run by people who, no matter how justly they feel they are performing their jobs, serve as gatekeepers of public discourse (Hilgartner and Bosk 1988). The space in the editorial pages is quite finite, and decisions must be made. There is mixed evidence regarding whether or not this gatekeeping is biased (Sigelman and Walkosz 1992; Renfro 1979). For the two newspapers in my content analysis, different levels of gatekeeping occurred. The *Spokane Spokesman-Review* publishes an average of eight to twelve letters per day, and it is estimated that around 40 percent of the letters the editorial staff receives eventually make their way onto the editorial pages. Because the *Seattle Times* serves a larger population base and generally prints fewer letters per day (four to six), around 10 percent of the letters make the final cut. To make these difficult decisions, the editorial staff uses a wide variety of screening mechanisms (length, use of profanity, etc). For example, the proportion of anti-gay letters that the editorial staff *prints* may differ from the proportion of anti-gay letters that the editorial staff *receives*. Regardless of these possible biases, it is the letters that get printed that ultimately affect the climate: they are the ones that gays and Christian conservatives read, process, and discuss with friends.

Before I turn to the type of coverage received by the two groups on the editorial pages of these two newspapers, I analyze the level of coverage. As I argued in chapter 1, an important way to read the political climate toward a group is the extent to which its issues have permeated public discourse. Of the 6,930 pieces my research assistants and I coded, 5,453 pieces concerned Christian conservative issues, and 1,811 pieces concerned gay and lesbian issues.[1] Of the pieces that concerned Christian conservative issues, the most frequent topics were abortion (2,009 pieces), youth/school issues (456), Christian conservative organizations (331), church/state separation (322), censorship (308), and declining morality (258). Of the pieces that concerned gay and lesbian issues, the most frequent topics were AIDS (514 pieces), gays and lesbians in the military (126), antidiscrimination bills (120), media coverage (110), statewide voter initiatives (103), and gay marriage (93). The prominence of these issues lines up nicely with the major issues discussed in mainstream and academic literature on these two groups.[2]

Christian conservative issues seem to have taken the spotlight more frequently than gay and lesbian issues, but the size of this difference is not constant over time, as figures 2.1 and 2.2 illustrate. In the *Seattle Times,* since the early 1980s, there has been a dramatic increase in the coverage of gay and lesbian issues, showing the entry of gay topics into mainstream discourse. Since the late 1980s, the amount of editorial coverage has ricocheted up and down, based on what was going on in the political sphere at the time. For example, the peak in 1993 was due mostly to pieces about gays in the military and an anti-gay ballot initiative. Coverage of Christian conservative issues on the editorial pages of the *Seattle Times* has been erratic as well, yet has consistently (except for 1993 and 1997) remained at a higher level than coverage of gay and lesbian issues.

The *Spokane Spokesman-Review* tells a somewhat different story. While

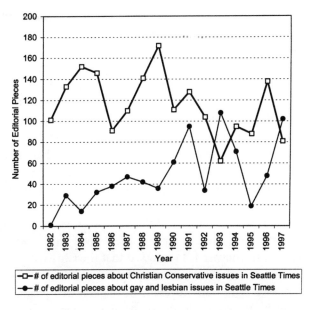

Figure 2.1. Editorial Pieces in the *Seattle Times,* 1982–1997.

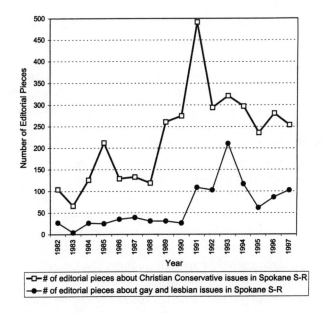

Figure 2.2. Editorial Pieces in the *Spokane Spokesman-Review,* 1982–1997.

there has been an increase in editorial coverage of gay and lesbian issues, this increase began later than in Seattle: in 1991 compared to 1985. While this is only a six-year difference, it does illustrate the later entry of gay and lesbian issues into mainstream discourse in Spokane. This level of coverage peaked in 1993, but has since remained at higher levels than in the 1980s. However, coverage of Christian conservative issues on the editorial pages of the *Spokesman-Review* has remained consistently at higher levels than coverage of gay and lesbian issues. Though this trend holds for both papers, it is more exaggerated in the *Spokesman-Review* than in the *Times*. For example, in the 1990s, the ratio of Christian-oriented to gay-oriented editorial pieces in the *Times* was approximately two to one. In the *Spokesman-Review*, it was approximately four to one.

I grant the possibility that this difference between the two groups is due to the simple fact that Christian conservatives have a wider variety of issues to cover. In chapter 1, I discussed that the Christian conservative movement is active in many different causes simultaneously. Many of these issues receive significant coverage in the editorial pages, which is a good sign that the issues are on the political and social agendas of these two cities. But what kind of coverage is it? I now address how much of this coverage is hostile toward the two groups.

I begin with the stances taken in the *Seattle Times* toward Christian conservative issues. Over the sixteen-year period my content analysis covers, the paper's editorials and cartoons have most often been in opposition to a typical Christian conservative viewpoint. While 55 percent of the editorial pieces were hostile in the early 1980s,[3] this number climbed to 68 percent in the late eighties, 70 percent in the early nineties, and then fell somewhat (to 64 percent) in the later nineties. Christian conservative readers of the *Times*, on a regular basis, are supplied with evidence that their newspaper does not share their views. However, they will find some solace in the letters that make the editorial pages, for a consistently lower proportion of these letters is hostile: 34 percent in the early eighties, 43 percent in the late eighties, and 46 percent throughout the 1990s. While voices espousing views in opposition to Christian conservatives are present, pro-Christian-conservative voices get roughly equal billing. The paper's editorial staff, when they are writing themselves, may let it be known that their views are contrary to Christian conservative stances, but these views do not seem to prevent Christian voices from being heard on the editorial pages. The climate faced by our Christian conservative reader is decidedly mixed, though leaning toward the hostile.

But what about a lesbian *Seattle Times* reader? What sort of climate does she most likely perceive? If she is looking for hostility, she'll hardly find it in the paper's editorials. Until the mid 1990s, less than 10 percent of the *Times*'s editorials took an anti-gay stance. In the later nineties, this proportion increased to 15 percent, but still remained far below the level of hostility toward Christian conservatives. Looking at the letters to the editor, the proportions have gone up and down, but have again remained relatively low: 27 percent in the early eighties, 19 percent in the late eighties, 30 percent in the early nineties, and back down to 20 percent in the later nineties. A large proportion of these hostile letters actually comes from towns neighboring Seattle, making Seattle seem that much more a safe haven. In contrast to the level of hostility faced by Seattle Christian conservatives, Seattle gay men and lesbians should come away from the editorial pages feeling pretty good about the climate of their city.

If the political climate in Spokane is indeed more conservative, this should be observable in the editorial pages of the *Spokesman-Review*. The first evidence for this is the relatively more hospitable treatment of Christian conservative issues in both the paper's editorials and the letters to the editor. Where the level of hostility in the *Seattle Times* has increased over time, the proportion of pieces in the Spokane paper that are hostile toward Christian conservative issues has decreased from 54 percent in the early eighties to 44 percent in the later nineties. While hostility seemed to be increasing among the Seattle letters to the editor, hostility among the Spokane letters hovered consistently at around 30 percent (ranging from 26 percent in the late eighties to 34 percent in the later nineties). Putting all of this together, we again see a mixed climate in the editorial pages toward Christian conservatives, but it leans toward the hospitable side, opposite from the *Seattle Times*.

A gay or lesbian reader of the *Spokesman-Review* experiences the most confusing climate of all. In the early eighties, very few hostile editorials or cartoons appeared (though bear in mind that there was hardly any coverage of gay issues in the early eighties in Spokane). This remained low (around 10 percent) through the late eighties and early nineties, but rose in the later nineties to 27 percent. Although it is a positive sign that the paper is covering gay issues more often, the editors are increasingly willing to take an anti-gay stance when they feel it is necessary (though this chance is still fairly low). The letters to the editor have made a significant shift over time toward the pro-gay side. In the early eighties, 49 percent of the letters about gay issues took an anti-gay stance. This proportion dropped to around 45 percent in the late eighties and early nineties, and then dropped further (to 36 percent) in the later nineties. With increasing hostility from the paper itself, yet decreasing hostility from the letters to the editor, the gay reader in Spokane has reason to scratch his head in bewilderment. There are other signs of an increasingly hospitable climate, though. For example, gay and lesbian letter writers in Spokane began to identify themselves in their letters *as* gay or lesbian in the 1990s, whereas this happened hardly at all in the 1980s (that is, you could not tell if a pro-gay writer was himself or herself gay or lesbian).

In the public space that is the editorial pages, we can also observe the increasing intersection of the two groups. In the coding of each editorial piece, we were careful to observe any mentions of the opposing group. For example, during the course of supporting a gay or lesbian issue, an editor, cartoonist, or letter writer might make a hostile comment directed at Christian conservatives. Over time, the trend is obvious. During the early eighties, there were twenty-three pieces in the two newspapers that simultaneously supported gay issues *and* explicitly expressed hostility toward Christians. There were 30 such pieces in the late eighties, 73 in the early nineties, and 101 in the later nineties. Increasingly, Christian conservatives have found hostility toward themselves couched within a pro-gay context. They leave the editorial pages with a clear message: pro-gay equals anti-Christian. This theme will arise again later in this chapter and throughout the rest of the book.

The editorial pages serve as a microcosm of the larger political and social environment. However, these pages are just a single section of the newspapers, and the newspapers are just a single part of larger systems of media. While Christian conservatives and gay men and lesbians think about the editorial pages, they also very closely scrutinize these other aspects of the media. In addition, they may have oppositional readings of these texts. I now turn to the interview data to assess the specific ways members of each group process these media.[4]

Christian Conservative Interpretations of the Media

Christian conservatives, in general, revile the media. In my interviews with Christian conservative community leaders and ordinary citizens in Seattle and Spokane, the respondents made a total of 143 claims about the media. Of these claims, ninety-five (or 66 percent) regarded a hostile climate while a mere twenty-nine of them (or 20 percent) regarded a hospitable climate. With regard to distinctions between the two cities, there was very little overall difference with regard to these claim proportions: 66 percent of the Seattle claims and 67 percent of the Spokane claims regarded hostility. Also, the themes that arose in the two cities were quite similar. While other chapters, as well as the gay section of this chapter, will focus more on inter-city differences, this section will not. Christian conservatives feel attacked from numerous angles when it comes to the media, resulting in a situation where they can seldom succeed. I discuss here the three dominant themes that I feel represent these claims as a whole. A general problem they discussed regarded a pervasive slant combined with a lack of understanding of their group. This led to two other problems: a lack of coverage of Christian-oriented events and sensationalistic coverage of the events or people that *were* covered.

The major source of hostility they describe was a consistent slant against Christian issues that colored all of the coverage of such issues. The source of this slant, according to the respondents, is a fundamental lack of understanding of the Christian conservative point of view. If reporters cannot understand Christian conservatives' issues and their stances on such issues, some of the respondents asked, how can they expect to report on these topics fairly? Below, I offer several examples of this concern, using interview data from both cities. In all of these examples, the respondents were making reference to the treatment their group receives from their city's newspaper. The first example comes from a Seattle pastor:

(TL: Do you feel the *Seattle Times* treats Christian issues fairly?) No. Both the *Times* and the *P.I.* are owned by the same company.[5] They both tend to, they don't tend to, they *have* a historical track record of distorting views, of minimizing numbers. (TL: Like when?) Like a rally at the legislature of several thousand people would be called several hundred in the press. And vice versa. A rally of several hundred people on the other team on moral issues would be exaggerated. And this has happened. We've participated in many, many Christian demonstrations, and to date, I have not seen an accurate statement in the press. And I don't know whether this is by design or just careless reporting. That's one thing. The press has its bias. The press is extremely secular. When it comes to Christians in public, the press doesn't get it. So they tend to, you know, when you're actually reporting on issues that you don't understand, it tends to distort your ability to report on it. (TL: Yeah, it helps to understand what you write about.) Right. They don't understand. As a general rule. Now, there are a few in the press that would understand.

Just as it wouldn't make sense to have a nonscientist report on nuclear physics, such is the case with non-Christians reporting on Christian conservative issues. No matter how hard they may try to be objective, reporters are inexorably biased due to their lack of understanding of one side of the argument. Another Seattle pastor made a similar point: "I think if you're in the world and you write a newspaper article about a Christian issue but yet you don't know all the background or what God says about this issue. So you're bringing it from a worldly point of view versus a Godly point of view." In Spokane, this same theme arose: putting non-Christian reporters in charge of representing the Christian community is just a bad idea. The following example comes from a charity director:

> (TL: Do you think the *Spokesman Review* treats Christian issues fairly?)
> No I don't think they do, because I don't think they have anyone to represent the Christian community that understands the Christian community. (TL: So it's the fact that they don't have anyone on staff there?) Yeah. Well, you know, their religious editor or one of their key writers isn't a born-again Christian. Now you're asking someone to go in and write about the church and write about Christians that doesn't even understand what true Christianity is. They are going in with the perspective, a lot of their articles, their latest way of dealing with it is to try to present issues that are related to Christianity, that are controversial and pit one Christian group against the other. That's the latest thing they are doing. And I've been caught in the midst of that twice, so I know the strategy.

In this example, Christians suffer because of the paper's need for exciting copy. Typical of movement coverage, the only time the readers see something about Christians in the paper is when there is controversy, helping to perpetuate the stereotype of the contentious Christian. Combating this stereotype is a major goal of the Christian conservatives I interviewed.

Christians sometimes try to do something about this problem. A nonactivist Christian woman, responding to the same interview question about the paper, recounted a failed attempt at activism. On a flight, she found herself seated next to one of the editors of the *Spokesman-Review* and decided to do her part to make the editorial pages a better place for Christians:

I sat with Scott Peck on a flight up to Edmonton. He's one of the editors of the editorial page, and I asked him why the Spokane paper had to be so biased. Some of the Priggee cartoons are absolutely awful. I don't think that they're fair. There hasn't been an issue recently, and I'm trying to think of some of the issues that have happened in the past. The *Spokesman Review*, though, seems to be very, very opinionated. It's my sense that they slant the news, they're not reporting it. (TL: What kind of a slant do they put on it?) [Pause] That's hard. But I remember in talking to Scott Peck, he just didn't understand what I was talking about.

The frustration in her voice was obvious to me. The paper's staff is so far removed from the Christian conservative perspective that they cannot even begin to comprehend what they are doing wrong. As a result, the persecution will persist, regardless of what Christians do. A Spokane pastor seems to have had a little more luck in pursuing changes in the *Spokesman-Review*'s policies, but the effect of his efforts were short lived:

I was appointed to a committee that was meeting for a while, and I think it was an undeniable factor as we laid down story after story and just showed them the obvious bias and slant that was there. There was a conscious effort of the paper to do something about it, and at least we were told, to bring it more balance, both in their editorial approach, and in the coverage that they give, the way they cover stories. But I have to be honest, it lasted for a little while, but I perceive no permanent change. I could take the paper in any week, sit down and show that obvious bias. (TL: So they made an attempt, but,) It was an attempt made because there was so many people canceling their subscriptions. And when you get a whole bunch of people writing in and canceling their subscriptions, not that the subscriptions mean much to a paper, but their advertising revenue is based upon what their subscription basis is. So it cuts into their advertising revenue as well.

Although I will deal with various types of activism separately in a later chapter, this serves as a good initial example: Christian conservatives try to effect change in their paper by canceling their subscriptions and by directly addressing the problem through meetings with the paper's staff. Unfortunately for them, such efforts do not produce the level of change they desire.

Christians are so concerned about this slant because its implications are enormous. For example, it can dampen the effectiveness of social movement activity. A pro-life clinic director in Seattle recounts a specific incident in which the media's liberal slant worked against their cause:

> I have seen occasions when conservative groups have tried to make a statement or gather as a group and there is an incredible amount of hostility. Groups will come and form to combat them and there is a lot of media given to them, to the hostile groups, and there's a lot of, really depending on how PC your movement is, it depends on how much PR you're going to get. (TL: So the more PC you are the more PR you get?) Yeah. And that's not always the case, but I've seen it happen. I saw it happen. I went down to Olympia [the state capital] a couple of years ago to the pro-life rally in January. And there were about four to five thousand people down there, they were just down there on the pro-life side, they just wanted to make a stand and then some of them would go talk to their legislators about what they would like to have supported. And there was a group of about fifteen young people in a group that were kind of heckling, not really bad, but just kind of heckling and chanting some stuff. . . . [Y]ou could see the news media was over there talking to this group of hecklers and had their cameras going and all this and they interviewed them and viewed them for probably half the time we were there, and there was a little bit done on the crowd, and when it came on the news later, it was like a thirty-second thing on it. Twenty seconds of it was the hecklers, and ten seconds was "Here's some people doing this." You would think they would say, yeah, there were some hecklers, but you would think they would have given the time to why are these people here, why were there five thousand people?

The interviews with Christian conservatives are peppered with such instances in which the media do not notice Christian activism as much as Christians feel they should. This bias makes Christian activism seem insignificant and ineffective.

This last example leads to the second general theme that upsets Christian conservatives. Because of their slant, the papers do not allot Christian events sufficient levels of coverage. Scholars generally agree that media attention is critical to a social movement's success (Oliver and Myers 1999; Gitlin 1980). This is particularly true if a movement seeks to attract new members, for media exposure is a major way new members can find out

In discussing the content analysis of editorial pieces, I spoke of the increasing tendency for pro-gay sentiment to be combined with anti-Christian sentiment. Christian conservatives notice such occurrences. A pastor in Spokane recounts a story involving the *Spokesman-Review*'s editorial cartoonist, whose work many Christians found offensive:

He says things that are not just kind of cutesy, they're inflammatory. Let me give you an example, one of them he put, it was a couple of years ago, when the gay issue, when the homosexual issue was still going on. Well, right at Eastertime he did a cross scene with a man hanging on a cross and he labeled him a homosexual and I think the guard there, or something, was the Christian community, so it was like we were crucifying the homosexual. Well, first, that grossly misrepresents how every evangelical Christian I know of feels toward those people. They don't hate them. They don't harbor anger at them. We've got them in our community. We've got them in our churches. We love them, but we don't agree with the position. To put, at a time when that is a Christian holiday, an individual on a cross that is a sacred symbol and you compare that with the crucifixion of Jesus Christ, and those two issues. If you had done that to the Muslim world, they'd've had a bomb at your door the next day, and they would, no doubt about it, that's why they don't do it. If you'd have done that with the Jews, you would've been called into court. I mean, you would have an incredible uproar. But you do it with evangelical Christians, and it's OK. It's expected.

Christian conservatives feel that very few groups in society are subject to ridicule like they are. Some of this ridicule is connected to the progress the movement is making. As gays and lesbians become more accepted, those who continue to speak out against them—such as some Christian conservatives—are shunned.

This last interview excerpt introduces the third major theme. Christian conservatives are upset not only about the lack of coverage of their issues. They are often equally upset when they do receive coverage because it is not the *kind* of coverage they want. Again and again, Christian conservatives say, the media paint them as foolish and dangerous extremists. Often, they say, when Christian conservatives are discussed in the media, only the most extreme people, attitudes, and behaviors are mentioned. This phenomenon comes in basically two forms. First, Christians are lumped together with truly extremist groups. Second, the media sensationalizes Christian activities in order to attract readers.

about the movement. Christian conservatives, with their evangelistic impulse, consider such matters to be extremely important. This concern is often connected with disappointment in a media system that has let Christians down in this respect. No matter how attention-worthy their events, Christians seem to be denied coverage. There were many examples of this. Below are two of them. The first is from a pastor of a large church near Seattle, the second is from a Spokane activist:

For example, every year, we have a big production here: the Living Christmas Tree. And we have thirty-five to forty thousand people come here to see it. It's basically the biggest Christmas show in town. But they wouldn't dream of coming out and covering any of that. They'll cover some Hanukkah, some people downtown with AIDS lighting a candle or something, but they would never think of coming to cover something like this, even though it's bigger and more spectacular.

You know, I think that it's sad that they don't give, I think when they see something come across their table that's strictly Christian, I think the media sets it aside and doesn't give it coverage. For instance, we've got the Christian Worker's Conference here in town. It's the largest Christian training conference in the country. Well, Spokane doesn't have, well, it has the largest Bloomsday [a running race], it has the largest, and look what they do with Bloomsday. And with the 3-on-3 [basketball] tournament. I mean, the media covers it like crazy. Well, you know anything that is the largest in the country should be covered very well. I don't care what it is. It should be covered. But we don't. I mean, we send them media kits and we send them information on it and we offer them interviews with the speakers. They come from all over the world. They don't do anything on it. And I am convinced it's because it is strictly Christian. There's nothing else it's about; it's just Christian. It's training Christian leaders to be good leaders. But it's the largest one in the country. There's 7,000 people coming here from like nine different states and like three countries or more. And 1,400 churches are represented. That's a big thing, and they don't cover it at all.

Each of these events, as well as those recounted in other examples, has specific purposes within the Christian conservative movement: to build solidarity, to train people to be more effective in their activism. However, an additional goal is to garner media attention in order to show that

Christians do play vital roles in their communities, and to bring more people to the Christian community. The local media, according to some of my respondents, do not believe that Christians play an important enough role in their communities to warrant such attention, angering some Christians terribly.

A feeling of relative deprivation produces even greater frustration. Christian conservatives see themselves as an oppressed minority group that receives far less media attention than other minority groups. The group that is used most commonly as a reference point? Gay men and lesbians. Here is the first example of a recurrent theme of the book: Christian conservatives think a lot about gays and lesbians, interpreting gay progress as a sign of anti-Christian hostility. They compare and contrast the reception of their activities with the reception of the activities of the gay and lesbian rights movement. With regard to the media, their conclusion is simple: the gay movement receives an inordinate level of media coverage when contrasted to the coverage received by Christian conservatives.

This contrast appeared in interviews in both cities, sometimes in very detailed ways, providing evidence that this is a lightning rod for Christian conservative attention. For example, a pastor in Spokane told the following story:

> But I don't think their editorial staff, I know almost all of them, and sat in meetings with them. I don't think they're out to get us. I do think they come with a very liberal bias, however. So that when they frame an issue, they often frame it so that the liberal bias looks better than the conservative bias. You know, case in point, a couple of weeks ago there was a gay pride march. It had about a hundred, no, how many did they say, maybe this year it had a thousand, five hundred, I don't know, it was less than a thousand, I know. Well they've got, you know, you get a picture of it as an entire group, as many of the people as you can see, you know, filling the street, front page of the "IN" section, which is the regional section. However, the pro-life march, which occurs annually as well and draws anywhere from three to five thousand, never once in the four years that I've been here have I seen a picture of the entire group, it's always one or two individuals. It's usually buried somewhere back in the section. They will say, well, because it's not newsworthy, it happens every year, it's nothing new. Not much difference with gay pride. It happens every year, not terribly new. So, and then they will run not only that, but several articles usu-

ally about the gay and lesbian debate that is going on, an framed from the gay and lesbian position. It will hardl framed from an evangelical perspective.

This pastor's observation almost resembles an equa various factors (size of event, annual nature), the key is highly significant, and biased against Christian cons gelical perspective—that homosexuality is a sin—has alized that it is no longer worthy of mainstream news state in Seattle, the respondents made the same kinds contrast in Seattle is particularly striking since the Se and the annual March for Jesus tend to fall around th tle charity organizer, and then a Seattle pastor, explai

> I didn't pay a lot of attention to how it was covered l two years ago, for example, there was the opposites of and there was also, I don't know if it was the same same day, there was also a gay pride march and the not covered. Not at all and there were hundreds, th people getting out and marching and not being of public march. I guess there was some music involve have been offensive for some people [laughs] I gue key. But that was, that wasn't equally covered.

> I don't think they treat Christians or Christianity f know, there can be a demonstration downtown of there will be fifty in the demonstration, and they'll page. You know, we can have a youth group here like we had here last Friday night, and the media ig of thing where the obvious is basically ignored. The parade and make headlines out of that, but they tians march in the general Praise March and neve the newspapers.

In Christian conservative minds, their moveme are roughly opposites. And for the opposite to g amount of the finite media space is completely u two groups are engaging in what they perceive to

Concerning public image, Christian conservatives are sensitive to denominational and philosophical differences and take great offense when they are wrongly connected to a group whose ideology they do not espouse. They believe that in the eyes of the media, they are often guilty by incorrect association. This is especially true in Spokane, which is geographically quite close to Hayden Lake, Idaho. Hayden Lake gained a notorious reputation in the 1990s for being home to numerous white supremacist and militia groups. Sometimes, these groups ride under the banner of the Christian Identity movement (Aho 1994). The Christian conservatives I interviewed in Spokane took pains to distance themselves from these groups. The media, they claim, did not help in this matter. Here are two examples of this: the first from a pastor and the second from a political activist:

> I think we'll get probably blamed for a lot of stuff that a lot of kooks, you know, the right wing racist groups. (TL: Do you see these people becoming more closely associated with you?) I see that, yeah, I think, in the media, that's what they're doing, they're tying us with those people, and that is simply not true. Those groups are very fringe. I don't know of a single evangelical Christian that would support those causes or those groups.

> So the media has done a very good job of painting the Christian community as this radical abortion burning, I have a feeling that many of the abortion clinics that are bombed are bombed by the people who want to keep providing abortion because that's the way to get attention, and they blame it, that's the way Hitler did it in Germany. He blamed the Jews, only he did it. And it's an excellent example of what may be happening here. That's pretty strong stuff. I don't know if I could say that for public comment. It *is* a rather strong opinion.

At this point in the interview, I couldn't help scooting a little farther away from her on the park bench we were sharing. To be fair, though, this respondent was the only one to make such a claim. Although discussion of extremist linking was more common in Spokane, it occurred in Seattle as well, as one does not need to be geographically close to an extremist group in order to be connected to it. These extremists do exist, my respondents admit, but it is wrong to use such a large brush to paint all Christians in a negative light. Below are two Seattle examples of this juxtaposition, the first from a pastor, the second from the director of a pro-life clinic:

The press, of course, tends to, they tend to give voice to the vocal minority. They write down their words. So it's not so much the press itself, even though sometimes the press also uses inflammatory words to describe Christians. And then of course also in our ranks there are a few people who, who I would have to carefully call idiots who are very loud-mouthed, are insensitive, who speak too strongly without discretion. So within the ranks of the Christian community, there's always this fringe element. (TL: So the press tends to focus on them more?) Oh yes, the press *loves* those elements. It's drawn to them. But that happens on the other side as well. Within organizations, those people who speak radically tend to get a lot of press.

Well, for instance, there was a, up on Capitol Hill, at Planned Parenthood up on Capitol Hill, there was a big news thing about an explosion, and the right-wing extremists were blowing up the abortion clinic. And within a couple of days they found out that some guy several houses away had had a backfire on his car, and somebody had left a backpack against the wall at the clinic, and so everybody assumed that there was an explosive in this and this guy didn't even know. And it was on the news, and there was all this, the right-wing extremists have done this again, and he didn't even know until he turned on the news, that it was his little explosion, and he called in and told them that, and there was this little article a couple of days later, like a one-inch article about ten pages in, that said, oh by the way, it was just a little bloop. But when it came on, there was a big thing, front-page news kind of thing about all the right-wing Christian extremists had done this, and that's pretty typical, that they didn't go back and make it right, nor did they even check out their facts before they flipped out, and so there's kind of a sad atmosphere of make assumptions, blame, and then if you have to go back and retract, just do it very tiny. Which is too bad. So people get the wrong idea. Not that there aren't people out there that do that, whatever flag they choose to come under, but it's sad that you see that slant.

The other major factor that paints Christian conservatives in a bad light is the media's tendency to engage in sensationalism. In this age of five hundred channels, the media do have a penchant for the extreme story. Such attention paid to extremism and sensationalism, Christian conservatives argue, disadvantages Christians in the public sphere. Both Christian politicians and Christian social movement organizations pay a dear price.

I illustrate this connection by discussing two specific topics. The first is the political campaign of Ellen Craswell, a Christian conservative who won the Republican gubernatorial primary in Washington State in 1996. She was the subject of intense media scrutiny, and eventually lost the election by a decisive margin (60 percent/40 percent). Many of the respondents in both cities felt that Craswell was treated unfairly by the press, which concentrated on areas Christians felt were inappropriate. A nonactivist Christian in Spokane waxed philosophical:

> But every time I listened to her speak, I thought she was very eloquent and articulate and everything else, and intelligent, but when you watched the news, it was about what a radical Christian she was. . . . I'm not sure if my perspective is sound, but I do recall . . . listening to her speak and thinking this is a wonderful woman, you know, who could do our state a lot of good, and then you watch the news, "Well this is a radical Christian Bible-thumping woman who wants to shove her ideology down everyone's throat."

Other Christian respondents were similarly befuddled: what they saw as a woman with conservative yet reasonable views was being painted as an extremist by the press, and painting *them* as extremists by extension. In Seattle, a woman who recently ran her own unsuccessful campaign (for the local school board) empathized with Craswell's plight:

> You look at the government, the gubernatorial election, between Locke and Craswell, and they were asking, they were nailing Craswell on issues that they weren't mutually asking Locke about, like they kept getting hung up on the role issues between her and her husband. Nobody asked Locke about how he and his wife divided power in their family. So, no, I don't think it's a fair shake. I'd like to see Christians being able to run on a platform where Christianity isn't the issue. You know, I'm not running because I'm a Christian, I'm running because I have something to say and would be able to represent some constituencies and I don't see that happening.

Politicians who just happen to be Christian conservatives find this aspect of their lives flung into the forefront as they try to accomplish their political goals; their religious identity is given master status, and they feel this is unfair.

It is not only individuals who are subject to such scrutiny, but also entire social-movement groups. While I was conducting my interviews, Promise Keepers was one of the key Christian conservative groups. This group is made up of Christian men who attended both small support groups and large stadium-sized rallies with the goal of becoming better husbands and fathers. Many progressives saw the group as a strategic attempt to put women back into a barefoot and kitchen-bound place (Messner 1997). While Promise Keepers garnered major media attention, much of it was not positive. The media, Christian conservative respondents maintained, predictably sided with the progressives. Below are two versions of this story, the first from a youth pastor in Seattle and the second from a church administrator in Spokane:

> A good example would be that men's thing, the Promise Keepers, and just the antagonistic report on that that would just from the very word go, and of course there would be a battle in the editorials but I would think they generally have a negative view toward that. . . . I thought that generally of all the articles that I read, I think they all, most of them had a negative tone. About the dangers of this. They may say, "This is a good thing BUT." There's always a big BUT.

> I am not one of those radical-right guys who say that the media is out to destroy America, but I think that there is a certain, you know, I was thinking even with the Promise Keeper agenda. Which was just last weekend. And I think it was promoted the way a non-, someone who doesn't know anything about Promise Keepers, would look at it, you would get the view from the opponents, instead of, what I didn't like, they allow for example NOW, other organizations, to interpret the intentions of Promise Keepers instead of letting Promise Keepers explain their intentions. And so you go away with the feeling that Promise Keepers was a bad thing because NOW says they are. . . . (TL: So they would report of the weekend's events, but they wouldn't have representatives from Promise Keepers there?) Oh, no, no, no. They would have, they would have a Promise Keeper, but it would be: "This is what people say about Promise Keepers, defend yourself about *this*." On the defense, instead of saying: "Tell us about Promise Keepers."

Roughly an equal number of respondents praised the media for their coverage of recent Promise Keepers events. Many were pleasantly surprised by what they saw as increased and higher-quality coverage.

In fact, as I mentioned at the beginning of this section, there were a significant number of Christian conservative media claims that illustrated a hospitable climate. Some pointed to the presence of Christians within the local media organizations. Others pointed to the media's increasing tendency to feature Christian-oriented shows on TV such as *Touched by an Angel* or *Seventh Heaven*. Others offered examples of positive coverage. However, for the most part, Christian conservatives in both cities felt constantly betrayed by the media. According to most respondents, if given the chance, the media moved the climate in a hostile direction rather than a hospitable one.

Gay and Lesbian Interpretations of the Media

Like Christian conservatives, gay men and lesbians pay very close attention to how they are treated by the media. Unlike Christian conservatives, gay men and lesbians often perceive the media climate as hospitable. In my interviews with gay men and lesbians, both activists and nonactivists, the respondents made a total of 121 claims about the media. Of these claims, forty-three (or 36 percent) felt there was a hostile climate and fifty-three (or 44 percent) thought it was a hospitable climate. Thus, while gays and lesbians still sense a fair amount of hostility coming from the media, this level is markedly lower than that perceived by Christian conservatives.

Another general contrast to the Christian conservative claims was the difference between the amount of hostility perceived by Seattle and Spokane respondents. While the difference is not huge, it is the *direction* of the difference that is striking. Spokane respondents perceived a more hospitable climate than those in Seattle. Among the Spokane claims, 32 percent were hostile, compared to Seattle's 40 percent. This finding is counterintuitive, especially given the clearly more hospitable climate in the editorial pages of the *Seattle Times*. To understand what is going on, we must consider the historical context and the pace of social change in these two environments. As I'll show in coming chapters, life is changing quickly for Spokane gay men and lesbians. The gay rights movement in Spokane is relatively young and has experienced a fair amount of success in its few years of activity. One of these successes is better coverage, in both quantity and quality, from the media. A full third of the hospitable media claims from Spokane respondents concerned *increasing* hospitableness. The Spokane gay rights movement is like the unpopular child on the playground who has finally found a friend, and that new friend is the Spokane media. Overcome with gratefulness, such a child is unlikely to say anything bad about his new friend, especially since that friend has the power to influence the other children. In contrast, Seattle gay respondents seemed to have the luxury of looking at the media with a more critical eye.

A number of specific themes arose frequently in the gay and lesbian interviews. I begin with comparisons to Christian conservative themes. One theme the two groups shared was their concern with sensationalism. Gay men and lesbians in both cities often felt that their media succumbed to sensationalism in their coverage of their group. However, whereas the most common concern to Christians was abortion-clinic bombing, Idaho-dwelling extremists, gay men and lesbians had a far different attention-grabbing nemesis: drag queens. Again and again in the interviews, especially in Spokane, the respondents pointed out the extent to which the media would spotlight drag queens at the annual gay pride parade, often at the expense of covering other aspects of the gay and lesbian community. I illustrate this concern with two examples. The first is from the organizer of the Spokane pride parade, and the second from one of Spokane's all-around gay activists:

> Channel 6 has a tendency to sensationalize. Channel 4 we get nothing. Channel 2 is pretty good. (TL: Sensationalize meaning?) Well, like at the pride march they searched out the one lone drag queen in drag. You know, we have two thousand people there and, you know, they go find the drag queen. Things like that.

> Traditionally, Q6 has been horrible. But this last year was the first year in which we got positive coverage of the pride march. Q6 was, it was hysterical, a couple of years ago, when we were meeting at the beginning of the march. And there were protesters there. And one of the marchers, you could tell he had been drinking, and they got into an altercation. I mean, some punches were thrown. But, it was broken up really, really quickly, because we had all these peacekeepers there. It barely had time to start before they were in there, and then the police came and arrested them both. So Q6, which usually focuses on drag queens, which we have hardly any of in the Spokane pride march, I mean, we'll have one thousand people, and maybe one or two drag queens. And maybe two or three people in leather. And that's *all* you'll see on the coverage. But another thing too, that year

about the movement. Christian conservatives, with their evangelistic impulse, consider such matters to be extremely important. This concern is often connected with disappointment in a media system that has let Christians down in this respect. No matter how attention-worthy their events, Christians seem to be denied coverage. There were many examples of this. Below are two of them. The first is from a pastor of a large church near Seattle, the second is from a Spokane activist:

> For example, every year, we have a big production here: the Living Christmas Tree. And we have thirty-five to forty thousand people come here to see it. It's basically the biggest Christmas show in town. But they wouldn't dream of coming out and covering any of that. They'll cover some Hanukkah, some people downtown with AIDS lighting a candle or something, but they would never think of coming to cover something like this, even though it's bigger and more spectacular.

> You know, I think that it's sad that they don't give, I think when they see something come across their table that's strictly Christian, I think the media sets it aside and doesn't give it coverage. For instance, we've got the Christian Worker's Conference here in town. It's the largest Christian training conference in the country. Well, Spokane doesn't have, well, it has the largest Bloomsday [a running race], it has the largest, and look what they do with Bloomsday. And with the 3-on-3 [basketball] tournament. I mean, the media covers it like crazy. Well, you know anything that is the largest in the country should be covered very well. I don't care what it is. It should be covered. But we don't. I mean, we send them media kits and we send them information on it and we offer them interviews with the speakers. They come from all over the world. They don't do anything on it. And I am convinced it's because it is strictly Christian. There's nothing else it's about; it's just Christian. It's training Christian leaders to be good leaders. But it's the largest one in the country. There's 7,000 people coming here from like nine different states and like three countries or more. And 1,400 churches are represented. That's a big thing, and they don't cover it at all.

Each of these events, as well as those recounted in other examples, has specific purposes within the Christian conservative movement: to build solidarity, to train people to be more effective in their activism. However, an additional goal is to garner media attention in order to show that

Christians do play vital roles in their communities, and to bring more people to the Christian community. The local media, according to some of my respondents, do not believe that Christians play an important enough role in their communities to warrant such attention, angering some Christians terribly.

A feeling of relative deprivation produces even greater frustration. Christian conservatives see themselves as an oppressed minority group that receives far less media attention than other minority groups. The group that is used most commonly as a reference point? Gay men and lesbians. Here is the first example of a recurrent theme of the book: Christian conservatives think a lot about gays and lesbians, interpreting gay progress as a sign of anti-Christian hostility. They compare and contrast the reception of their activities with the reception of the activities of the gay and lesbian rights movement. With regard to the media, their conclusion is simple: the gay movement receives an inordinate level of media coverage when contrasted to the coverage received by Christian conservatives.

This contrast appeared in interviews in both cities, sometimes in very detailed ways, providing evidence that this is a lightning rod for Christian conservative attention. For example, a pastor in Spokane told the following story:

> But I don't think their editorial staff, I know almost all of them, and sat in meetings with them. I don't think they're out to get us. I do think they come with a very liberal bias, however. So that when they frame an issue, they often frame it so that the liberal bias looks better than the conservative bias. You know, case in point, a couple of weeks ago there was a gay pride march. It had about a hundred, no, how many did they say, maybe this year it had a thousand, five hundred, I don't know, it was less than a thousand, I know. Well they've got, you know, you get a picture of it as an entire group, as many of the people as you can see, you know, filling the street, front page of the "IN" section, which is the regional section. However, the pro-life march, which occurs annually as well and draws anywhere from three to five thousand, never once in the four years that I've been here have I seen a picture of the entire group, it's always one or two individuals. It's usually buried somewhere back in the section. They will say, well, because it's not newsworthy, it happens every year, it's nothing new. Not much difference with gay pride. It happens every year, not terribly new. So, and then they will run not only that, but several articles usu-

ally about the gay and lesbian debate that is going on, and it will always be framed from the gay and lesbian position. It will hardly ever, if ever, be framed from an evangelical perspective.

This pastor's observation almost resembles an equation: controlling for various factors (size of event, annual nature), the key variable (the cause) is highly significant, and biased against Christian conservatives. The evangelical perspective—that homosexuality is a sin—has become so marginalized that it is no longer worthy of mainstream news coverage. Across the state in Seattle, the respondents made the same kinds of observations. The contrast in Seattle is particularly striking since the Seattle gay pride march and the annual March for Jesus tend to fall around the same time. A Seattle charity organizer, and then a Seattle pastor, explain:

> I didn't pay a lot of attention to how it was covered last year, but I know two years ago, for example, there was the opposites of the March for Jesus and there was also, I don't know if it was the same weekend or even the same day, there was also a gay pride march and the March for Jesus was not covered. Not at all and there were hundreds, there were *hundreds* of people getting out and marching and not being offensive. It was just a public march. I guess there was some music involved, I guess that could have been offensive for some people [laughs] I guess, if they weren't on key. But that was, that wasn't equally covered.

> I don't think they treat Christians or Christianity fairly. I think that, you know, there can be a demonstration downtown of pro-homosexuals, and there will be fifty in the demonstration, and they'll put that on the front page. You know, we can have a youth group here of seven hundred kids, like we had here last Friday night, and the media ignores that. It's the type of thing where the obvious is basically ignored. They can have a gay pride parade and make headlines out of that, but they can have 15,000 Christians march in the general Praise March and never barely mention it in the newspapers.

In Christian conservative minds, their movement and the gay movement are roughly opposites. And for the opposite to garner a disproportionate amount of the finite media space is completely unfair, especially when the two groups are engaging in what they perceive to be parallel activities.

In discussing the content analysis of editorial pieces, I spoke of the increasing tendency for pro-gay sentiment to be combined with anti-Christian sentiment. Christian conservatives notice such occurrences. A pastor in Spokane recounts a story involving the *Spokesman-Review*'s editorial cartoonist, whose work many Christians found offensive:

> He says things that are not just kind of cutesy, they're inflammatory. Let me give you an example, one of them he put, it was a couple of years ago, when the gay issue, when the homosexual issue was still going on. Well, right at Eastertime he did a cross scene with a man hanging on a cross and he labeled him a homosexual and I think the guard there, or something, was the Christian community, so it was like we were crucifying the homosexual. Well, first, that grossly misrepresents how every evangelical Christian I know of feels toward those people. They don't hate them. They don't harbor anger at them. We've got them in our community. We've got them in our churches. We love them, but we don't agree with the position. To put, at a time when that is a Christian holiday, an individual on a cross that is a sacred symbol and you compare that with the crucifixion of Jesus Christ, and those two issues. If you had done that to the Muslim world, they'd've had a bomb at your door the next day, and they would, no doubt about it, that's why they don't do it. If you'd have done that with the Jews, you would've been called into court. I mean, you would have an incredible uproar. But you do it with evangelical Christians, and it's OK. It's expected.

Christian conservatives feel that very few groups in society are subject to ridicule like they are. Some of this ridicule is connected to the progress the gay movement is making. As gays and lesbians become more accepted, those who continue to speak out against them—such as some Christian conservatives—are shunned.

This last interview excerpt introduces the third major theme. Christian conservatives are upset not only about the lack of coverage of their issues. They are often equally upset when they do receive coverage because it is not the *kind* of coverage they want. Again and again, Christian conservatives say, the media paint them as foolish and dangerous extremists. Often, they say, when Christian conservatives are discussed in the media, only the most extreme people, attitudes, and behaviors are mentioned. This phenomenon comes in basically two forms. First, Christians are lumped together with truly extremist groups. Second, the media sensationalizes Christian activities in order to attract readers.

Concerning public image, Christian conservatives are sensitive to denominational and philosophical differences and take great offense when they are wrongly connected to a group whose ideology they do not espouse. They believe that in the eyes of the media, they are often guilty by incorrect association. This is especially true in Spokane, which is geographically quite close to Hayden Lake, Idaho. Hayden Lake gained a notorious reputation in the 1990s for being home to numerous white supremacist and militia groups. Sometimes, these groups ride under the banner of the Christian Identity movement (Aho 1994). The Christian conservatives I interviewed in Spokane took pains to distance themselves from these groups. The media, they claim, did not help in this matter. Here are two examples of this: the first from a pastor and the second from a political activist:

I think we'll get probably blamed for a lot of stuff that a lot of kooks, you know, the right wing racist groups. (TL: Do you see these people becoming more closely associated with you?) I see that, yeah, I think, in the media, that's what they're doing, they're tying us with those people, and that is simply not true. Those groups are very fringe. I don't know of a single evangelical Christian that would support those causes or those groups.

So the media has done a very good job of painting the Christian community as this radical abortion burning, I have a feeling that many of the abortion clinics that are bombed are bombed by the people who want to keep providing abortion because that's the way to get attention, and they blame it, that's the way Hitler did it in Germany. He blamed the Jews, only he did it. And it's an excellent example of what may be happening here. That's pretty strong stuff. I don't know if I could say that for public comment. It *is* a rather strong opinion.

At this point in the interview, I couldn't help scooting a little farther away from her on the park bench we were sharing. To be fair, though, this respondent was the only one to make such a claim. Although discussion of extremist linking was more common in Spokane, it occurred in Seattle as well, as one does not need to be geographically close to an extremist group in order to be connected to it. These extremists do exist, my respondents admit, but it is wrong to use such a large brush to paint all Christians in a negative light. Below are two Seattle examples of this juxtaposition, the first from a pastor, the second from the director of a pro-life clinic:

The press, of course, tends to, they tend to give voice to the vocal minority. They write down their words. So it's not so much the press itself, even though sometimes the press also uses inflammatory words to describe Christians. And then of course also in our ranks there are a few people who, who I would have to carefully call idiots who are very loud-mouthed, are insensitive, who speak too strongly without discretion. So within the ranks of the Christian community, there's always this fringe element. (TL: So the press tends to focus on them more?) Oh yes, the press *loves* those elements. It's drawn to them. But that happens on the other side as well. Within organizations, those people who speak radically tend to get a lot of press.

Well, for instance, there was a, up on Capitol Hill, at Planned Parenthood up on Capitol Hill, there was a big news thing about an explosion, and the right-wing extremists were blowing up the abortion clinic. And within a couple of days they found out that some guy several houses away had had a backfire on his car, and somebody had left a backpack against the wall at the clinic, and so everybody assumed that there was an explosive in this and this guy didn't even know. And it was on the news, and there was all this, the right-wing extremists have done this again, and he didn't even know until he turned on the news, that it was his little explosion, and he called in and told them that, and there was this little article a couple of days later, like a one-inch article about ten pages in, that said, oh by the way, it was just a little bloop. But when it came on, there was a big thing, front-page news kind of thing about all the right-wing Christian extremists had done this, and that's pretty typical, that they didn't go back and make it right, nor did they even check out their facts before they flipped out, and so there's kind of a sad atmosphere of make assumptions, blame, and then if you have to go back and retract, just do it very tiny. Which is too bad. So people get the wrong idea. Not that there aren't people out there that do that, whatever flag they choose to come under, but it's sad that you see that slant.

The other major factor that paints Christian conservatives in a bad light is the media's tendency to engage in sensationalism. In this age of five hundred channels, the media do have a penchant for the extreme story. Such attention paid to extremism and sensationalism, Christian conservatives argue, disadvantages Christians in the public sphere. Both Christian politicians and Christian social movement organizations pay a dear price.

I illustrate this connection by discussing two specific topics. The first is the political campaign of Ellen Craswell, a Christian conservative who won the Republican gubernatorial primary in Washington State in 1996. She was the subject of intense media scrutiny, and eventually lost the election by a decisive margin (60 percent/40 percent). Many of the respondents in both cities felt that Craswell was treated unfairly by the press, which concentrated on areas Christians felt were inappropriate. A nonactivist Christian in Spokane waxed philosophical:

> But every time I listened to her speak, I thought she was very eloquent and articulate and everything else, and intelligent, but when you watched the news, it was about what a radical Christian she was. . . . I'm not sure if my perspective is sound, but I do recall . . . listening to her speak and thinking this is a wonderful woman, you know, who could do our state a lot of good, and then you watch the news, "Well this is a radical Christian Bible-thumping woman who wants to shove her ideology down everyone's throat."

Other Christian respondents were similarly befuddled: what they saw as a woman with conservative yet reasonable views was being painted as an extremist by the press, and painting *them* as extremists by extension. In Seattle, a woman who recently ran her own unsuccessful campaign (for the local school board) empathized with Craswell's plight:

> You look at the government, the gubernatorial election, between Locke and Craswell, and they were asking, they were nailing Craswell on issues that they weren't mutually asking Locke about, like they kept getting hung up on the role issues between her and her husband. Nobody asked Locke about how he and his wife divided power in their family. So, no, I don't think it's a fair shake. I'd like to see Christians being able to run on a platform where Christianity isn't the issue. You know, I'm not running because I'm a Christian, I'm running because I have something to say and would be able to represent some constituencies and I don't see that happening.

Politicians who just happen to be Christian conservatives find this aspect of their lives flung into the forefront as they try to accomplish their political goals; their religious identity is given master status, and they feel this is unfair.

It is not only individuals who are subject to such scrutiny, but also entire social-movement groups. While I was conducting my interviews, Promise Keepers was one of the key Christian conservative groups. This group is made up of Christian men who attended both small support groups and large stadium-sized rallies with the goal of becoming better husbands and fathers. Many progressives saw the group as a strategic attempt to put women back into a barefoot and kitchen-bound place (Messner 1997). While Promise Keepers garnered major media attention, much of it was not positive. The media, Christian conservative respondents maintained, predictably sided with the progressives. Below are two versions of this story, the first from a youth pastor in Seattle and the second from a church administrator in Spokane:

> A good example would be that men's thing, the Promise Keepers, and just the antagonistic report on that that would just from the very word go, and of course there would be a battle in the editorials but I would think they generally have a negative view toward that. . . . I thought that generally of all the articles that I read, I think they all, most of them had a negative tone. About the dangers of this. They may say, "This is a good thing BUT." There's always a big BUT.

> I am not one of those radical-right guys who say that the media is out to destroy America, but I think that there is a certain, you know, I was thinking even with the Promise Keeper agenda. Which was just last weekend. And I think it was promoted the way a non-, someone who doesn't know anything about Promise Keepers, would look at it, you would get the view from the opponents, instead of, what I didn't like, they allow for example NOW, other organizations, to interpret the intentions of Promise Keepers instead of letting Promise Keepers explain their intentions. And so you go away with the feeling that Promise Keepers was a bad thing because NOW says they are. . . . (TL: So they would report of the weekend's events, but they wouldn't have representatives from Promise Keepers there?) Oh, no, no, no. They would have, they would have a Promise Keeper, but it would be: "This is what people say about Promise Keepers, defend yourself about *this.*" On the defense, instead of saying: "Tell us about Promise Keepers."

Roughly an equal number of respondents praised the media for their coverage of recent Promise Keepers events. Many were pleasantly surprised by what they saw as increased and higher-quality coverage.

In fact, as I mentioned at the beginning of this section, there were a significant number of Christian conservative media claims that illustrated a hospitable climate. Some pointed to the presence of Christians within the local media organizations. Others pointed to the media's increasing tendency to feature Christian-oriented shows on TV such as *Touched by an Angel* or *Seventh Heaven*. Others offered examples of positive coverage. However, for the most part, Christian conservatives in both cities felt constantly betrayed by the media. According to most respondents, if given the chance, the media moved the climate in a hostile direction rather than a hospitable one.

Gay and Lesbian Interpretations of the Media

Like Christian conservatives, gay men and lesbians pay very close attention to how they are treated by the media. Unlike Christian conservatives, gay men and lesbians often perceive the media climate as hospitable. In my interviews with gay men and lesbians, both activists and nonactivists, the respondents made a total of 121 claims about the media. Of these claims, forty-three (or 36 percent) felt there was a hostile climate and fifty-three (or 44 percent) thought it was a hospitable climate. Thus, while gays and lesbians still sense a fair amount of hostility coming from the media, this level is markedly lower than that perceived by Christian conservatives.

Another general contrast to the Christian conservative claims was the difference between the amount of hostility perceived by Seattle and Spokane respondents. While the difference is not huge, it is the *direction* of the difference that is striking. Spokane respondents perceived a more hospitable climate than those in Seattle. Among the Spokane claims, 32 percent were hostile, compared to Seattle's 40 percent. This finding is counterintuitive, especially given the clearly more hospitable climate in the editorial pages of the *Seattle Times*. To understand what is going on, we must consider the historical context and the pace of social change in these two environments. As I'll show in coming chapters, life is changing quickly for Spokane gay men and lesbians. The gay rights movement in Spokane is relatively young and has experienced a fair amount of success in its few years of activity. One of these successes is better coverage, in both quantity and quality, from the media. A full third of the hospitable media claims from Spokane respondents concerned *increasing* hospitableness. The Spokane gay rights movement is like the unpopular child on the playground who has finally found a friend, and that new friend is the Spokane media. Overcome with gratefulness, such a child is unlikely to say anything bad about his new friend, especially since that friend has the power to influence the other children. In contrast, Seattle gay respondents seemed to have the luxury of looking at the media with a more critical eye.

A number of specific themes arose frequently in the gay and lesbian interviews. I begin with comparisons to Christian conservative themes. One theme the two groups shared was their concern with sensationalism. Gay men and lesbians in both cities often felt that their media succumbed to sensationalism in their coverage of their group. However, whereas the most common concern to Christians was abortion-clinic bombing, Idaho-dwelling extremists, gay men and lesbians had a far different attention-grabbing nemesis: drag queens. Again and again in the interviews, especially in Spokane, the respondents pointed out the extent to which the media would spotlight drag queens at the annual gay pride parade, often at the expense of covering other aspects of the gay and lesbian community. I illustrate this concern with two examples. The first is from the organizer of the Spokane pride parade, and the second from one of Spokane's all-around gay activists:

Channel 6 has a tendency to sensationalize. Channel 4 we get nothing. Channel 2 is pretty good. (TL: Sensationalize meaning?) Well, like at the pride march they searched out the one lone drag queen in drag. You know, we have two thousand people there and, you know, they go find the drag queen. Things like that.

Traditionally, Q6 has been horrible. But this last year was the first year in which we got positive coverage of the pride march. Q6 was, it was hysterical, a couple of years ago, when we were meeting at the beginning of the march. And there were protesters there. And one of the marchers, you could tell he had been drinking, and they got into an altercation. I mean, some punches were thrown. But, it was broken up really, really quickly, because we had all these peacekeepers there. It barely had time to start before they were in there, and then the police came and arrested them both. So Q6, which usually focuses on drag queens, which we have hardly any of in the Spokane pride march, I mean, we'll have one thousand people, and maybe one or two drag queens. And maybe two or three people in leather. And that's *all* you'll see on the coverage. But another thing too, that year we had the altercation, their little teaser . . . the only year we got a front spot with them: "Gay pride march turns ugly, film at 11." I laughed so hard because it was a *nothing* story. It was, like, such a dumb story. Most people who were even there, lined up, didn't even know it happened because it happened so quickly. And that was the total focus of Q6. Last year, though, was the first year that it was a little more positive. Channel Two has always had the better stuff. Better coverage. This year, their stuff was great. They had a group from North Idaho marching, they had the woman with the stroller telling why she's bringing her little baby there, because the day-care worker that she takes her daughter to is a lesbian and she wanted to teach her tolerance and respect. I mean, it was great. Great sound bites. You know, stuff that we like. Film of drag queens is great, but sometimes they're so stupid, just "Woo Woo!" Well, that's neat, but. . .

Coverage of the pride activities is so crucial in Spokane because it is often the best chance for the general public to stop and contemplate gay and lesbian issues. And if all the public will see is drag queens, oozing with otherness, then it is unlikely that they will be able to relate to gays and lesbians. Better coverage, this last activist suggests, is the less exciting stuff: women pushing strollers, "normal"-looking people.

Gays and lesbians, like Christian conservatives, paid attention to the level of coverage their activities garnered from the media. Unlike Christian conservatives, though, most gay men and lesbians were at least satisfied if not quite pleased with the level of coverage their group received. Spokane respondents were particularly impressed by the increased frequency with which the media covered their increasing level of movement activity. While the feelings of the Spokane respondents are predominantly positive, there is some difference of opinion, depending on whether the respondents are looking at it currently or retrospectively. If they looked at it retrospectively, they were more likely to speak positively. If they focused only on the present, they were likely to speak more negatively. Here is an example of each, the first from an activist, the second from a nonactivist:

(TL: Do you think the *Spokesman Review* treats gay and lesbian issues fairly?) They've come such a long way, it's remarkable. They still have quite a ways to go, but given the readership they represent and the regional interests, I think they really do make an effort, and I'd give them, probably, a B– or a C+. It's amazing how much you read about the issues now compared to when I was in high school. I graduated and left in '85, and you may have gone six or seven weeks, at least, before you read anything. And now it's rarely more than two or three days, very rare.

The only real way I could gauge that is during the yearly parade. We're so starved, we're like, "Oh, the camera coverage is adequate," but then they only have two stories the entire year in Spokane, you know, they're not going out and looking for anything in the community to find. When they have the parade you channel-switch between all three because you know all three of the stations were there. OK, who gives us better time, who gives us better coverage? But I think they're probably all pretty equal. Equally, minimally.

The Seattle respondents were in general more critical of the level of coverage, as these representative quotes suggest:

They're pretty good. KING5 is always really good with gay and lesbian stuff. They support AIDSWalk and talk about Dine out for Life [an AIDS fund-raiser] stuff. KIRO covered our rally in Red Square and the decision on domestic partnerships. At the same time, I don't know how good their research is, but I don't know how good any of their research is.

I feel that it has a few writers that treat it fairly but on the whole I think it sort of skirts issues more so than anything. It tries not to say too much about it. Avoidance is the best tactic, or saying just as little as possible so that you don't offend.

As suggested by the first quotation, Seattle has a lot more movement-oriented events to cover, so the media must pick and choose. Perhaps it is this high level of activity that explains the pessimistic attitudes among the Seattle respondents, as the media cannot possibly cover everything and must therefore displease at least some people. However, I think the most appropriate explanation is the newness of the issue in Spokane, and the corresponding new level of coverage. Gay and lesbian progress is still new (and thus news) in Spokane. In Seattle, it is old hat.

As with Christian conservatives, it is not just level of coverage that is important. The quality of that coverage can also make or break a movement's progress. The Spokane gay and lesbian respondents paid much more attention to this than the Seattle respondents. And again, there was more emphasis on change in Spokane: the quality of the coverage has markedly and quickly improved in recent years. In the past, the gay and lesbian community was treated as a stigmatized minority, and sometimes still is. But recent coverage has been more positive. Two activists from Spokane explain:

> It's taken a while for us to be noticed by the media. A few years ago, the TV media would show our feet walking at the pride march but not our faces. They'd say things like, "Well, four thousand feet were out there." Where's our faces? It's a march to be seen, not to admire our shoes. Now our faces are in the paper. And there's always something in the paper about gays or lesbians or AIDS. Sometimes they sort of roll it all into one, which needs some work, but at least there's a recognition on some level that this part of the community needs to be acknowledged.

> (TL: So it's level of coverage?) Even the quality. I mean, I remember that when I came out in '92 or '3, shortly before that time if a man was picked up for molestation of a boy, they would usually, in their headlines or taglines include, you know, "Gay man arrested," something to that effect. You don't see that hardly occurring anymore. Still, in terms of what they choose to cover, it can be somewhat stereotypical or limited. They've done a good job, though. They've tried to cover some of the family issues and larger-perspective issues, custody issues, things I would have never expected them to.

Old-style coverage painted gays as a hidden oddity that needed to be feared. New-style coverage paints gays as people with faces that need domestic partnership benefits. Seattle respondents, as before, were more critical about the quality of coverage. Some of them, such as this student activist, picked up on subtleties in the coverage. He is commenting on two public figures: Margarethe Cammermeyer, a Washington resident who was drummed out of the army for being a lesbian, and Gary Locke, the first Asian-American governor of Washington (and in the country).

> I remember particular ways in which they're very quick to stereotype. So there was an article two or three years ago on Margarethe Cammermeyer and it was some important decision about her case and it was, you know, "Margarethe Cammermeyer, this, duh, duh, duh, duh, duh, see LESBIAN page 5." It's not like if it were Gary Locke wins the election, "See ASIAN page 5." It seems like they are more willing to stereotype and group

together gays and lesbians than other groups of people. So that is one thing I have noticed.

Another respondent, a nonactivist woman, also stressed that the coverage had subtle negatives:

They coat everything with a fine veneer of phobia. It's very subtle. (TL: Why do you think this way? Can you offer any specific examples?) I'm trying to think of a recent one [pause], like the domestic partnership thing over at the UW. They basically make sure that the people who do not like the concept get lots of column space, whereas they minimize the people who are fighting for it to a few choice sound bites, and if they can find one that's not very complimentary, or very well thought out before it was uttered, that's the one they'll use. They'll at least put one in that's kind of whiny.

This example compares well to the concerns of some Christian conservatives: political activists are unfortunately portrayed as unpleasant people who have an axe to grind.

A final theme that gays had in common with Christian conservatives was their occasional focus on national media, particularly prime-time television. In addition to being exposed to ideas through the news media, Joe Public may also experience these two groups while watching television shows, especially since the average American watches around four hours of television per day (Putnam 2000). This exposure has consequences, as Larry Gross argues: "On issue after issue those who watch more television are more likely—whatever their background—to project television's versions of reality on to their conceptions about the world, its people, and how they function" (Gross 2001). The example brought up most frequently by gays and lesbians was Ellen DeGeneres, who, during the time I conducted my interviews, came out as a lesbian in her real life and on her self-named sitcom. Within a year, *Ellen* was canceled. However, while it played, there was much talk of the significance of these developments. Respondents in both cities spoke of how it had touched them. For example, here is an activist in Seattle and a nonactivist in Spokane:

I think the example of *Ellen* is a good one about how Americans deal with this, because as expected there were certain companies that wouldn't advertise on *Ellen,* but it was also the most watched show and boosted

CBS's, or whoever it was, ratings tremendously. And Oprah, who has not always been supportive of gay and lesbian issues, came on the show and was very supportive and then was very staunch in her defense of her appearing on that show. What she said to the people in her audience who were not comfortable with it was excellent. And so, because those people really represent the center, they represent the dynamic change which America and Americans are capable of, I'd like to think that there is some hope out there: we're not inexorably homophobic, just uncomfortable.

Ellen and some other TV characters that are prominently gay have brought out some more talking about it and I think that talking about it is good. You know, I think every time you have a sore subject and you start talking about it, you can arrive at understanding why certain things are the way they are, just by talking about it. (TL: OK, so even though *Ellen* was canceled, you still think that that one year of talking about it was . . .) I still think it helped. I was sad to see it happen but, you know, I can't do anything about it except for voice my opinion to the network. Done that. (TL: You have?) Yeah, I've e-mailed them. Basically specifically citing the same kiss that didn't get a parental warning, I thought it was more of a kiss on *Spin City* when the black gay guy kissed Mike but it was a joke. When it's a joke, it's OK. But the serious kiss on *Ellen*, which was really no big deal, got a big parental warning: this is adult matter. Blah blah blah. (TL: Because it was real?) Right, right. Cause it was serious.

To these respondents and many others, prime-time media matters: the American public gets an idea, if only for a season or for a moment, of what it's like to be gay or lesbian (Gamson 1998). However, as the last quote above illustrates, gay and lesbian life is still sometimes played for laughs. As Suzanna Walters argues in her incisive critique of gay and lesbian media representations, this newfound visibility can be problematic progress, as old stereotypes are simply given new twists that have the potential to create new types of homophobia (Walters 2001). Some gays and lesbians are willing to put in the time to carefully monitor this progress.

A theme well represented in the Christian conservative interviews, yet conspicuously absent from the gay and lesbian interviews, was the comparison to the "opposite" group. Above, I discussed the propensity for Christian conservatives to compare the level of coverage they received to the level of coverage received by the gay movement. Such a phenomenon hardly exists in the gay and lesbian interviews. Of all the media claims, there was only one that sounded like these other claims. Uttered by an activist, here it is:

> I guess what annoys me is, it's like, they usually have this, this, oh, thirty-second blurb on "Oh, there was the parade today," and that was it, and it's like we're in the back, and you know, whereas if the religious right goes down and pickets Planned Parenthood, hey, that's the first story of the evening [laughs]. So I guess I sometimes feel like, you know, the community as a whole gets shortchanged on some of their events.

This quote sticks out for its uniqueness: no one else made such a claim. In talking about the media, occasionally a respondent would mention Christian voices as they appear in the editorial pages, but no other gay man or lesbian contrasted the levels of coverage the two groups received. This is an important point, and one that will come up again in future chapters: gays and lesbians don't think about Christian conservatives as much, or in the same way, as Christian conservatives think about gay men and lesbians.

A final theme is one that was very prominent in the gay and lesbian interviews but relatively rare in the Christian conservative interviews. Twenty-seven of the gay claims about the media (22 percent) concerned the editorial pages of the newspapers, while there were only six claims about the editorial pages in the Christian conservative interviews (only 4 percent). A fair number of gay men and lesbians pore over the editorial pages as a major way to assess their climates. As examples of this, I first offer some claims from Spokane respondents. The first two examples are from nonactivists who were responding to the general question: "How would you characterize Spokane in terms of issues pertaining to gays and lesbians: hostile, hospitable, or both? Why do you feel this way?" The third example is from a nonactivist who was responding to one of the specific media questions in the interview.

> Well, I'd probably say both, just by what I've seen in the paper, the editorial comments that people have wrote in. (TL: Letters to the editor?) Yeah. That's really the only way I can tell. But there does seem to be a lot of hospitality toward gay people. The letters seem to be more accepting than not accepting, but they do print both.

> Whew! Probably both. You take a look at the letters to the editor in the newspaper, and probably two-thirds of them are negative, one-third posi-

tive or at least neutral, so there's definitely a mix of opinions. (TL: So one-third are neutral or positive, and the rest are negative?) Yeah, roughly, roughly, of course there's always the people you don't hear about that don't take the time to write, but from time to time issues will come up and people will weigh in and there are some very, just awful diatribes out there . . . it's pretty scary. I've certainly appreciated reading the letters to the editor where the different people at least they have a neutral attitude of live and let live, or hey, it's OK, who are we to judge, or they're very affirming and they're saying look, treat all people with respect.

And they do print a lot of letters to the editor, that's always really colorful, on both sides. They don't hasten to print the ones from the type of people who just must be so inbred, you know, the people who write some of those, and you just read some of these really hateful letters to the editor. Oh my God. What a schmuck. I would hate to be on the other end of his, you know, hate stick. I'm really glad that they continue to print. (TL: So they do print those?) Oh, yeah. (TL: And you're really glad they print those?) I am. I am because they're just scary to any, I think, you know, the majority of the population just go, "Eww, yikes, we have to protect them against these people. I don't care, I don't have to love you but I've got to make sure *you* don't have power, I've got to make sure that, if you're the antimovement for these people, then I might be with these people over here."

In Spokane, particularly among the nonactivists, using the letters to the editor to gauge the city's climate is a common activity. Since gay and lesbian issues are relatively new in Spokane, it is hard for a lot of people, especially nonactivists, to accurately assess the attitudes of the public. We will see more of this in the next chapter, but this is one way Spokane respondents accomplish this: by reading the editorial pages, specifically the letters to the editor.

In Seattle, the gay and lesbian respondents were also likely to mention the editorial pages, but they were much less likely to talk about the letters to the editor. Instead, they would reference the staff editorials. Because most gays and lesbians in Seattle have a fairly good idea about how the public feels, they turn their attention to gaining institutional support. For better or for worse, the newspapers are major institutions in the city. For example, shortly before I conducted a good portion of my interviews, the *Seattle Times* reported on an attempt by a local gay rights organization to donate money to public school libraries for the purchase of gay-positive books. This created an uproar, and the paper did not consistently take a pro-gay stance. With that background, a couple of excerpts from Seattle respondents:

> Like with the Seattle schools thing, I did read those editorials, and I felt that they really got their facts wrong, so I don't think that was fair treatment, so that antagonized me a little bit. I guess I have really low expectations, though.

> And I guess this was a very telling incident, because initially the school board was supportive of it, indicating that the people in power are basically liberals and really don't have any problems. But then, a group of twenty parents found out, or one person found out and they got a group of twenty parents together, made a big fuss, and the school board, feeling some public pressure, said, "Well, we need to look into this, and we need to get a little committee to review exactly what's happened here." But then, push came to shove . . . and John Stanford [the school superintendent], turned around and said, "No, it's OK, we approve, this is not a problem, this is what's going to happen, the librarians are going to decide, end of story." And so the *Seattle Times,* they first had an editorial saying, "Hey, these parents have brought up this issue, this is a concern, we need to look into it," but they then did a second editorial saying, "Yes, these books should be in the schools, we really don't have a problem with this." So, I would say that the politics are, as politics always are, they go where public pressure is, and they will waver and they will sell out, but there is also balancing forces which bring it back to our side. (TL: So when the forces balance . . .) It's in favor of us.

These respondents obviously keep track of these things quite carefully. Many gay men and lesbians proved to be active consumers of the editorial pages. One Seattle nonactivist woman even went so far as to create a scrapbook of editorial pieces and other pertinent news items.

Why don't Christian conservatives put emphasis on these same editorial pages? One possible explanation concerns the feeling of resignation that many Christian conservatives have. While they are still willing to fight for balanced, objective coverage in the news sections, many of them feel that the editorial pages are a lost cause. This may be why they didn't bring up the topic as much: Why complain about something that isn't going to change? To provide evidence for this, I turn to one of the hypothetical scenarios that appeared near the end of the interview. For the Christian conservative respondents, the scenario read, "Your local newspaper features an editorial cartoon that makes Christians out to be small-minded." For the gay and lesbian respondents, the scenario was, "Your local newspaper features an editorial cartoon that pokes fun at gay men as being promiscuous." While these may not be completely equivalent, they both make reference to actual examples that had appeared in the papers in recent years. The dominant theme among the Christian responses was resignation and lack of surprise. Twenty of forty-one respondents (nine in Spokane, eleven in Seattle) said they fully expected this kind of thing to happen in the editorial pages. Below is an example from a Spokane church administrator:

> They already do that. It wouldn't surprise me that the *Spokesman-Review* would do it. They editorialize, again. Would I write anything? I have only really been tempted to write a couple of things, and it goes back to an issue I can speak to. In the editorial section, they don't, they very, very seldom publish Christian views on a controversial subject, and I think that's a rub that's bothered me about the *Spokesman-Review*. (TL: You think they get the letters, but they choose not to run them?) I believe, I have to assume that, I mean, there is always Christians who want to voice their opinion. So I just notice that they don't present a balanced view.

Notice the contrast between his perceptions and the results from the content analysis. This theme of resignation appeared hardly at all in the gay and lesbian respondents' reactions to their parallel scenario. In fact, a more common theme was surprise. Such a cartoon would be breaking a norm in the editorial pages. This is all the more striking because the idea for the gay scenario was based on an actual cartoon that appeared in the *Seattle Times* a couple of years before I conducted the interviews. Gays and lesbians have progressed to a point where a media attack like this seems improbable. One can judge the climate, then, by what people think is possible or impossible.

Conclusion

In this age of media saturation, being part of a movement for social change is inherently frustrating. Social movement organizations have become increasingly savvy in their efforts to attain media attention, knowing when the "news holes" are largest and how to reduce their messages to ten-second sound bites (Salzman 1998). Unfortunately, the corporatization of the media has led to an increasing need for eye-catching copy, and the occasionally mundane activities of movements often do not muster media support. Gaining exposure becomes a Faustian bargain, with activists engaging in increasingly bizarre behavior to get their voices heard. The line between fame and infamy is a difficult one to walk.

But is this walk the same for Christian conservatives and gay men and lesbians? On the surface, yes. Both face the problem of sensationalism. Both would like more coverage. But delve deeper into their critiques and differences in their oppositional readings of the media become apparent. The major difference can be summarized by a word that appears repeatedly in Christian conservative discussions of the media but is conspicuously absent from the gay and lesbian interviews: "perspective." Christian conservatives are more critical and demanding of the media. They want their news (about themselves and about the social issues important to them) reported from a particular Christian conservative perspective that they feel few media outlets can provide. To them, those in charge of the media are so liberally biased that they cannot even begin to see how they are maligning the Christian community. To effectively report about such a perspective, they argue, one would need to be living this perspective.

One could imagine what news covered from a "Christian conservative perspective" would look like, however unlikely this scenario is to happen in the mainstream media.[6] To say that gay men and lesbians would like their news covered from a "gay perspective" doesn't make as much sense. For example, one does not need to live a gay life in order to write effectively about gay issues. Certainly there are details that only a gay or lesbian reporter could effectively understand, and the respondents did say that the details were sometimes incorrect. However, they were hopeful that with time, a greater level of understanding would be reached. There was no such hope among the Christian conservative respondents. I make this observation not to belittle the concerns of Christian conservatives. I believe that much of the hostility they sense from the media is real. I have seen with my own eyes the cartoons and editorials about which my respondents spoke. But Christian conservatives do have great expectations of the media, and such expectations are not likely to be met.

Regardless of how they feel about the attention they receive, both groups realize that they need the media to accomplish some of their goals and are therefore bound into a relationship with them. Because media representations affect how the rest of the general public thinks about these two groups (if they think about them at all), members of the groups take these representations very seriously.

3

Reading the Public Mind

George Herbert Mead, one of the founders of American sociology, argued that a critical developmental stage in a child's life happens when she internalizes the *generalized other*: she understands how she is viewed—and *that* she is viewed—by society and learns to act accordingly (Mead 1934). It is sociology's answer to the conscience, or Freud's superego. Not far from the generalized other is the common phrase *general public*. The fact that many people use this phrase, rather than simply saying "public," is telling. It means that however diverse our society may be, we think that there is one public, a general public, that forms coherent attitudes, passes judgment, and influences leaders' political decisions.

As I described in the introductory chapter, there is some evidence that people have an uncanny sense of knowing what the general public thinks about certain issues at any given time. Yet there has been very little research that examines how people do this. Most studies of people's perceptions of public opinion have tried to assess simply whether people can adequately gauge public opinion (Taylor 1982; Fields and Schuman 1976). Because these studies rely almost exclusively on quantitative experiments or surveys, they cannot assess the intricate processes people use to gauge opinion.

A recent study by Susan Herbst (1998) is on the right track in this respect, taking the field of opinion perception beyond experiments and surveys. Herbst conducted in-depth field interviews in order to understand what people mean when they speak of public opinion. Her interview subjects were all ensconced in state politics in the state of Illinois: legislative staffers, journalists, and political party activists. For all of these groups, public opinion is an important part of their daily lives in that it affects what policies they pursue or what stories they cover. Herbst shows that people's conceptions of public opinion vary from group to group, even from time to time. When assessing public opinion on a particular issue, a legislative staffer may consider certain perceptual resources that are easily available to her, while a journalist may use a completely different set of perception tools. A single political actor may use one measure at one stage in her career, but develop further measures as she becomes savvier in her political relationships. In Herbst's words:

> Among political practitioners we see several conceptions of public opinion at work simultaneously, and hence we find more evidence that the notion of public opinion is an extraordinarily malleable sociolinguistic construction. Many different social indicators and many cultural artifacts seem to "count" as public opinion. (Herbst 1998, 78)

This fluid nature of individuals' perceptions of public opinion raises interesting theoretical and empirical questions. On what does a person focus in order to conclude "the general public hates my group"? This is especially important during times of social change: what metaphorical fingers do people hold up into the air to judge these winds of change? How do you know when the public has started or stopped despising you?

Such questions are of great concern to both Christian conservatives and gay men and lesbians. In this chapter, I examine the variety of ways in which members of these groups try to address such questions. Each group focuses on different aspects of their relationship with the public. This leads to important differences with regard to how these groups perceive social change concerning the public. Before I address these interpretive processes, I use a more conventional approach to studying public opinion by examining some of the public opinion data regarding these two groups. Such an exploration of objective data serves three purposes. First, it provides a backdrop for these subjective interpretive processes. Second, it illustrates the relative support that each group receives from the public. Finally, it shows that opinion climates do differ by region, a claim that is central to my analysis.

Nation, State, and Local Opinion Climates

Opinion Climates on the National Level

While the movement for gay and lesbian rights has had some success, it is still a long way from purging national public opinion of anti-gay sentiment (Loftus 2001; Yang 1997). The following results from an analysis of

General Social Survey (GSS) and American National Election Studies (ANES) databack up this assertion in many ways.[1] American attitudes toward homosexuality *are* becoming more accepting. However, Americans distinguish between approval of behavior and approval of civil rights. It is clear that many Americans disapprove of homosexual behavior, yet agree that homosexuals should not be denied certain rights. Ever since the GSS began asking questions in 1973 about homosexuality, a consistently low percentage of Americans have claimed that homosexual behavior is *not* wrong. Since the end of the 1980s, though, there has been a marked increase in this percentage, more than doubling (from 12.8 percent to 28.2 percent) from 1990 to 1996. A full 60 percent still believe that such behavior is "always wrong."[2] With regard to the three civil rights questions that the GSS consistently asks, there has been steady liberalization. In 1973 fewer than 50 percent of Americans thought that a "man who admits that he is a homosexual" should be allowed to teach at college.[3] In a span of twenty-three years, that proportion has risen to over 77 percent. The question concerning a homosexual giving a public speech has risen from just over 60 percent to over 80 percent. Regarding the possibility of allowing a book espousing homosexuality into the public library, attitudes have liberalized more slowly: from 55 percent in 1973 to just over 70 percent in 1996. I discuss this exception in my analysis of the interview data later in this chapter.

The ANES, using quite different questions, offers similar evidence. Unfortunately, the ANES did not begin asking questions related to the issue until 1984. Using the ANES feeling thermometer as a measure of an overall reaction to gay men and lesbians shows the same trend in attitudes as the GSS: a steady 40 percent rated gays and lesbians somewhere between fifty (neutral) to one hundred (very warm) in the 1980s. The 1990s brought a liberalization of attitudes, with this same proportion rising to 50 percent in 1992 and 55 percent in 1996. Although the percentage of ANES respondents giving gays and lesbians a zero on the thermometer (implying that they felt extremely cold toward that group) has dropped from 35 percent in 1988 to 20 percent in 1996, this 20 percent is at least *five* times higher than the figure for most other groups the survey mentions. The next closest group—with only 4 percent of Americans giving them a zero—is Christian Fundamentalists.

Regarding specific gay and lesbian issues, the ANES has limited data. One question, concerning job discrimination, was asked in 1988, 1992, and 1996, with the percentage of Americans favoring a law barring job discrimination against gays and lesbians rising from just over 50 percent in 1988 to just over 60 percent in 1996. The most seriously anti-gay opinions are found in a question asked only in the 1992 ANES: "Should gay or lesbian couples be permitted to legally adopt children?" Seventy-two percent of respondents asked this question were against such adoptions, 62 percent strongly so. In summary, national opinion toward gay men and lesbians has liberalized in recent years, but it is by no means completely hospitable.

Christian conservatives face a relatively more hospitable national opinion climate. As I already mentioned above, very few ANES respondents rate them at zero on the feeling thermometer.[4] Unfortunately, using the feeling thermometer to examine trends concerning Christian conservatives is difficult because the ANES has changed the wording of the questions over time. In 1980 and 1984 the ANES asked respondents to rate "evangelical groups active in politics, such as the Moral Majority." In 1988, this changed simply to "evangelical groups active in politics." In 1988, the ANES also began asking about "Christian Fundamentalists." Two things arise from an examination of these data. First, the general public feels warmer toward Christian conservatives than toward gay men and lesbians: in 1996, 70 percent of the respondents rated Christian Fundamentalists at neutral or warmer (in contrast to 55 percent for gays and lesbians). Second, focusing on 1988 data, when the NES asked about both political evangelicals and Christian Fundamentalists in the same survey, the American public *does* distinguish between these two groups. They express considerably more disfavor when religion and politics are mixed. While fewer than 50 percent of Americans were neutral or warmer toward evangelical groups active in politics in 1988, 70 percent were neutral or warmer toward Christian Fundamentalists.

I return to GSS data in order to examine a couple of specific topics of concern to Christian conservatives: abortion and school prayer. Over the years the GSS has been conducted, there has been relatively little change in attitudes concerning these topics. Consistently, around 50 percent of respondents say that abortion should be legally available in the case of "soft" reasons (woman does not want any more children, family cannot afford more children, etc.). For "hard" reasons (the woman's health is seriously endangered, the woman was raped), the percentages are consistently around 90 percent.[5] There are also consistent patterns regarding school prayer, with around 40 percent of Americans agreeing with the Supreme Court decision to remove prayer from public schools. This consistency in national opinion is in marked contrast to the attitudes toward gay and lesbian issues, which are moving in a liberal direction at a fairly rapid pace.

The religious behaviors of the American public also remain at a constant level. Americans, relative to European countries, are quite religious in both their behaviors and their beliefs (Lipset 1996). Consistently, over 50 percent of the GSS respondents claim they pray every day, and between 30 and 40 percent attend church on a weekly basis. Around a third of the GSS respondents claim that the Bible is to be taken literally, and a similar percentage identify themselves as fundamentalist in their religion. ANES statistics corroborate these findings. In terms of mere numbers of people like themselves, Christians face a more hospitable national climate than gay men and lesbians. While the percentage of the population that is gay or lesbian is hotly contested, recent scientific studies estimate that between 2 and 5 percent of the American population is homosexual (Laumann et al. 1994). For both groups, though, these national percentages are not evenly distributed across the entire United States. It is necessary to look at more localized levels of opinion climates.

Opinion Climates on the State Level

While national climates are important, many interesting patterns occur at a more localized level. In this section, I briefly contrast the opinion climate of Washington State with that of the rest of the United States. The GSS allows the researcher to determine only the general geographical region of the country in which the respondent is living, hence it cannot be used for this comparison. In contrast, the ANES identifies the state of residence of each respondent. Unfortunately, the ANES samples include a limited number of Washington State residents, and not all of these respondents were asked the pertinent questions.

First, regarding Washingtonian attitudes toward gay and lesbian issues, it is clear why Washington State may be perceived as having a more hospitable opinion climate for gay men and lesbians than many other parts of the country. Sixty-four percent of Washingtonians feel neutral or better toward gay men and lesbians, while less than half of other Americans (47 percent) feel similarly. Sixty-nine percent of Washingtonians favor job discrimination legislation compared to 59 percent of other Americans. Where only 27 percent of other Americans support adoption by gays and lesbians, almost half (49 percent) of Washingtonians do.[6]

The case for Christian conservatives is the opposite: they face a more hostile opinion climate in Washington State. Washingtonians are more supportive of abortion: 60 percent of them say that abortion should always be available compared to 41 percent of other Americans. Washingtonians are considerably less likely than the rest of the country (50 percent versus 72 percent) to rate Christian Fundamentalists as neutral or warmer on the feeling thermometer. Very few of them (19 percent) describe themselves as born-again Christians or biblical literalists.

Due to the small samples of Washington State residents, I analyze these ANES data for trends only in the most speculative sense. The mean of Washingtonians on the feeling thermometer toward gay men and lesbians has climbed from 48 in 1984 to 54 in 1996. Where 65 percent of Washingtonians favored antidiscrimination laws in 1988, that number has risen to 77 percent in 1996. Interestingly, the mean for Washingtonians with regard to the Christian Fundamentalist feeling thermometer seems to be rising steadily (from 35 in 1988, to 47 in 1992, to 53 in 1996).

Opinion Climates on the City Level

Though Washington State opinion is considerably more liberal than the rest of the country, this liberalness is in no way constant throughout the state. The findings of a statewide survey conducted in the spring of 1996 illustrate this. For the survey, six hundred Washington State residents were interviewed, including ninety-four from Seattle and fifty from Spokane. Unfortunately, this survey did not ask any questions specifically relating to gays and lesbians. However, there were several questions pertinent to Christian conservative issues.

The results from two of these questions expose striking differences between the two cities. While 54 percent of Spokanites agree with "stands taken by Christian conservatives," only 19 percent of Seattlites do so. While 85 percent of Spokanites agree that America is "getting too far away from God," only 47 percent of Seattlites agree with this statement. Even though these results are based on a small sample, both of these differences are statistically significant ($p < .001$).[7] According to the survey results, there is a small difference between the church attendance of the two cities: 32 percent of Spokanites say they attend church once a week or more, while 23 percent of Seattlites say the same. This is interesting given that Seattle is generally believed to be far less churched than Spokane (as we will see in the interviewees' perceptions below). There is also no significant difference between the cities' responses to a question regarding where they perceive the largest threat, in the moral or in the economic climate, with slight majorities in each city claiming that the moral climate is more threatening. This finding easily could be a result of the booming economy in Seattle, as it becomes more difficult to claim that the economic climate is threatening when the economy is doing so well.

All of the statistics presented in this chapter so far paint fairly clear portraits of the opinion climates on the national, state, and city levels. While these statistics are important, the fact remains that everyday people do not have easy access to such statistics. Yes, a savvy enough person can locate some of these statistics on the Internet if she knows where to look, but how many average people (i.e., not social scientists) really do this? Very few Christian conservatives and gay men and lesbians know these statistics, but this does not mean that their lives are unaffected by public opinion. For them, public opinion is a perceptual and lived phenomenon. They see public opinion when they talk to their neighbors, they sense it in their parent-teacher conferences at school, they feel it on the street as strangers walk by. When I asked the respondents in my study to assess how the public feels about them, very few of them were stumped by the question. On the contrary, members of both groups identified well-developed techniques by which they judge the public's level of support. However, the strategies used by the two groups differ substantially.

Christian Conservatives and the General Public

Recall that in the previous chapter on the media, there were no significant overall differences in the feelings toward the media between Christian conservatives in Seattle and those in Spokane. Such is not the case with feelings about the general public in the two cities. Here, the expectation that Seattle is more hostile and Spokane more hospitable rings true in the minds of the respondents. Of the sixty-eight claims that Spokane respondents made about the Spokane public, 52 percent concerned a hospitable environment, 41 percent a hostile environment. Of the eighty-three claims about the Seattle public made by the Seattle respondents, only 24 percent concerned hospitableness, and 69 percent concerned hostility. What specific aspects of the public's opinions and behavior are more hostile in Seattle than in Spokane?

Rather than gauging the public's support by poring over public opinion statistics, some Christian conservatives simply look out their windows, as did this charity director who had recently moved from Minneapolis to Seattle:

> That was one of the interesting things when I moved out here. In Minneapolis, as I mentioned earlier, seems like everyone goes to church. Sunday morning you see everyone coming out of their houses and trucking in their cars and going to church. When I moved out here and we moved into our new home in _____ and we live on a corner house and the first four or five Sundays we were settling in and we really didn't go any place and I made the observation, being a good sociology major, to Shirley, my wife. I said, "No one is going anyplace. It's Sunday morning and no one is going anyplace." . . . They are out cutting grass, they are doing their cars, football games come on television at ten in the morning. In Minneapolis, it is noon or 1:00 but here it is ten in the morning and everything seems to be against at least the traditional church and its time and its services and everything else. Kids' soccer games are on Sunday. That would never happen, at least not nine years ago in Minneapolis. You would just not do anything on Sunday like that.

One of the most prominent themes about the public in both cities regarded church attendance. Spokane Christians perceive their city's church attendance rate to be somewhat low compared with the rest of the nation. Christians in both cities perceive Seattle's church attendance rate to be very low indeed. What is interesting about these claims is that no respondent seemed to care what church was being attended, or what specific religious beliefs people had. They simply made general references to how much of the population goes to church regularly. Of concern here is how church oriented the public is, how much the culture of the city is willing to revolve around a religious axis. As the quote above illustrates, Seattle does not really make room for churchgoing: it is simply not part of the city's psyche. By extension, religion is not important in Seattle, and therefore religious people should not play an important role in civic life.

The respondents gauged church attendance in numerous ways. Some cited statistics. In response to the general question about what it is like to be a Christian in Spokane, an evangelical pastor replied:

> I'd say Spokane is a pretty positive religious environment to be in. You don't really face a whole lot of slack for being a Christian in this city. . . .
> I think that church attendance is higher here than it is on the west side,

significantly higher, probably about 10 percent higher. The statistics over there are anywhere from 4 to 8 percent regular church attendance, which is one of the lowest in the nation. Over here it's probably more around 20 percent. So, there's more of a church environment citywide here.

This reference, like others, regards a general religious environment, not specific churches or denominations. In contrast to the common notion that Christian conservatives maintain a "my way or the highway" philosophy, my interview data and other recent national research on evangelicals (Smith 2000; Wolfe 1998) show that many of them do not really care about the specific flavor of Christianity that is practiced, only that you can taste a general religiosity. People's lives should be faith centered, but what this faith looks like is up to them.

In Seattle, regardless of the denomination, Christians perceive a faulty state of affairs. An evangelical pastor in Seattle explains:

(TL: How supportive of Christian causes is the general population of Seattle, do you think?) I don't think they are very supportive at all. Simply because, the latest stat that I have is about four years old from the National Association of Evangelicals that only about 9 percent of the population in King County [in which Seattle is located] goes to church on a weekly basis. So that lets you know that about 91 percent of the people don't give a rip about Christianity or the church. A lot of them are good quote-moral-unquote people, but not sympathetic toward Christians.

Notice how this respondent connects the actions of people (or in this case, lack of action) to their attitudes: a lack of action is indicative of a lack of sympathy. In want of concrete attitudinal data on the public, Christians use church attendance as a reasonable proxy.

Closely related to this theme is some Christians' emphasis on the number of churches. Here, the importance is placed on the public's ability to go to church if they so desired. A Christian activist in Spokane replied to a general question about living in Spokane as a Christian with: "I was counting, and I can't remember the exact numbers, I think it's somewhere only 9 or 10 percent of the people in Spokane could get into a church if they wanted to on any given Sunday, because there isn't enough churches here." His eye on evangelism, this respondent sees a need for more places of worship for the people he hopes to bring into the fold. Yet he is very vague regarding the type of churches these would be. A nonactivist Christian in Spokane, looking at the number of churches, had a different perspective:

> (TL: What is it like to live in Spokane as a Christian?) I was amazed when I first came to Spokane because there were so many churches. Tons and tons of churches. Before I came here, I really wasn't familiar with the myriad of the denominations that were out there. . . . So I came here, and I look into the phone book, and not only are there a hundred Assembly of God churches, there is a hundred denominations. . . . There's a lot of churches here, there's a lot of opportunity to express your faith as a Christian.

The contrast between the two claims illustrates the relative nature of perceptions. As a nonactivist simply looking for a church, having come to Spokane from a religiously homogeneous environment, the latter respondent is optimistic. The former respondent, looking at things from a more activist viewpoint, is more pessimistic about the possibilities.

Even if Christians were dismayed by the church attendance of their fellow citizens, some of them looked at this as a challenge put before them by God to evangelize. They used the term "mission field," especially when talking about Seattle. The Seattle charity director from Minnesota, whose quote began this section, responded to the general question "What is it like to live in Seattle as a Christian?" as follows:

> I find it exciting, coming from the Midwest which is a very highly churched population. Seattle is not a churched community and in many ways I find that exciting because it is a challenge and you have to question your faith, I think, and make sure that you know what you believe in. Where in the Midwest, everybody went to church. So you have a lot of "churchianity" but maybe not Christianity. So, I find that exciting and I find that because the climate, at least the people I meet are very open to discussion. I am able to talk about my faith and people don't just turn you off or they don't just say, "Well, I am Lutheran" or "I am Baptist," because a lot of the folks I talk to are nothing and so they are very open. So I find it an exciting place to be and at the same time a real challenge, and I like challenges.

Others laughed as they spoke of Seattle. There's so much work to be done, they really don't know where to begin. They feel that God has called them to the Northwest for a reason, but the job ahead of them is difficult indeed.

Christian conservatives use church attendance as an indicator of how open their city's culture is to them and their views. A youth pastor in Seattle expressed what his city is lacking in these terms:

> Just people born, bred, raised in church and that's their worldview. Doesn't seem to be that's the way things work out. . . . Like northern California, or some areas that are really the Bible belt. Where that seems to be their general frame of mind. Whereas in the Northwest, I think that's not the general frame of mind.

To him, and to other Christian conservative respondents, things are better for Christians if churchgoing is institutionalized within the climate in which they are living, if the public simply takes it as a given that many people go to church on Sunday morning. But, as one Spokane respondent remarked, "I do know that on Sunday morning, you leave your house to head for church, you're amazed at how easy it is to get around this city."

Another action that Christian conservatives closely observe is the participation of the general public in charitable causes. During the interview, if there was one question that the Christian respondents found confusing, it was, "How supportive is the general population of Christian causes?" When asked this, many of them stopped and asked for clarification, or answered the question in two different ways, such as this Seattle charity director:

> Christian causes? Well, that is the key, I think, is what the cause is. We have huge response around Christmas for adopting families for Christmas, helping out with Thanksgiving dinner, we send things out over United Way Network, and get a lot of response for something like that. . . . Now if we were to ask for a response on something that will be more emotionally charged, and more around morality issues than a good-neighbor issue, I guess that's really what determines your response.

This was a common response to this question in both cities: charitable causes received great support, moral and political causes generally did not. The public's responses to Christians' charity efforts offered one of the main forms of hospitableness to Christians in both cities, with only slightly more hostility arising in the claims from Seattlites, such as this response from a pastor in Seattle, who noticed a change in the nature of charitable support within his city:

> We have a lot of philanthropists in the city and they're not interested in Christian causes, when you look at the Bill Gateses or Nordstrom's, the Nordstroms are Christian guys. The whole family. They have given generously to Christian causes. But even now the face of Nordstrom's is changing to the political climate. Now it's a general benevolence rather than any kind of specific support of church causes. And that's a change because ten years ago their monies went to causes that were sponsored through the church specifically, but now Nordstrom's gives a lot to causes that are sponsored through government agencies.

With regard to noncorporate charity, though, most Seattle respondents were quite pleased with the level of support they witnessed. Even though most Seattle residents are not churchgoing Christians, they're still good people, and that makes Christians' charity work easier. As a Seattle shelter director explains: "There's a heart, there's a personality to the city, to its people. I think that compassion flows, maybe sometimes to a fault. There's enough compassion right now. We have three people for every homeless."

In Spokane, the respondents felt that their fellow citizens were very much in support of their various charity works. A pastor explains:

> (TL: How supportive of Christian causes is the general population of Spokane, do you think?) I think very supportive. Things that are done in the community that are done by Christians have received the support of the whole community, whether it be public services which we've done a number of things, the fifth Sunday nights of the month in the old arena, things like basketball camps, Christian schools, things like that. I think that we've received good support from the community. I've never felt like . . . it was ruled out just because Christians were leading it.

Charity is one of the main ways Christians feel they have a major effect on the general culture of their cities. When asked about "Christian causes," then, this is immediately what came to mind for many of them, rather than causes of a more political nature. Because charity is such an important way for Christians to feel vital to their culture, some of them are particularly sensitive when the city does not pay this aspect of their activities due attention. Sometimes, some Christians commented, their good works are overlooked, or they are not given credit for these works. A charity organizer whom I have already quoted earlier brought up this aspect when I asked her the question, "Are there any Christian elements that are not represented in Seattle that you would like to see represented?" She replied:

> I think that the Christian community is underrated. I guess because of my work I get the sense from agencies or school districts or whatever that they don't think we're doing anything. In reality, a lot of churches are doing a lot of things on a very small scale. Were we to tally how many bags of groceries are handed out, just out of pastor's pantries or whatever with no folderol, no fanfare, we find that the churches are doing a significant amount of work.

Christian conservatives want to feel that they play a vital role in their communities. In addition, they want the general public to *perceive* them as vital. Charity work is the main way they experience this feeling. But sometimes they feel they do not get credit where credit is due.

Up to this point, I have discussed how Christian conservatives perceive the public's level of support by looking at the *actions* of the public: going to church, participating in charity. Indeed, observing action is one of the major ways that Christians read the public. They also attempt to observe the attitudes of the public. It is from looking at such attitudes that Seattle Christians perceive more hostility than Spokane Christians. Among such claims from the Seattle respondents, nineteen out of twenty-one concerned hostility. Among similar claims from the Spokane respondents, ten out of sixteen concerned hostility. Seattle Christians spoke about such topics more often and were more likely to relate stories of hostility.

In the previous chapter, I showed that Christian conservatives feel that the media stereotype them. This stereotyping crosses over into their feelings about the general public, especially the Seattle public. They see the public applying an oversimplified stereotype to Christians. In general, they think they are stereotyped as brash, unthinking, intolerant, and judgmental persons. While I was sitting with an elderly Christian woman in a coffeehouse in West Seattle, she tried to explain why it was hard to be a Christian in Seattle:

> You have this enormous gap between the vast majority thinking of Christians as this very conservative, destructive conservative. And then the rest of the Christian community over here is this far left, and somehow, most

of us that are neither camp find ourselves being lumped there and so the results of that are, there is a certain persecution that goes with being a Christian. (TL: OK. If you don't see yourself as part of the Christian Left and you don't see yourself as part of the Christian Right, you see yourself somewhere in the middle but more conservative?) More conservative than liberal, I think. (TL: But you feel that the majority of the Seattlites, if you would say to them that you were a Christian, they would automatically assume . . .) That you are over there in the far right. Yeah, they would. (TL: What effect does that have, that kind of assumption, what are the implications?) It is hard not to become defensive. (TL: It's hard for Christians to not become defensive?) Yes, I think it is. Or to be so intimidated by that labeling to say I don't want to be a part of that so therefore I am not willing to declare my faith. (TL: Do you think a fair number of Christians actually . . .) Back off. (TL: Back off?) I do. I really do. And you can turn that part around because there have been so many foolish things that has been labeled under the umbrella of God and Christians, you know, like the burning of abortion clinics or the shootings or something like that. And those are the kinds of things that just really bother me. They really do. Because I tend to think that that's the way that all Christians are labeled.

What she describes is reminiscent of the spiral of silence theory developed by Noelle-Neumann (1993): dominant public opinion marginalizes certain groups until they are no longer willing to state their views in public.

When I asked her whether the hostility she feels had increased over the years, she immediately brought up homosexuality. She specifically referenced the pro-gay job discrimination initiative that had recently been on the statewide ballot but was shot down by a wide margin:

I don't think it has become more or less. I just think that it has been in there and whether that will increase now with some of the issues that are coming up, regulations of various sorts of the, the discrimination kinds of thing, I don't know whether that will increase in hostility toward Christians or not. (TL: What things are you talking about?) Well, you know, when government begins to deal with issues and passing laws and that sort of thing and equal access to whatever health care or whatever. As a Christian, if you start speaking out, either for or against, you are going to antagonize somebody. Usually, if they realize you're a Christian, then that puts you in this camp of nonunderstanding, nontolerance, etc.

(TL: So you think that there is growing hostility, and it has to do mainly to the types of issues that we are starting to deal with?) Exactly . . . because I am thinking in terms of, do we recognize homosexual marriages, do we have access to health care, do we hire, I mean the fact that we had this on the ballot about the, you know, and it was defeated or whatever, you know. When any of these things come up and you are talking with someone who is on the far left, then they immediately assume that you are the intolerant one.

For this woman, the fact that homosexuality has become a social issue is causing greater hostility toward Christians. As shown in the previous chapter, homosexuality plays a major role in Christians' perceptions. A different twist on this perspective comes from a student who grew up in Seattle but attends a Christian college in Spokane. I interviewed her because I thought she would be able to make some interesting contrasts between the two cities. She did not let me down. Here, she talks about being a Christian in Seattle:

If I just tell a person I'm a Christian, there's a lot of rolled eyes, things like that. (TL: Not the same in Spokane?) No. It's a lot more conservative there, so it's not even an issue to tell someone you're a Christian. It's just like, oh great. (TL: So it's a nonissue in Spokane, but in Seattle?) Yeah. (TL: Any other stories?) The only thing I can think of, in terms of the differences for me is that in Spokane, there's less to know, just because, for instance, homosexuality is not as much of an issue there. So if they were to see, it always seems like I'm in situations where *I* have to explain things to people, because I'm from Seattle. If I see a sticker on a car, they usually don't know what it means in Spokane. (Like what?) Like the rainbow sticker, or upside down pink triangles, no one knows what they mean. Or certain initiatives, a lot of times the political climate is really different there and people aren't as aware. So just because there's not as much to know, they're more accepting of what they already know, which is religious beliefs or whatever. [In Seattle] there's such a wide variety of beliefs in political terms and religious terms, that there's usually more of an opinion on them too. And I've noticed that. Just there's more to choose from, so people do that. They do pick and choose. When there's less to know, it's just not as much of an issue. So the ignorance in Spokane is almost a relief sometimes.

For this student, homosexuality and other related issues merely serve to complicate matters, thus making life for Christians more difficult. Life as a Spokane Christian is easier because it's simpler. Most people just don't talk about such things. A final example regarding homosexuality concerns the way that Christians are treated by the public in contrast to how they treat gay issues. A pastor from Seattle made this contrast quite explicit:

> And many Christians are persecuted because we're perceived as intoler-
> ant. You know, we're narrowminded, we think in terms of black and
> white, not in gray. A Christian is not a person who's going to say, "Yeah,
> everyone's OK and what everybody does is OK." We're bound by beliefs
> and that's not how we view life. We feel that there's one road to destruc-
> tion and there's one road to life. (TL: That's the perception?) Right. (TL:
> And do you call that a misperception?) Of Christians? (TL: Yes.) Oh no, I
> don't think that's a misperception. I think tolerance needs to run both
> ways and there's tolerance for everything *but* Christians. So if I went
> down to the HUB [the Husky Union Building on the University of Wash-
> ington campus] and I was talking about traveling in the Castro [a gay
> neighborhood in San Francisco], I would be undisturbed and would
> cause no debate. If I went there and started preaching Jesus, first of all the
> administration would ask me to leave, and secondly, the people would be
> disturbed, so there's no tolerance.

Thirty years ago, a speaker talking about homosexuality might have caused debate on the University of Washington campus. Today, that is not likely at all. What *is* likely to disturb the public? Vocal Christians.

Christian conservatives feel stereotyped as judgmental, even though many of them try very hard to not come across that way. We heard a little of this in the excerpts from the elderly woman and the pastor above. Two of my younger respondents—the first from Seattle, the second from Spokane—spoke of their reactions to this dilemma:

> I would still, even if I didn't completely avoid it [Bible study], sometimes I
> would change my, the way I would say it, like I would say, "Well, I have a
> function tonight," or "I have a class tonight." And if they asked me, then I
> would tell them. (TL: But you give them that one more chance?) I never
> wanted people to think I was preaching them, or judging them. And I was
> always worried about that. I thought well if they're not a Christian, I don't

want them to think that I'm judging them so I'm going to say, "Well, I'm going to Bible school." (TL: So if you came out right away and said, "Well I'm going to Bible study," that would sound like preaching to some people?) I thought some people might look at it like they would feel that I would then look at them differently and more through judgmental eyes. And I wanted them first to get to know me to realize that I'm not that way, not judgmental. And so I worried about that.

But I think, in general, probably in Spokane, it's kind of "Oh, man, Christians. Just a group of people, just as long as they don't bother me with their fanatic ideas." (TL: Do you think that's the general perception? That Christians are fanatics?) Well, yeah, sometimes, I don't know, it's hard. I don't really know what the general climate is, but I think that one thing, sometimes Christians are, you know, I can't really say especially in Spokane, I don't know for sure, but that we're, like, self-righteous.

Though the presence of stereotypes was more commonly perceived by the Seattle respondents, it was a significant problem in both cities. Christian conservatives feel misunderstood by the public. This makes their evangelistic duties more difficult, as it makes the rest of the public that much harder to reach. While some Christians said they did not interact with the general public (one respondent said he lived in a "Christian cocoon"), most would like to be fully engaged with the general public, seeking to form relationships with them that could lead to evangelistic opportunities. As illustrated in numerous ways above, sometimes the hostile nature of the climate prevents them from doing this.

While the majority of the interview dealt with the respondents' views of their cities' climates, I also asked the respondents some questions about the state and national publics. These questions are important with regard to the general public because when public opinion "acts" in a legislative sense, it is usually at the state or national levels. Thus, while local public opinion is likely to affect the experiential lives of the respondents, state and national public opinion is likely to affect the lives of the respondents by governing what they can and can't do, legally (for example, pray in school or prohibit abortions). Some respondents had a difficult time gauging public opinion on these vast levels. But an overview of the findings is still illuminating.

The Christian conservative respondents in the two cities differed with regard to their assessments of Washington State as a whole. Sixty-five percent of the Spokane respondents' claims about the state public concerned hostility, while only 36 percent of the Seattle respondents' claims did so. Objectively, since the respondents from each group were assessing the same entity, these percentages should be nearly the same. However, these statistics show that the local climate in which a person lives affects his or her subjective evaluations of the state. For example, a Seattle Christian conservative will contrast the rest of the state with Seattle and have no trouble finding it more hospitable.

When I asked Christian conservatives to think about Washington State, the dominant theme by far was church attendance. Again and again, respondents in both cities made reference to the fact that Washington State is one of the least, if not *the* least, churched states in the country. This implies both a lack of Christians and a lack of churches to put them in. As a Spokane nonactivist said: "I know we're an unchurched state, probably more than any other state. We're one of the most unchurched and most liberal states and so from that I would say we're probably more hostile toward Christians. I mean, no one's threatening me, no one's writing stuff on my door. I don't think it's that bad, yet." When you get them to talk about the climate on the state level, many Christians in Washington State definitely have a minority mentality.

There was more agreement between the Christian conservatives in the two cities about the nation as a whole: 59 percent and 70 percent, respectively, of the Spokanites' and Seattlites' claims about the U.S. public concerned hostility. The main concern of Christian conservatives at the national level was the stereotypes they believed the American public holds of them. A fair number of the respondents had serious problems with the national leadership of various Christian conservative entities, whether they are televangelists or heads of political organizations. One of the more striking moments during my interviews in Spokane came near the end of my time there. I was talking with an administrator at a conservative church about the direction of the national climate. At first it was rather difficult to make out what he was saying. But eventually, with some probing questions on my part, I think his point became clear:

And I think the Religious Right has been painted in such a bad light. . . . There is an increasing number of people who are supporters of [abortion], there's an increasing number of supporters or increasing numbers of gay and lesbian people. Christians or the Religious Right are against that. So, again, it's translated the Religious Right as Christians. Even though I wish that were not the case. (TL: So ideally what would you like to see, separation of Christian beliefs with the Religious Right?) I don't know if we can have that because some of those are the same. What I would like to see, what I would like to see is people who understand that Christians have, I guess, what I really would like to see, is that the Religious Right, quote-un-quote, very quote-un-quote religious, represent Christianity in a better light. That's what I would like to see. I am 100 percent against homosexuality, but if I am going to be like Jesus Christ, then I am gonna have to love that person. And treat him as he is my brother. And the very same as if I think I am 100 percent against adultery. But I am not gonna banish the person who commits adultery to an island. We have to love the individual. And that doesn't mean saying it from afar behind my Bible, that means getting in that person's face and saying, "You know I really love you," and showing him so that he knows that I love him, or she knows that I love her, and I wish the heart of Christ would be represented instead of the Religious Right banging on walls, and Christ never protested the society, so . . . (TL: So, for example, while you would share the belief with the Religious Right that homosexuality is wrong, the implications of that for the Religious Right, their course of action, and *your* course of action . . .) Are very very very different. At [my church] we don't really get involved in a lot of that social agenda kind of thing.

This man's frustration was palpable. He desires many of the same things that the Religious Right desires, but he wants to achieve these goals in a different way. One can see how this lack of solidarity could cause confusion among observers. The Christian respondents perceive the public wondering: "What exactly *is* a Christian conservative?" As one Seattle nonactivist explained about the national public:

I really think that right now they're puzzled. (TL: That Christians are puzzled?) No, I think the U.S. population is puzzled because Christians are so, I mean, you want Christians to be this nice little, you know, let's define Christians and they'll all fit right here and when they don't, well gosh, then what do we do, you see? (TL: People are realizing that there are many different flavors?) Yes! Absolutely! And I think a lot of this has come about because what you hear on "The 700 Club" may not necessarily be what you hear about [her church], and for a lot of people, they'll say, well, it doesn't matter. But for the most part, people are saying, "Now wait a minute. Are these both Christians? How do we define these persons?" It comes to that. So I don't think that the whole population is necessarily more hostile, I just think that they're more confused about what Christians are.

Unfortunately, as one can glean from these responses, eradicating this misunderstanding is a daunting task that Christians don't really know how to accomplish. Their primary problems with the public are extremely difficult to overcome.

Gay Men, Lesbians, and the General Public

As the expected climate difference between the cities was perceived by Christian conservatives, it also was perceived by gay men and lesbians, though the difference is not as severe. Of the city-level claims the Spokane respondents made about the general public, 48 percent of them concerned a hostile public, 33 percent a hospitable public, and an additional 12 percent an increasingly hospitable public. In Seattle, 33 percent of the claims regarded a hostile public, 46 percent a hospitable public, and 8 percent an increasingly hospitable public.

In order to contrast gays with Christian conservatives, I first identify the extent to which the prominent themes in the Christian conservative interviews were manifested in the gay and lesbian interviews. The first theme I described above was church attendance. For obvious reasons, this didn't come up very often in the gay and lesbian interviews. But it did come up in talking to a couple of people—in rather notable ways. In Spokane, a nonactivist used this theme to characterize a hostile climate: "Spokane seems like a big place for the Christian Right, not extremists, but it has that big Christian flair to it here. (TL: How do you know that?) From what I hear and read, and there are a lot of churches here." Just as Christian conservatives perceived the climate through the mere number of churches and the people inside them, a few gay and lesbian respondents used these numbers to characterize the climate toward themselves. In Seattle, a nonactivist used the lack of religiosity to characterize a hospitable climate:

If I remember correctly, one of the selling points of Seattle is that they have one of the lowest church attendance rates in the U.S. (TL: Selling point for you?) Yeah. (TL: What does that imply?) It implies that organized religion was not very entrenched. I think that the rest of the state clings to these kinds of things a little bit more.

While such excerpts are interesting, they were infrequent. Most of the gay and lesbian respondents did not mention church presence at all. In general, gays and lesbians do not use the public's Christianity to characterize their climate.

Another theme prominent in the Christian interviews regarded charity. Because charity plays a relatively smaller role in gay life (most gays and lesbians don't see it as one of their defining roles in their communities), few gay men and lesbians discussed this. When they did discuss it, they generally spoke of a hospitable public, such as this Seattle AIDS Walk coordinator:

(TL: How would you characterize Seattle in terms of issues pertaining to gays and lesbians: hostile, hospitable, or both?) I would say hospitable. I think working on the AIDS Walk, we had so many people from the non-gay community participate and everyone really seemed to show their support. So it seems pretty hospitable. (TL: So you think the rate of non-gay participation in the AIDS Walk here in higher than in other cities?) We don't have those kind of stats, but I worked on the organizing committee for the AIDS walk and that had a lot of non-gay participants as well, but it just seems as more of a community effort than the one in Austin did.

On the other side of the state, in Spokane, when charity came up, the tone was positive but not entirely so:

(TL: How supportive of gay and lesbian causes is the general population of Spokane, do you think?) Hmmm. Knowingly? Spokane Aids Network gets a lot of support, but . . . (TL: From the general population?) Yeah, pretty much, I've, I, I mean, being a fund-raising coordinator for EMCC [the local gay and lesbian church], I look at who's supporting them in their ads, and their fund-raisers, and they have a broad spectrum of support. But you know, not just homosexuals get AIDS, so that's why it's OK.

Where the Christian conservative respondents talked a lot about action as well as attitudes, the gay and lesbian respondents concentrated mainly on attitudes. While this emphasis on attitudes may at first sound like a similarity between the groups, the ways gays and lesbians think about the attitudes of the general public differ markedly from Christian conservatives. As I showed above, Christians concentrate on stereotyping. Gay men and lesbians talk about stereotypes but they equally bring up other themes: the public's level of awareness and the public's support for gay issues. In addition, they employ the strategy of illustrating the public by making reference to specific people in their lives.

The dominant theme in the gay and lesbian interviews concerning the public was awareness. In addition to *what* the public thinks about gays and lesbians, equally important is *that* the public thinks about them at all. For a person to change his mind about a group, he must have that group in his mind. So the fact that homosexuality has become a social issue, that people even recognize it as an important issue, is an accomplishment in itself and a sign of social change. Awareness of gay and lesbian life is growing in Spokane, but according to many respondents, there remains a long way to go. Summing up this sentiment is this amusing quote from an activist regarding the rainbow symbol of gay and lesbian pride:

> A couple of years ago, one of the Kentucky Fried Chickens had, like, three or four rainbow flags out in front of them, and somebody made a remark about them, and I said, "They don't know. They think it looks good. I mean, I guarantee it, they think it looks good."

The Spokane public's ignorance of such symbols and gay catchphrases sometimes manifests itself in rather odd ways, as this organizer of the annual Pride parade explains:

> Last year, have you seen the *Inlander* magazine that comes out on Wednesdays? Last year on April Fool's Day we tried to do a "Send Your Friend to Jail" thing: we'd go pick them up and have a fake jail and they would have to raise bail as a fund-raiser for us. And we put it in the *Inlander* under the calendar under "Benefits" so we got a whole bunch of calls. . . . So I started calling people back and mentioned the gay pride march and nobody wanted to do it after that. (TL: So they didn't understand what it was for?) No, they didn't understand what Pride was for. So I called the *Inlander* and told them what was going on. And the associate editor said, "Well, I knew what Pride was, so I guess I just thought that everybody knew what that meant." I'm like, "No they don't! Gotta put that in there!"

This example is also telling of a hostile climate in Spokane, as it illustrates not only the public's ignorance, but also their reluctance to support the gay movement. Almost equaling in number such claims of ignorance were claims regarding the increasing awareness of the Spokane public. Some respondents thought that the Spokane public was well on its way to figuring things out. A steadfast activist compares present-day Spokane to the Spokane of ten years ago:

> There wasn't even visibility, you know. Like, the pride march started in '92. That kind of stuff. So, there's a lot more visibility than there used to be. There's now recognition that there are gay and lesbian people in Spokane. And most people know that now. I think ten years ago, people would have said, "There's a few freaks in the closet," or something. But then you have 1,500 people marching down the street, and you've got all the policies out there, it raises people's consciousness.

Across the state in Seattle, respondents in general were pleased with the public's level of awareness and saw it improving. A businessman who by night was one of Seattle's premier drag queens explains the effect of people living their lives out in the open:

> But I think people are becoming more accepting, and more understanding, and I think a lot more straight people are finding out that they do have more gay friends than they realized. That doctor that they've always loved, that dentist they have always loved, and then they go to find out this person's gay. I think in their own minds they realize that this person's been a friend of mine for all these years. I am not going to give this up. And I think a lot more people are coming to realize that.

However, being aware of gay and lesbian *issues* is different from being aware of gay and lesbian people. Others were more pessimistic about the public's awareness of the political issues that gays and lesbians confront. Here are two such thoughts from Seattlites, the first a longtime activist and the second a relatively uninvolved African American lesbian:

> If you would ask a typical straight person here, they don't feel affected by the issue, and they don't feel that gay people are, you know, they would say, "Oh, there's no problem, there's no discrimination problem." And I don't believe that's true, I believe that there still are people out there that

are facing discrimination, and that legal protection would be helpful for them. So, I think those people are educable, but I don't think that they're already at the point where they're going to come out and support. I mean, even in Seattle, if the marriage issue was on the ballot, it could face some problems. Because the people who, like half the population who, if they voted, would vote our way, but they wouldn't bother to vote.

(TL: How supportive of gay and lesbian causes is the general population of Seattle, do you think?) I wonder that the general population is actually aware. (TL: OK, so it's not even something they're aware of?) I think that there are people who make it a point to be aware of certain things, but overall I don't know how much they see it or want to see it as existing. I mean, there are people who, like you say, if you never come to Capitol Hill [the gay neighborhood], don't know anyone that's gay, so it's not an issue for them in their lives.

Closely connected to awareness is the issue of support. Just because a public is aware of you doesn't mean that it will support you. Here, there was a difference between the two cities: Seattle respondents found mostly hospitableness in this respect, while Spokane respondents found a mixture of hostility and hospitableness. In Seattle, an interesting perception came from a nonactivist who, because of her job as a temp, was exposed to a wide variety of the public. She made the following observation:

I think they are quite supportive. I have worked temps recently and that means I do a lot of floating around a whole lot of organizations and I haven't found anyone who has a problem with gays or lesbians and it is not necessarily that I come out to them but they just sort of mention things, attend the AIDS Walk or whatever. They seem like a whole different philosophy or mindset that they have been either raised with or reprogrammed or something (laughs). So just the number of people who have it as part of their consciousness. (TL: So, it's part of their consciousness here?) It's part of their consciousness. I guess I'm just kind of thinking of urban Seattle. I view it as kind of this slick, urban, educated city. And with education comes the coolness of being gay. (TL: So one of the ways to show you're hip is to be cool with being gay?) Yeah, right, hip to be even appearing gay, even if you're not. That's probably the ultimate show of entering the mainstream, that actually we're some kind of watermark for being hip. We're what you aspire to.

Now this respondent may be taking things a little far, but other respondents had plenty of examples of the support that gays and lesbians get from the general public. From the general public's attendance at the Seattle [Gay] Men's Chorus concerts to their patronage of a new gay-owned restaurant in the gay part of town, from being gay-friendly neighbors to supporting gay-themed books in the schools, heterosexuals in Seattle are consistently coming through for the gay and lesbian community.

In Spokane, the picture painted by the respondents was mixed. One of the respondents at first replied, "There's a strong and supportive non-gay community here," but moments later commented, "We just had a pride parade, there wasn't really anybody out to support it."[8] Or, if there is support, it is not exactly the kind of support that the gay community wants, as these activists suggest:

> The perception is still that it's a choice to some degree. I think that there would be more of a kind of condescension sense of sympathy from the general populace. More folks are starting to think that, well, maybe if it's not a choice, they're still diseased individuals who deserve empathy.

> The liberals in this town who like gay people are upper-middle class white liberals with a condescending "Let's be charitable to those poor people who are homosexual or HIV+ or both." The form takes this sort of '50s-'60s notion of liberal charity. In this town that is rampant. None of the idea of let's stand *with* each other.

Finally, as in Seattle, there is increased straight patronage of gay spaces, but even this sends mixed messages to Spokane gays and lesbians, as this nonactivist explains:

> That's one thing, there's so many straight people being OK with it, and so they're all, like, coming out into the [gay] bars. (TL: There are more straight people in the bars?) Oh, *God* yeah. [My girlfriend] did her [class] video on straight people coming into the bars and at first we were all so up in arms about it, this cultural imperialism, that they can come into our bar and there we were with our tail between our legs and like Native Americans running away, running away fleeing instead of standing up and saying, "Look, don't come in here and stare at me, asshole! Get the hell outta my bar!" (TL: And that's not why they were there?) Oh, well, some of them were. A lot of them, you know, it's been a whole meta-

morphosis . . . (TL: So do you think you consider that a good change?) I think I did originally. Like, isn't this the way we're supposed to want it, gay, straight, everybody dancing together? And then I kind of got mad, because I was like, where do we go now? What do we do just to go and be with other straight people, I mean gay people, where do you go for support?

In Spokane, gay men and lesbians aren't quite sure what to make of the newfound support they feel from some of the general public. Some support is better than no support, but they are not sure that they have achieved the ideal type of support that symbolizes the public's full acceptance of the gay and lesbian community.

Another way gay men and lesbians offer examples of a hospitable public is through stories about specific people who are supportive or who have become supportive. This is a theme that was not present in the Christian conservative interviews: the embodiment of public opinion within a specific member of the public. One of the more moving examples of this comes from a woman in Spokane who had recently spoken at a town meeting about a proposed ordinance to outlaw anti-gay discrimination. A few years back, this woman had been brutally beaten in a gay bar in Spokane and went to the meeting to tell her story. After the meeting, a man approached her:

This really nice man came up to me and said, "You know, I'm straight and I really didn't know how I felt about this issue, but I just had to tell you that as a straight man, I am so sorry these guys just beat the snot out of you, for one, and you've really changed my mind. I'm going to go home and talk to my wife and tell her that I think we should support this because I don't think you should be fired from your job just because you're a lesbian. And I don't think that you should be pulled out of your apartment just because you're a lesbian. And I think that's wrong. I really think that's wrong." He says, "I don't really believe in the gay marriage thing but, you know, hey, you changed my mind on *these* things."

Although this is only one man, it is easy to see how the profound nature of his attitude change could affect how this woman feels about the greater public. A gay man in Spokane had a less dramatic, but no less meaningful example that he used to confront what he saw as misconceptions about Spokane:

It's probably more widely accepted than what most people would like to believe, or what the conservative community would like to believe, I think it's more accepted. (TL: OK, so you think among the conservative community there's not a whole lot of acceptance, but you think that . . .) I think the community is not as conservative as it used to be, and therefore there is a greater variety of acceptances of everything. (TL: OK, what makes you think that it's more liberal than it was?) Because, just listening to people talk. (TL: OK, and it's day-to-day conversation.) Day-to-day conversation, meeting people. In the mornings I go have my coffee at McDonald's and there's a group of older people in there and we discuss things in the newspaper and there's not any gay bashing or anything when there's gay articles discussed, and these are construction people, and business people, and . . . (TL: And people do discuss this?) We discuss them. I've not come out and said, "Well, I'm a member of the gay community," although I've made some very leading comments, that if somebody was smart enough they'd probably ask the question.

One could argue that this strategy of embodying the public in a single person or set of persons is a form of selective perception. If someone wants to believe that the public is supportive, he can easily find a single example to illustrate this support. One could just as easily use a single story of prejudice to argue that the climate toward gays is not improving. However, the tendency for the Spokane respondents was to tell stories exemplifying an improving climate. Seattle respondents had similar stories to tell, such as this activist:

A good example would be the rest of my family, my siblings, and my mother, they probably wouldn't know anything about gay issues, they might even be a little hostile on gay issues, except, since [my partner] and I have been part of their lives for over twenty years now, even though they're not a very educated group of people, their viewpoint has changed dramatically to the point where they would be defensive. Well, I know my nieces and nephews, now that they're in high school, they'll argue with people that call gay and lesbian as derogatory comments, and that's kind of a tough thing to do as a high school kid because they'll probably be accused to being gay or lesbian right on the spot. But I've heard enough reports of them doing that. It proves to me that with education, most people are going to develop a more rational viewpoint.

The theme to come out of these excerpts regards the malleability of the public's attitudes. These individual members of the public have adjusted their attitudes, meaning that others, given the right information and experiences, could do the same. It is the feasibility of social change, rather than the actual existence of it, that creates a hospitable climate here. It is the duty of the movement and of individuals to make sure that the public gets the information and exposure they need in order to change their attitudes.

According to some respondents, if people do not develop pro-gay attitudes, it helps if they at least hold disdain for anti-gay attitudes and behavior. In other words, it is not so much that they are pro-gay, but that they are "anti-anti-gay." This attitude was a sign of a hospitable climate among a few of the respondents, mostly in Spokane. A Spokane activist explains how the public there reacted to anti-gay ballot initiatives in recent years:

A poll was done showing that Spokane County would have voted overwhelming against the anti-gay initiatives, more so than King County [where Seattle is located] or any of the other counties in the state. That was a bit of a shock to me and to a few of us, a delightful shock. We were real proud of the work we had done. I think it symbolizes that people here are not going to tolerate intolerance. They may not be very accepting and nurturing of gays and lesbians, but they're not going to tolerate overt bigotry. They may not get a lot of things, but they won't put up with the overt stuff. We got to the muddled middle and convinced them that this was indeed bigotry. That's nice.

A woman active in the local gay church in Spokane echoes the same theme, though in response to anti-gay violence:

There are times when they amaze you. When they come, you know, together in a time of need, and it's like they crawl out of the woodwork and while they don't necessarily maybe agree with it, but they don't like what ended up happening, you know, as far as people being hurt or whatever. They still shun the idea of, say, homosexuality, but they don't like the fact that somebody got beat up because of it, you know, that's not necessarily cool.

In lieu of the public's full acceptance of gays and lesbians, some Spokane respondents settle for their nonacceptance of anti-gay behavior. For some of the key goals of the gay movement, this is enough. For example, with regard to anti-gay violence, if enough of the general public strongly feel that gay bashing is deplorable, the increased stigma attached to such behavior could be enough to prevent it from happening.

A final interesting theme on the city level regards the Seattle gay and lesbian responses to my question about the general public's position on teaching about gay issues in schools. The Seattle responses were striking because of their uncharacteristic nature when compared to the rest of their comments. While most perceptions of Seattle were of a hospitable opinion climate, when it came to the questions regarding gay issues in the schools, many of the respondents turned around and said that the public would be hostile. According to the respondents, there are limits to the public's acceptance of gays and lesbians, and the schools issue is beyond those limits. Below is an excerpt from a Seattle activist that gets to the heart of the issue:

> (TL: What about teaching about gay/lesbian issues in school? How supportive is the general population of Seattle?) You know, that's interesting. That would almost contradict what I've been saying, what a wonderful place Seattle is. I sometimes get the sense that there's a line that people don't want to cross, either, that most people consider themselves, who consider themselves very liberal, that that's a difficult one for them. (TL: That would be a difficult issue?) Yeah, I think people are mixing up sexuality too much, there's a lot of people who think that sexuality should be taught at home, so I think the point that they're missing is that they don't understand what it's like to grow up gay. . . . I heard some people calling in on that radio show, well, they called in and said, "Well, I was fat in school and,"—maybe it wasn't that program—it was on KIRO, Dori Monson, he's kind of conservative, I heard him when I'm in the car and he was having trouble with this Kent student that came out in the school district. He was having a big problem with that and his listeners were calling in and saying, "I don't know why he's having such a big problem. It seems like he's being a baby about it. I was fat throughout high school and I suffered a lot too, and I got over it. I didn't sue the school district because all these kids teased me because I was fat. What's the difference?"

The Seattle respondents were particularly strong voiced about this topic as it represents the homophobia that remains among an otherwise gay-positive public. They see the public as still buying into the notion that gays and lesbians actively seek new recruits:

> Even the very liberal people that I am talking about that, they accept me as a lesbian as their receptionist or something. That is probably a line they would draw. I think that they do have the belief that it can be taught just as they have been teaching us heterosexuality and that it is just too dangerous, you know, just kind of the deep emotional charges that come out of people and their children. You are fucking with their children and they are very vulnerable and they are very impressionable and you may make them gay. (TL: So that's still a fear?) I think so, yeah, I think so, that it can be something taught. It is a choice, people still view it as a choice. This seems attractive, they don't want it to be as equally attractive.

In Spokane, the responses were similar. The theme of predatory recruitment, of people choosing to be gay because they learned about it in school, came up repeatedly:

> (TL: Or teaching about gay/lesbian issues in school? How supportive is the general population of Spokane?) I'd say probably only about twenty to thirty percent. (TL: Why would that be so low?) Oh, cause we have these little wands and, gosh, if we tell our kids about it you know they just might become gay because it might be the cool thing to do. The people that think we have these little wands and run around and go, "Oh, you're gay and they're not. Poof, now they're gay!" I just find that comical and I kind of see that really a lot of people think that way.

But in Spokane, there was no "this is the exception to the rule" rhetoric as found in the Seattle interviews. In Spokane, where the attitudes of the public are mixed, anti-gay attitudes regarding schools were not all that surprising.

Just as Christian conservative claims about Washington State differed between cities, gay claims at the state level were also markedly different in the two cities: Seattlites argued (in 70 percent of their claims) the state was hostile, while Spokanites were much less likely to do so (only 36 percent of their claims involved hostility). Again, we see that one's local experience colors one's perceptions of the state. As on the city level, the gay and lesbian state-level claims were primarily concerned with awareness, which most saw as growing throughout the state. For example, a nonactivist in Spokane, when asked if the state is changing, replied: "More people are talking about it, which is good, that more people are talking about it, and that's a step in the right direction. Get more people to talk about it and we can see where we can go from there." However, a Seattle activist illustrates a more demanding take on awareness as we discussed the public in Washington State:

> People just don't know how we live. We're still invisible. And then I think with education, people are openminded about it. This one guy I was talking to was like, "Well, what is all this stuff about gay marriage? What are you trying to pull?" Well, what we're trying to *pull* is I'd like to visit my partner in the hospital and make decisions for her if she is ill. I want a car insurance policy that automatically covers both of us, so we don't have to pay for a second policy. And when I told him this, he was like, "No *way!*" And I'm like, "Yeah, it's a total ripoff." And he responded to that. *That* made sense to him. And he's like, "Well, you can go to another state, which state provides?" "*None.*" I'm like, "Hello?!" *That's* what I'm talking about. They have no idea.

Making the public realize that gays and lesbians exist is only part of the battle. Getting the public to understand the full complexity of gay issues is quite another thing.

The gay and lesbian national-level claims were similar across the two cities and were evenly divided between hostility and increasing hospitableness. In Spokane, 34 percent of the claims provided evidence of hostility at the national level, while 49 percent concerned increasing hospitableness. In the Seattle interviews, 49 percent of the national-level claims regarded hostility, while 40 percent concerned increasing hospitableness. In the Christian conservative interviews, very few of the national claims (only 7 percent) regarded increasing hospitableness. Clearly, concerning the national public, gay men and lesbians are much more optimistic than Christian conservatives.

Regarding the content of these national claims, gay men and lesbians once again concentrate on awareness. The increased level of national dialogue about gay and lesbian issues is, in many respondents' minds, very important. As a Seattle activist put it: "It's on their radar screens more than it used to be." An activist in Spokane describes the personal nature of this awareness:

I think there's more awareness. People have been made more aware, in Spokane, in WA, in the U.S. And people are having to listen to it a little bit more. They have to take a look at it and kind of develop their own thoughts that they didn't have to acknowledge before. I mean, twenty years ago, it wasn't out there, at least to my knowledge. I mean, it wasn't in your face. You didn't have to acknowledge it or even worry about it, but now you've got to at least make up your mind on what you're going to think about it. . . . I think the thing that's making a lot of difference and that people are slowly realizing is that you *do* know a lot of gay people, you just don't know who they are. And the U.S. as a whole I think is going through that too. People *do* work with gay people and there *are* gay people in every family and there *are* gay people in the schools. They teach your kids, they pump your gas, they do everything and people are starting to realize that. A lot of it is because of information, I guess, that is out there now. And becoming more and more acceptable because they do know these people as a contributing part of society, not as people that march in parades.

On the local, state, and national level, the gay and lesbian respondents feel that one of the major accomplishments of social change has been the public's recognition that gay people exist. Pessimism still reigns for some, though, such as this Spokane nonactivist:

It's been a subject of quite occasional interest on magazines and TV and whatnot so people know about it, they think about it, but I don't think they necessarily want to think about it. I don't think they want it to be an issue. (TL: So, it's like an itch?) Yeah, I think so. (TL: A cultural itch.) Yeah, really, that's a good way to describe it.

Conclusion

Open up the scholarly journal "Public Opinion" and you will find that the majority of the articles analyze various national data sets. This work, which usually involves examining opinion trends among social groups, is important and necessary. The science of opinion polling has come a long way since its development in the early part of the twentieth century. It has become a vital part of the American political system, and a social institution unto itself (Beniger and Herbst 1990). Newspapers and newsmagazines have their own polling offices that release survey results on an almost daily basis. Politicians are criticized for their addiction to polls.

However, when the topic shifts to real people trying to make sense of opinion change, especially at the local level, few researchers have tried to understand how these opinion trends are experienced. The findings in this chapter show that most people have clear ideas about the opinions of their local public. The techniques they develop have important implications. If a group demands a lot of the public, odds are good they are setting themselves up for disappointment. A group that sets realistic expectations for the public is likely to fare better, creating an optimism that itself can bring about further social change. The attitudes and behavior of the general public weigh heavily on the minds of Christian conservatives and gay men and lesbians. But the nature of this weight looks different for the two groups: Christian conservatives focus on the actions of the public and the stereotypes they hold; gay men and lesbians concentrate on awareness and support for gay issues. Therefore, in terms of improving the climate for Christian conservatives, the road is longer, for it involves more serious readjustments of the public's lives: going (back) to church, developing deep religious faith, giving more to charity, spending time understanding the subtle differences between different types of Christians. For gay men and lesbians to feel better about the public, less is required on the public's part: a recognition that gays exist and a willingness to consider and understand their issues. This may explain why more gay men and lesbians are far more optimistic about the public than are Christian conservatives. These differences in goals for the public will also become apparent later in the book, as they affect each group's strategies for achieving social change.

4

Engaging the Government

In this chapter, I address the most political component of climates: perceptions regarding the actions that occur within the governmental sphere itself. One indicator of a social movement's power is its ability to permeate this sphere (McAdam 1982). If a climate is hospitable toward a particular group, then the group should have at its disposal numerous means through which it can enter the political arena and effect political and social change. For example, representatives of a group can exercise power through citizen participation in local governmental bodies, such as school boards and town meetings. Or they could get some of their own elected as policy makers. If this is not possible, the group may still have political power if it has access to politicians who may not be official members of the group, but are willing to lend a sympathetic ear. This willingness can be due to politicians' perceptions of an important voter base, or an ideological identity that predisposes them to coalition-building efforts on the part of the movement (Bawn 1999). In some states and localities that allow voter-led initiatives, a group may completely sidestep the conventional political process if it is able to collect enough signatures and votes to pass such an initiative.

At the other extreme, a hostile political climate may be perceived when these various avenues to political voice are blocked: members of the group are not allowed, or at least are severely discouraged, from participating in the political process. Perceptions play an important role here: a political structure that is quite open may be perceived to be closed, or a closed structure may be perceived to be open (Kurzman 1996). An overall finding from analyzing this set of climate claims remains the same as in previous chapters: Christian conservatives perceive a more hostile climate than gay men and lesbians. However, the different emphases of the two groups offer insight into the distinct roles that Christian conservatives and gay men and lesbians play in political arenas.

Christian Conservatives and the Political Sphere

In a recent interview, openly gay congressperson Barney Frank said, "Why do you think [Pat] Robertson got rid of the Christian Coalition? He doesn't need it anymore; he has the Republican Party" (Bull 2002). Numerous scholars have chronicled the rise of Christian conservatives as a force in American politics, both at the local level (Rozell and Wilcox 1995) and at the national level (Watson 1999; Hardisty 1999; Martin 1996). Upon hearing my findings, some may scoff at my Christian conservative respondents' claims that they face hostility in the political sphere. In a country whose currency states "In God We Trust," how can such perceptions possibly be correct? Regardless of their accuracy, I argue, such perceptions of hostility have real consequences.

In the respondents' voices as reported below, the reader will hear the palpable frustration that causes Christian conservatives to mobilize politically to fight what they see as a very hostile political climate, especially in Seattle. They feel that, at many junctures, they are blocked from adequately participating in the democratic process. Before I examine this situation more fully, I will give an overall breakdown of the Christian conservative climate claims regarding the government. In Seattle, 84 percent of the claims made about the city government concerned hostility. Only five claims out of sixty-one (or 8 percent) concerned a hospitable climate. In Spokane, the picture was markedly more positive. A slight majority of the claims (56 percent) concerned hostility, and 36 percent of the claims had to do with hospitableness. At the state and national levels, there were no overall differences between the claims made by the two cities' respondents. Around 70 percent of the Christian conservative claims about the government at both the state and national levels regarded hostility.

At multiple sites, the city government shapes the level of Christians' involvement in public life. Almost every time a church or religious organization tries to accomplish something outside of the confines of its building, it must interact with city officials of some sort, from politicians to police officers. Often, these interactions are strained at best, and Christian conservatives conclude that the city government is out to hinder their progress, not help it. This is especially true in Seattle, making this one of the main reasons why the Seattle respondents perceived their government to be more hostile than the Spokane respondents did. In the Seattle interviews, there were six references to the government's role in deciding how active Christians could be in the public sphere, and all of them regarded closest convention center that has any size that would make it bigger. I don't want to move it. But it is frustrating when you're doing something that's good like that and it's just a great event, people love it.

A similar space issue can occur when a church wants to expand and the ∨ does not allow them to do so easily. A Seattle pastor lamented over ious churches' moves to the suburbs:

I don't perceive the city of Seattle and King County having that kind of openness to Christians. At every level, the mayor's office and the zoning laws, even the way we do things politically, fund-raising, I do think that this is a whole other environment. I don't see the same openness to the Christian community in general. I don't think the city itself is generally hospitable towards growing churches. I think the city would rather have growing churches move out of the city. I think that's a huge mistake on the part of the city. All the churches have left the city. The latest one was Calvary Chapel which was in Wallingford at the old high school, now they've moved to Mountlake Terrace [a northern suburb].

A final way in which the government can make Christians feel welcome unwelcome to participate in civic life is when government-led social vices and religious charity intermingle. Unfortunately, my interviews ntained only a few examples of this. Two examples are extremely telling, ough. The first, from a Seattle activist, shows how the government can der Christians' attempts at such participation. The second, from a Spo-ne activist, illustrates how the government's call for Christians' assis-ice can be perceived as a sign of a hospitable climate:

There were a couple of ladies, single moms, in a low-income housing area who my wife knew, because she was working there through the church we were attending at the time. They had a women's ministry, trying to help the ladies get their lives together, teach them how to take care of the kids and their families, and bring them some biblical truth and help them get their lives together. And there were a couple of them who had their kids taken away from them by Child Protective Services, and we felt that the circumstances were not, did not warrant that, nor was CPS dealing fairly and honestly with them. They tend to go after low-income people who cannot defend themselves. We got involved in that, mainly because of our faith, but we ended up trying to help these ladies deal with CPS, and we

hostility. In the Spokane interviews, there were eleven references to this topic; only four of them regarded hostility.

Some Spokane activists felt they had adequate access to the inner eche-lons of city government. For example, an African American pastor de-scribes his influence:

There were no black policemen here. And the school board had no black council members. So we kind of organized ourselves, and went to the city council, to the city manager, and we told them what the issues were and some of the desires we had. We were very persistent. And out of that, there were six black people hired by the police department. And then we got the school board to kind of open up. And through that, we have made clear that we're going to be a part of this city. Consequently, in the last five years, the relationship with City Hall has increased. If you want to talk about a personal basis, I can get an audience with anyone here right now. And they call me on issues of this nature.

Another Spokane pastor described how the city included him in a special annual leadership program:

Most cities today have a chamber which is whatever the city's called, is called that city's name, plus "Leadership," and they teach leadership and they look for leaders in their community and I was chosen in this com-munity as a preacher to go through that with about twenty to twenty-five other community leaders, so I think that was a sign of openness of our community to Christians, and knowing where I was coming from to ask me to participate in that.

Community leaders in Spokane offered numerous examples of the openness of the city government. In contrast, Seattle respondents had no such stories. A Seattle charity organizer described the difficulty a pastor had at a community meeting:

There seems to be an assumption that if a Christian or a pastor would stand up and address an issue, they're going to address it uninformedly and from a religious perspective. I just heard from a pastor who was speaking on some of the new curriculum they're trying to propose to in-troduce into some of the school districts and they assume that because he's a pastor he's going to stand up and object to the material according to moral issues or religious convictions, and he didn't. He basically used the Center for Disease Control statistics and said, "We're talking about a health issue here, folks. If you're going to promote certain lifestyles that are going to create health risks to our kids." . . . So that to me is part of the hostility, is that there is this assumption that a Christian can't articulate intelligently based on the facts that if they're a Christian, that the issue is immediately categorized as a moral, religious one. That always puts us at a disadvantage in my mind, that we're not being heard as just a person bringing a concern to the school board or whatever.

Though the number of references to these types of occurrences is fairly small, their presence combined with the lack of hospitable references conveys the feeling that in Seattle, it is more difficult for Christian conservatives to achieve the political voice they desire.

Another point at which Christians need the attention of the government concerns public events, such as parades and marches. Because marches generally occur in public spaces, Christians, like any other group, must obtain permits and police help. In Seattle, Christians have found the police to be less than courteous. This is particularly annoying to Christians in Seattle because the annual March for Jesus has occurred right around the same time as the annual gay pride march. This provides Christians with an easy way to contrast the treatment the city gives the two groups. Below are two examples of this, the first from a pastor, the second from a charity organizer:

(TL: How would you characterize Seattle in terms of issues pertaining to Christians: hostile, hospitable, or both?) I think it hostile, basically. There's some exceptions to that, but I think basically it's a hostile climate. For example, when I was on the committee for the Praise March a couple of years ago, and we asked for some police help and they wouldn't give any. None at all. And yet they had over forty policemen helping with the gay pride parade, not a problem at all. People who parked down where the Praise Parade was got a lot of tickets because they were overparked on a Saturday.

Some of those little things, the March for Jesus. I think it was the March for Jesus, where the police officer wore his uniform and got chewed out and yet the Chief of Police wore his uniform in a parade, happened to be the gay parade down Broadway and he wore his uniform and that was

OK. I think that is a double standard and that is not community.

In Spokane, there were no such stories. While people b type of contrast, it was not imbued with perceptions o

(TL: How would you characterize Spokane in terms of to Christians: hostile, hospitable, or both?) Well, I don't an awful lot different than any other city. You've got y and people are going to line up on both sides. I believ able to express, we can have a Jesus march, as well as th gay pride march.

Christians often want the use of other public spaces nity centers or convention halls—for various reasons, give permission to use the space is taken as a sign of a Seattle, a woman described how a Christian group was community center:

I was involved in the opening up a few years ago of our center in Burien. . . . And they had a weeklong series of performing arts, and different kinds of activities that we there was a group from a local church out south here, wh play or something they wanted to put on, and they were d of separation of church and state. Because it was a schoo yet they had every kind of community group.

The excerpt recalls the "everyone is accepted *but* Chris has appeared previously. Through this example, this wor groups except Christians are allowed to appear in public feel that the use of the church/state separation rhetoric used to hide an ulterior motive. An activist in Spokane yearly conference had a similar complaint about the Spok

And in fact, the city tries to get rid of us. I mean, they bu and they made it hard to, we take the whole convention ce every bit of space that they had. In fact, it's not big enough anymore just because we don't have a big enough space know, our next best thing would be to move it to Chica found a lot of deceit, a lot of half-truths, a lot of lying in the courtroom. Things that we knew were absolutely not true. And our sense of fairness and rightness and truth, we determined that we were going to try to help these ladies as much as we could. But because of our faith, some of the people in social services, not all of them, but some of them are very antagonistic toward the faith, toward Christianity. . . . So they were antagonistic toward us, and I think to some degree because of our faith, because of what we stood for. And we were never that way with them. We tried to tow the line and walk on eggshells and treat them with respect and kept our mouths shut and didn't rail against them. But we sensed that antagonism toward us and, consequently, things turned out bad in both cases, but there wasn't anything we could do.

One day the Department of Social and Health Services called and asked me to come to this private meeting. I wondered what I was getting into. I went over there, the guy from Washington DC was there, the guy from Olympia was there, a woman also, and all these people, and me and they invited one other pastor, a black pastor. And there we were. They asked our opinion about what do you think about the government coming to the church and asking for help? I said, "Really?" They said, "We want to work a foster care program, we think Christians in churches would do a better job of being a foster parent than the druggies we got out here that are doing this to kids."

Government programs such as CPS and DSHS, often strapped for monetary and human resources, may see in Christians a viable source of help. On the other side, Christians see such programs as being representative of the government. Therefore, when these programs ask for help, Christians feel vital to their community and are likely to form more positive opinions about the political climate. However, such programs often employ politically liberal social workers who may have issues with conservative Christianity. Such a nexus may prove to be increasingly important in future years, as government programs continue to be reformed.

I now move on to the representative of the local government that touches the lives of the largest numbers of Christians: the public school system. For many Christian conservatives, this is the key state-run body with which they must interact. While some choose to send their children to private, Christian schools, and Christian conservatives make up the majority of home schoolers (Stevens 2001), many more Christians (either by choice or necessity) put their children through the public school system. In the public schools, many Christian conservatives feel that they face an overly secular culture run amok. In the interviews, I did ask specifically about the topic of prayer in schools, but usually in the context of assessing public opinion toward the issue. Often, the Christian respondents discussed how the local government treated the issue, or brought up school-related issues other than school prayer. Some of the references below come from my prompting. However, even more frequently, the respondents brought up the topic on their own. Fifty-three percent of the thirty-two references to treatment of Christians in the public school system were unprompted, pointing to the salience of this issue to Christian conservatives. Overall, the respondents in both cities perceived hostile treatment: thirteen of the sixteen references in Spokane and fourteen of the sixteen references in Seattle regarded hostility.

A number of these references concerned a perceived movement toward political correctness that tolerates every form of spirituality except Christianity. Most of these references came from Seattle. Here are two examples, both from Seattle activists:

> And I think that part of what is increasing the intensity of the debates, the Christian community to some extent is reacting against the double standard: no you can't have a Bible club at the school . . . but they'll let them teach chants. Or, no you can't put up a nativity scene at Christmas, or you can't talk about Christ as a Christmas tradition, and yet at Halloween we get occultic stuff all over the place and kids writing witch chants and spells and that kind of thing. Education has stepped back from remaining neutral.

> Another thing, too, is that school districts in the state, they spend money to erect totem poles on public school campuses, but they will not allow a cross or a Christmas tree or anything that even hints at Christianity. And yet, this other thing is cultural. Well, so's the other. Because not everybody is a true Christian who uses a cross or Christmas tree or anything like that. In fact, we don't even believe in Christmas trees ourselves. But the fact that they would spend taxpayer money for religious icons that they call cultural. There are other cultural things they could use besides those idols to demonstrate their concern for the native culture. The fact that the, in fact, I have books from the Superintendent of Public Instruction teaching kids in the schools—they're elective, according to the teacher, if

they wish to use them, but the fact is they are paid for by taxpayer dollars and they are available in the schools—where kids can learn to use Chinese prayer wheels, use horoscopes, use all sorts of other religious activities, actually engage them in religious activities, on the flimsy reasoning that it's a *cultural* thing. And yet they cannot say a prayer in school. I mean, give me a break. It blew me away when I saw it.

Some Christians feel that the school administrators, hiding behind the church/state separation rule, are on a veritable witch hunt to drum out every last Christian influence in their schools. One of the most vivid stories came from a Spokane nonactivist mother whose son brought candy canes to his kindergarten class one day:

My son, he's in kindergarten, and every week is a different letter of the alphabet, and it was J week and he brought candy canes, and the story of the candy cane to go with it. Do you know the story about the candy cane? (TL: No.) How the candy cane was made: an Indiana candy maker wanted to share his Christian witness at Christmastime, or just basically any time, and so he took white candy and formed it into a J. It was hard solid rock, white, pure virgin birth, pure life, and then the J for Jesus. And he said it looked pretty plain, so he decided to add some color, so he added one great big red stripe, meaning the sin of the world, and the three small red stripes, which represent the lashing, the slashing that He received on the way to the cross. . . . Anyway, he went to school with the story for J day, for his show-and-tell, and handed it out to all of his little classmates and they all brought them home. Well, the next day, unbeknownst to me, there was a meeting called between a couple of concerned parents and the principal and the teachers, of my son's class *and* my daughter's class because there were kids who had siblings in both classes, there were families with kids in both classes. And so they said look, separation of church and state, you can't do this, and all of this is unbeknownst to me, my son gave it out voluntarily at show-and-tell and show-and-tell is supposed to be a time when you can do whatever you want to. (TL: Now, did he give out the candy cane and the story?) Uh-huh, we had tied ribbons and attached the story to each candy cane to send home, and I guess some of the parents weren't real pleased. So, they had this meeting and they said, they told my daughter's teacher, don't let her do that. And my daughter's teacher happened to be a Christian, and she said, "____, don't bring the cards, you can bring the candy canes, and she can tell the story in her own words, but don't bring the cards." I said OK, I can handle that. So she did it, and once again, it hit the fan. Then, the principal called us in. (TL: This was the first time the principal called you?) Right . . . and we went into the principal and the first words out of her mouth were, "I hope you're not coming to tell us that you're pulling your kids out of our school." Why would I do that? The reason why, in my head, I'm thinking, "As much as it would be a relief to you, no, I'm not." And I said, "Not until my kids are completely persecuted for their Christianity would I even think about pulling them out because we're called to be," and I told her this, "in the Bible, we're called to be salt and light in the world, and I think that we can do our own little thing." And my son is the playground evangelist, he gets out there and tells his little friends about Jesus and if you don't have Jesus you're going to go to the, the devil, he calls it. Anyway, and it's cute, and I've made sure that that is OK, and basically she said, the reason why she agreed to have a meeting, was because, "Well, Christmas is all over, we don't need to have a meeting." And I said, "But Easter's coming," and she said, "Yes, maybe then we do need to have a meeting." And she tried to explain about how diverse the population at the school was, how strong the Jewish population was, how strong the Mormon, and how strong the Jehovah's Witness, and, you know, all this, and we can't have everybody. . . . And I wasn't willing to go to the cross for the candy cane, I wasn't willing to really pursue it really hard, but I did go in and have a meeting, and say, "OK, I understand where you're coming from, but if my kids get up at show-and-tell time and say something about their faith, that's allowable in my respect, and if you hold that from them, I might have to do something about that."

I quote this story at length because it illustrates so well how the public school can serve as a critical nexus for the intersection of Christianity and the state. It is easy to see how the circulation of such a story could create the perception of a hostile school system, and by extension, a hostile government and hostile general climate. The existence and circulation of such vivid narratives make it easy for Christians to claim a hostile climate.

And it is not just the Christian parents who have a difficult time. Christian teachers do as well, such as this man, who feels that he must be careful about what he says to his primary-school students:

The feeling is that there's school and then there's life, and the kids come here, you know, the kids know that God, that they believe in God and hostility. In the Spokane interviews, there were eleven references to this topic; only four of them regarded hostility.

Some Spokane activists felt they had adequate access to the inner echelons of city government. For example, an African American pastor describes his influence:

> There were no black policemen here. And the school board had no black council members. So we kind of organized ourselves, and went to the city council, to the city manager, and we told them what the issues were and some of the desires we had. We were very persistent. And out of that, there were six black people hired by the police department. And then we got the school board to kind of open up. And through that, we have made clear that we're going to be a part of this city. Consequently, in the last five years, the relationship with City Hall has increased. If you want to talk about a personal basis, I can get an audience with anyone here right now. And they call me on issues of this nature.

Another Spokane pastor described how the city included him in a special annual leadership program:

> Most cities today have a chamber which is whatever the city's called, is called that city's name, plus "Leadership," and they teach leadership and they look for leaders in their community and I was chosen in this community as a preacher to go through that with about twenty to twenty-five other community leaders, so I think that was a sign of openness of our community to Christians, and knowing where I was coming from to ask me to participate in that.

Community leaders in Spokane offered numerous examples of the openness of the city government. In contrast, Seattle respondents had no such stories. A Seattle charity organizer described the difficulty a pastor had at a community meeting:

> There seems to be an assumption that if a Christian or a pastor would stand up and address an issue, they're going to address it uninformedly and from a religious perspective. I just heard from a pastor who was speaking on some of the new curriculum they're trying to propose to introduce into some of the school districts and they assume that because he's a pastor he's going to stand up and object to the material according to

moral issues or religious convictions, and he didn't. He basically used the Center for Disease Control statistics and said, "We're talking about a health issue here, folks. If you're going to promote certain lifestyles that are going to create health risks to our kids." . . . So that to me is part of the hostility, is that there is this assumption that a Christian can't articulate intelligently based on the facts that if they're a Christian, that the issue is immediately categorized as a moral, religious one. That always puts us at a disadvantage in my mind, that we're not being heard as just a person bringing a concern to the school board or whatever.

Though the number of references to these types of occurrences is fairly small, their presence combined with the lack of hospitable references conveys the feeling that in Seattle, it is more difficult for Christian conservatives to achieve the political voice they desire.

Another point at which Christians need the attention of the government concerns public events, such as parades and marches. Because marches generally occur in public spaces, Christians, like any other group, must obtain permits and police help. In Seattle, Christians have found the police to be less than courteous. This is particularly annoying to Christians in Seattle because the annual March for Jesus has occurred right around the same time as the annual gay pride march. This provides Christians with an easy way to contrast the treatment the city gives the two groups. Below are two examples of this, the first from a pastor, the second from a charity organizer:

(TL: How would you characterize Seattle in terms of issues pertaining to Christians: hostile, hospitable, or both?) I think it hostile, basically. There's some exceptions to that, but I think basically it's a hostile climate. For example, when I was on the committee for the Praise March a couple of years ago, and we asked for some police help and they wouldn't give any. None at all. And yet they had over forty policemen helping with the gay pride parade, not a problem at all. People who parked down where the Praise Parade was got a lot of tickets because they were overparked on a Saturday.

Some of those little things, the March for Jesus. I think it was the March for Jesus, where the police officer wore his uniform and got chewed out and yet the Chief of Police wore his uniform in a parade, happened to be the gay parade down Broadway and he wore his uniform and that was

OK. I think that is a double standard and that is not a good sign for a community.

In Spokane, there were no such stories. While people brought up the same type of contrast, it was not imbued with perceptions of hostility:

> (TL: How would you characterize Spokane in terms of issues pertaining to Christians: hostile, hospitable, or both?) Well, I don't think Spokane is an awful lot different than any other city. You've got your moral issues, and people are going to line up on both sides. I believe that we've been able to express, we can have a Jesus march, as well as the gays can have a gay pride march.

Christians often want the use of other public spaces—such as community centers or convention halls—for various reasons, and the refusal to give permission to use the space is taken as a sign of a hostile climate. In Seattle, a woman described how a Christian group was denied the use of a community center:

> I was involved in the opening up a few years ago of our performing arts center in Burien. . . . And they had a weeklong series of different kinds of performing arts, and different kinds of activities that went on there. And there was a group from a local church out south here, who had some little play or something they wanted to put on, and they were denied it, because of separation of church and state. Because it was a school district facility, yet they had every kind of community group.

The excerpt recalls the "everyone is accepted *but* Christians" theme that has appeared previously. Through this example, this woman infers that all groups except Christians are allowed to appear in public space. Christians feel that the use of the church/state separation rhetoric is a legal cop-out used to hide an ulterior motive. An activist in Spokane who organizes a yearly conference had a similar complaint about the Spokane government:

> And in fact, the city tries to get rid of us. I mean, they bumped our dates and they made it hard to, we take the whole convention center and it takes every bit of space that they had. In fact, it's not big enough. We can't grow anymore just because we don't have a big enough space for it. But, you know, our next best thing would be to move it to Chicago: it's the next

closest convention center that has any size that would make it bigger. I don't want to move it. But it is frustrating when you're doing something that's good like that and it's just a great event, people love it.

A similar space issue can occur when a church wants to expand and the city does not allow them to do so easily. A Seattle pastor lamented over various churches' moves to the suburbs:

I don't perceive the city of Seattle and King County having that kind of openness to Christians. At every level, the mayor's office and the zoning laws, even the way we do things politically, fund-raising, I do think that this is a whole other environment. I don't see the same openness to the Christian community in general. I don't think the city itself is generally hospitable towards growing churches. I think the city would rather have growing churches move out of the city. I think that's a huge mistake on the part of the city. All the churches have left the city. The latest one was Calvary Chapel which was in Wallingford at the old high school, now they've moved to Mountlake Terrace [a northern suburb].

A final way in which the government can make Christians feel welcome or unwelcome to participate in civic life is when government-led social services and religious charity intermingle. Unfortunately, my interviews contained only a few examples of this. Two examples are extremely telling, though. The first, from a Seattle activist, shows how the government can hinder Christians' attempts at such participation. The second, from a Spokane activist, illustrates how the government's call for Christians' assistance can be perceived as a sign of a hospitable climate:

There were a couple of ladies, single moms, in a low-income housing area who my wife knew, because she was working there through the church we were attending at the time. They had a women's ministry, trying to help the ladies get their lives together, teach them how to take care of the kids and their families, and bring them some biblical truth and help them get their lives together. And there were a couple of them who had their kids taken away from them by Child Protective Services, and we felt that the circumstances were not, did not warrant that, nor was CPS dealing fairly and honestly with them. They tend to go after low-income people who cannot defend themselves. We got involved in that, mainly because of our faith, but we ended up trying to help these ladies deal with CPS, and we found a lot of deceit, a lot of half-truths, a lot of lying in the courtroom. Things that we knew were absolutely not true. And our sense of fairness and rightness and truth, we determined that we were going to try to help these ladies as much as we could. But because of our faith, some of the people in social services, not all of them, but some of them are very antagonistic toward the faith, toward Christianity. . . . So they were antagonistic toward us, and I think to some degree because of our faith, because of what we stood for. And we were never that way with them. We tried to tow the line and walk on eggshells and treat them with respect and kept our mouths shut and didn't rail against them. But we sensed that antagonism toward us and, consequently, things turned out bad in both cases, but there wasn't anything we could do.

One day the Department of Social and Health Services called and asked me to come to this private meeting. I wondered what I was getting into. I went over there, the guy from Washington DC was there, the guy from Olympia was there, a woman also, and all these people, and me and they invited one other pastor, a black pastor. And there we were. They asked our opinion about what do you think about the government coming to the church and asking for help? I said, "Really?" They said, "We want to work a foster care program, we think Christians in churches would do a better job of being a foster parent than the druggies we got out here that are doing this to kids."

Government programs such as CPS and DSHS, often strapped for monetary and human resources, may see in Christians a viable source of help. On the other side, Christians see such programs as being representative of the government. Therefore, when these programs ask for help, Christians feel vital to their community and are likely to form more positive opinions about the political climate. However, such programs often employ politically liberal social workers who may have issues with conservative Christianity. Such a nexus may prove to be increasingly important in future years, as government programs continue to be reformed.

I now move on to the representative of the local government that touches the lives of the largest numbers of Christians: the public school system. For many Christian conservatives, this is the key state-run body with which they must interact. While some choose to send their children to private, Christian schools, and Christian conservatives make up the majority of home schoolers (Stevens 2001), many more Christians (either by choice or necessity) put their children through the public school system. In the public schools, many Christian conservatives feel that they face an overly secular culture run amok. In the interviews, I did ask specifically about the topic of prayer in schools, but usually in the context of assessing public opinion toward the issue. Often, the Christian respondents discussed how the local government treated the issue, or brought up school-related issues other than school prayer. Some of the references below come from my prompting. However, even more frequently, the respondents brought up the topic on their own. Fifty-three percent of the thirty-two references to treatment of Christians in the public school system were unprompted, pointing to the salience of this issue to Christian conservatives. Overall, the respondents in both cities perceived hostile treatment: thirteen of the sixteen references in Spokane and fourteen of the sixteen references in Seattle regarded hostility.

A number of these references concerned a perceived movement toward political correctness that tolerates every form of spirituality except Christianity. Most of these references came from Seattle. Here are two examples, both from Seattle activists:

> And I think that part of what is increasing the intensity of the debates, the Christian community to some extent is reacting against the double standard: no you can't have a Bible club at the school . . . but they'll let them teach chants. Or, no you can't put up a nativity scene at Christmas, or you can't talk about Christ as a Christmas tradition, and yet at Halloween we get occultic stuff all over the place and kids writing witch chants and spells and that kind of thing. Education has stepped back from remaining neutral.

> Another thing, too, is that school districts in the state, they spend money to erect totem poles on public school campuses, but they will not allow a cross or a Christmas tree or anything that even hints at Christianity. And yet, this other thing is cultural. Well, so's the other. Because not everybody is a true Christian who uses a cross or Christmas tree or anything like that. In fact, we don't even believe in Christmas trees ourselves. But the fact that they would spend taxpayer money for religious icons that they call cultural. There are other cultural things they could use besides those idols to demonstrate their concern for the native culture. The fact that the, in fact, I have books from the Superintendent of Public Instruction teaching kids in the schools—they're elective, according to the teacher, if

they wish to use them, but the fact is they are paid for by taxpayer dollars and they are available in the schools—where kids can learn to use Chinese prayer wheels, use horoscopes, use all sorts of other religious activities, actually engage them in religious activities, on the flimsy reasoning that it's a *cultural* thing. And yet they cannot say a prayer in school. I mean, give me a break. It blew me away when I saw it.

Some Christians feel that the school administrators, hiding behind the church/state separation rule, are on a veritable witch hunt to drum out every last Christian influence in their schools. One of the most vivid stories came from a Spokane nonactivist mother whose son brought candy canes to his kindergarten class one day:

My son, he's in kindergarten, and every week is a different letter of the alphabet, and it was J week and he brought candy canes, and the story of the candy cane to go with it. Do you know the story about the candy cane? (TL: No.) How the candy cane was made: an Indiana candy maker wanted to share his Christian witness at Christmastime, or just basically any time, and so he took white candy and formed it into a J. It was hard solid rock, white, pure virgin birth, pure life, and then the J for Jesus. And he said it looked pretty plain, so he decided to add some color, so he added one great big red stripe, meaning the sin of the world, and the three small red stripes, which represent the lashing, the slashing that He received on the way to the cross. . . . Anyway, he went to school with the story for J day, for his show-and-tell, and handed it out to all of his little classmates and they all brought them home. Well, the next day, unbeknownst to me, there was a meeting called between a couple of concerned parents and the principal and the teachers, of my son's class *and* my daughter's class because there were kids who had siblings in both classes, there were families with kids in both classes. And so they said look, separation of church and state, you can't do this, and all of this is unbeknownst to me, my son gave it out voluntarily at show-and-tell and show-and-tell is supposed to be a time when you can do whatever you want to. (TL: Now, did he give out the candy cane and the story?) Uh-huh, we had tied ribbons and attached the story to each candy cane to send home, and I guess some of the parents weren't real pleased. So, they had this meeting and they said, they told my daughter's teacher, don't let her do that. And my daughter's teacher happened to be a Christian, and she said, "____, don't bring the cards, you can bring the candy canes, and she can tell the story in her own words, but don't bring the cards." I said OK, I can handle that. So she did it, and once again, it hit the fan. Then, the principal called us in. (TL: This was the first time the principal called you?) Right . . . and we went into the principal and the first words out of her mouth were, "I hope you're not coming to tell us that you're pulling your kids out of our school." Why would I do that? The reason why, in my head, I'm thinking, "As much as it would be a relief to you, no, I'm not." And I said, "Not until my kids are completely persecuted for their Christianity would I even think about pulling them out because we're called to be," and I told her this, "in the Bible, we're called to be salt and light in the world, and I think that we can do our own little thing." And my son is the playground evangelist, he gets out there and tells his little friends about Jesus and if you don't have Jesus you're going to go to the, the devil, he calls it. Anyway, and it's cute, and I've made sure that that is OK, and basically she said, the reason why she agreed to have a meeting, was because, "Well, Christmas is all over, we don't need to have a meeting." And I said, "But Easter's coming," and she said, "Yes, maybe then we do need to have a meeting." And she tried to explain about how diverse the population at the school was, how strong the Jewish population was, how strong the Mormon, and how strong the Jehovah's Witness, and, you know, all this, and we can't have everybody. . . . And I wasn't willing to go to the cross for the candy cane, I wasn't willing to really pursue it really hard, but I did go in and have a meeting, and say, "OK, I understand where you're coming from, but if my kids get up at show-and-tell time and say something about their faith, that's allowable in my respect, and if you hold that from them, I might have to do something about that."

I quote this story at length because it illustrates so well how the public school can serve as a critical nexus for the intersection of Christianity and the state. It is easy to see how the circulation of such a story could create the perception of a hostile school system, and by extension, a hostile government and hostile general climate. The existence and circulation of such vivid narratives make it easy for Christians to claim a hostile climate.

And it is not just the Christian parents who have a difficult time. Christian teachers do as well, such as this man, who feels that he must be careful about what he says to his primary-school students:

The feeling is that there's school and then there's life, and the kids come here, you know, the kids know that God, that they believe in God and they're Christians; that those things can't be spoken about in school. And that's a feeling that kids have. And that's a false perception, because for the kids, it's fine, and they can talk about it as much as they want, and they can pray as much as they want, but teachers are not supposed to. So, the whole attitude that you can't talk about God, and so you don't pray at school, well, here at home, it's very important, you do it all the time. And then you get to school, and you're having a hard day, or you're going through a tough time, or your friend may be hurt, and I can't talk about it there. (TL: So that feeling does come up a lot?) Yeah. (TL: What would you call it, frustration?) I don't think the kids even realize it. I think the kids realize it sometimes when I, you know, we'll just be talking, discussing things, and it will come up, things will come up where they want to share something, and one of them will say, "Oh, yeah, we prayed about that," and then all of a sudden the kids will start talking and then it's something to talk about. Or, "This is what I did at church this weekend," and then four or five of them want to talk about what they did at church. So, when they start talking about that, then I'm like, I'm going to share what I did, rather than think, oh, I can't share what I did. Just like if we went to the beach, if that's what we did over the weekend, if I happened to spend the weekend at church, then I don't have a problem talking about that.

Although it does not seem that he is overly hindered from discussing his Christian life, I certainly got the impression that the topic is on his mind on a regular basis.

Another aspect of the move toward political correctness in the schools concerns homosexuality. The candy-cane mother had negative feelings not just about the school administrators, but also the teachers' associations:

I think that the teachers' associations, rather than the schools, are setting the agenda. I think that they are way left, and I don't like what their agenda is. That's why I'm in my kids' school, I don't like the fact that they, well, they hired, for a very short time here, the equity person was an open lesbian. Excuse me?!? That's a real good, I mean, a Hispanic lesbian, I mean, she kind of hit all the little minority buttons that they needed to get. I think that it's going to take concerned parents to get in there and be on the PTAs.

Christians are especially sensitive when the discussion of homosexuality involves ridicule of Christians and their traditional values. One Christian father recounted the following story, and he mentions the Hispanic lesbian as well:

> When they start making policies or when things go on at school that make it so that my job—which I feel is to raise my children to know God is my first thing, number two would be to make them successful adults— when they interrupt my ability or my thought process or my feeling that I can do that well, then it starts making me angry and maybe hostile towards them. Or at least aggressive in trying to do something about it. So those kind of things would be a lot bigger to me than the things I see that don't affect them because sometimes I feel like I can't do anything about it. The school board, well, like, for instance they did just do one, where they hired this lady that even in the newspaper said she feels like she was hired, her job is to make young men curtsy and young girls to spit. She is wanting to gender bend, she is wanting to make, she was a gay rights person. She's gay. And she was wanting to make sure that gay kids had a better feeling in school and that kids understood it's OK to be gay. And that was her agenda, and they *hired* her for that agenda. And the school was paying her to do that. I went straight to the superintendent and got a meeting with him and said, "You know, if you ever want a lawsuit, just keep her on and let her keep saying those things in the newspaper and let it ever affect my child, because I won't have that." And they actually hired a group of kids to come in the disguise of wanting people to be racially accepted. To be accepting of people who are different. Well, the whole assembly was about gays being different and how you should treat them the same. And my son came home and said that was sick, you know, I mean those people, and they were making fun of the Bible, saying it was an abomination unto God, and all that, well those are things that move me and make me call the superintendent and say, "Dr. _____, we're going to meet."

Putting all of these stories together, it is easy to empathize with Christian conservative parents who have children in the public school system. At every turn, according to such respondents, their children are faced with temptation that goes against Christian conservative beliefs. Such temptation comes not just from other kids, but from the school programs themselves. So why do these parents keep their kids in the public schools? As I mentioned above, for some it is a financial necessity. For others, such a move fits with their calling to be "salt and light" in the world: God does not want them to shut themselves off from the secular world; He wants them to be in it and change it. This philosophy applies to Christian children as well, even though it may cause their parents endless distress.

The final major way in which Christians assess their relationship to the political system is to focus on politicians. Just as I asked in the interview about prayer in schools, I also asked about "conservative Christian politicians" and how they were received. In contrast to the school issue, most of the responses about politicians resulted from my specific questions; there were few unprompted responses. Of the thirty-nine references to the topic, twenty-nine were a result of my questions. Also in contrast to the school issue, there was a large difference between the two cities when the respondents talked about local politicians. In Seattle, seventeen of the twenty-one references about the treatment of local politicians regarded hostility; in Spokane, only nine of the eighteen responses did so.

So what is the source of the additional hostility in Seattle? Why is it so much more difficult to be a Christian politician there? According to the Seattle respondents, the problem is stereotyping, on the part of the media and the public (as I discussed in previous chapters) and also on the part of the candidates' opponents. A politician's Christianity (especially if he or she is outspoken about it) in a Seattle political race can prove to be an Achilles heel that the opponents can exploit, as this Seattle pastor explains:

> Actually, in general and having been politically active at one time, watching the reaction of the whole political arena towards Christians, there was a time that if you were a "born-again evangelical Christian" that was a nonissue in a political campaign. Well if you are a born again, to say that I'm a born-again evangelical Christian, and run a political campaign, is like committing political suicide. (TL: So it didn't used to be political suicide?) No. (TL: And now it is?) Right. (TL: How long ago?) That's happened in the last twenty years. It's taken twenty years for that to develop. Candidates tend to now keep their religion a very personal private matter, they tend to avoid questions about it. You know, they're usually not going to come out and make spiritual statements in a political campaign. . . . You can still win an election as an outspoken Christian outside of King and Pierce County. Some people, some Christians, have actually *moved* to run in outlying areas. They move to the suburbs purposefully in order to make their political efforts successful. (TL: They weren't willing to suppress their views . . .) Well, even if you're willing to suppress, you know there are elements in the political arena, whatever you were involved in

twenty-five years ago is an open book. There's diggers. There's nothing, I mean, you can't hide. You can pretend that you don't even believe in God anymore but it's too late, you have been active in Christian circles. It's like, you know, if you've ever smoked marijuana [laughs].

This "Christianity as liability" theme was echoed by numerous Seattle respondents. In Seattle, it is best not to advertise one's religious beliefs, especially if one is a Christian conservative. There was particular concern in Seattle over the treatment of Ellen Craswell, the 1996 Republican gubernatorial candidate who was a Christian conservative from the west side of the state. Several respondents, such as this executive of a worldwide relief organization, thought her campaign offered a textbook example of how *not* to run as a Christian conservative:

> Christian politicians in general have given Christianity a bad name, that's a broad statement. But the Christian politicians are all characterized, and I think that Gary Locke [the Democratic candidate who beat Ellen Craswell] is a Christian politician, nobody knows he's Christian, and I'm not saying that because I voted for him, because I didn't vote for him, maybe I did vote for him, yeah I *did* vote for him. And the reason I didn't vote for the other person is I thought she was treading on a narrow format of Christian beliefs and didn't have the other stuff to go with it, to make it credible. What's her name, Ellen, and there are a lot of folks who will run on a very narrow Christian platform here, and I think probably to the point where they could be divisive.

Respondents in both cities believed that one must be a good politician first and a Christian second. Some even thought Christians shouldn't vote for a Christian candidate who has not proven himself as a worthy politician. Here are two examples of this, the first from a Seattle activist, the second from a Spokane nonactivist:

> They would have to be very careful about how they dealt with it, because people don't want to see someone today considered to be a fanatic, someone who is much more concerned about publicly espousing Christianity rather than what he's going to do for you on the job. They want someone who has the right qualifications for a job first. And if they're Christian, great. Some of the hard-core Evangelicals aren't going to agree with me, but I'm talking from a majority voter here. I think it's great that they have

faith, I think that's great. If you want to let that be known, but every other word out of your mouth shouldn't be, "Well, you're going to hell, and the Bible says this." You know, you shouldn't come off like a preacher. You should come off like a public servant, with these qualifications, and you understand the issues, and people can tell when they listen to you that you're a Christian by the way you're conducting yourself, the stories you use from your life, but you can't quote the Bible every other line. That is a believable Christian, the other kind kind of turns people off. And they don't feel like you know what you're doing, and in today's world, politics is so confusing, and the problems are huge, that we have to have some idea that the person that we're electing has some idea of what they are getting themselves into.

(TL: What about conservative Christian politicians, how supportive is the general population of Spokane?) It depends on how good a politician they are [laughs]. I think they're supportive, I really do. (TL: So a Christian politician could make it?) I think they could. However, there have been some that have been politicians and all, or wanted to be politicians, and all they have espoused is Christianity and they haven't made it, it doesn't fly. So I want Christians in politics, but I want them to be smart and as-tute and upbeat and positive and, you know, the things that we want to see in our nation's politicians, hopefully. Just because they bear the name Christian does not mean I will automatically say, "Oh, I'll vote for you."

Such quotes point to a savvy Christian conservative voter, one who recog-nizes the need for compromise in politics. This stands in marked contrast to the common stereotype of the Christian conservative who is willing vote for anyone who has claimed that he or she represents conservative Christianity.

While the prognosis in Seattle was grim, Spokane respondents were somewhat more optimistic about Christian politicians' chances in their city. First, they could point to a number of politicians within the city that were openly Christian and politically unharmed:

There are several people here that would call themselves conservative Christians, who have been elected to political office. Well, I'm thinking all the way to Nethercutt nationally. Nethercutt would be, I mean, the only person ever in the history of the United States that unseated a sit-ting speaker. The only time it has happened in the history of the country happened when Nethercutt defeated Foley, and was a conservative Christian candidate defeating a liberal candidate, and had the strong backing of the newspaper and the establishment. So I think it tells you that the people of our community are smarter than the newspaper gives them credit. Yeah, I think they were looking for a man with integrity and character, and I think those are values in this community yet.

In the Spokane area alone I think we have at least four key representatives that are all professing Christians. Top people. Senate, same way. At this point we had one Christian guy was defeated here, but the margin was like one hundred votes. It was so close, which indicated the people were not that rebellious, they just felt the other guy was more experienced, which he was.

So Christians do lose Spokane elections, but one does not get the feeling from the Spokane interviews that they lose *because* they are Christians. Rather, if they are good politicians, Spokane Christian conservatives can do quite well.

Several Spokane respondents, such as this evangelical leader, did feel that there was a lack of Christian leadership within the Spokane government:

I don't think the Christian community has produced leadership within our city, city government and other positions, people that have had a strong impact for Christ that the Christian community can look at and say, "That's what I'm proud to be a part of." We have lacked that over the years in our community. You go to some communities and they have a strong Christian mayor, or they have strong Christian city council members, board members, all that. You go, when you look at leadership in Spokane and you pull out who they are identifying as leaders, the Christians, there might be five and you wouldn't even necessarily know for sure they are Christians.

Implied here is that the cause of this problem is Christians themselves, rather than a hostile political climate. Being active in Spokane's public sphere, then, has its ups and downs. But Christians there do not feel as unwelcome there as they do in Seattle.

The respondents' state and national-level claims essentially reiterated themes present at the city level, with one notable exception. At the city and state levels, respondents made very few comments about the mayor's or the governor's lives or policies. Like their thoughts about the general public, they seemed unwilling to let a single individual represent the climate. However, during the section of the interview about the national climate facing Christian conservatives, a number of the respondents talked about Bill Clinton's embodiment of the hostility Christians face. They made reference to both the policies they see him backing and the lifestyle that he leads. Many Christians did see him as a representative of the national character. When I asked an African American pastor from Spokane, "How would you characterize the U.S. in terms of issues pertaining to Christians: hostile or hospitable?" he replied:

> Well, the big picture, when I think about that, I immediately think of our servant leader, Clinton. I think he is, now, this is kind of hard for me to say, because I've had a close association with Clinton, I have, and he's been very cordial, even to the body of Christ. Although, some of his participation and involvement kind of bashes Christianity. And so, it kind of gives you a mixed feeling of what the overall concept of our national, of the United States approach to Christianity really is. That's coming from the chief down. (TL: Like what kind of things are you talking about?) Well, the military gay issue. That's one. And I think the public accusations that have been brought against him, even though he hasn't been convicted of anything. Somebody said if there's some smoke, then there's a fire someplace. And there's a lot of smoke.

In response to the same question, a young man who works at a conservative Christian university in Seattle said:

> We're looking for leadership that's going to speak about basic values for human people. But then, at the same time, there's a huge issue with sexual morality now, with President Clinton. But then, to see his poll numbers so high. (TL: What does that tell you?) It tells me that we just want a good person in leadership, someone who cares about people. We separate the two. So that's a concern.

Christian conservatives were rather befuddled by the lack of seriousness most of the American public brought to the Clinton-Lewinsky accusations. The public's lack of condemnation makes Christian conservatives feel all that much more marginalized.

Gay Men, Lesbians, and the Political Sphere

While some of the themes that arose in the Christian conservative interviews also arose in the gay interviews, gays and lesbians had additional issues as well. In fact, the gay and lesbian claims about the government are notable for their diversity. Before we get to these themes, here is an overview of the claims. Of the forty-seven claims the Seattle respondents made about their city's government, 68 percent of them concerned a hospitable climate and only 21 percent concerned hostility. Of the fifty-six claims made by the Spokane respondents, they were evenly divided between the hospitable and the hostile (39 percent each, with 21 percent mixed claims). It is worthwhile noting that, of the twenty-two hospitable claims in Spokane, ten regarded increasing hospitableness. As before, with the media and the public, Spokane gay men and lesbians optimistically perceive an improving governmental climate on a variety of fronts.

At the state level, quite a large difference exists between Seattlites' and Spokanites' claims. As with the state-level claims about the public, Spokane respondents perceived more hospitableness than Seattle respondents. Seventy-two percent of the Spokane state-level claims regarded hospitableness, compared to only 32 percent in Seattle. At the national level, there was less of a disparity, with 29 percent of the Seattle claims and 50 percent of the Spokane claims concerning hospitableness. In the twenty-six city-level claims, the most common theme was schools. This is not surprising, given that I specifically asked about schools. While some respondents discussed the public's reaction to this issue (I covered such claims in an earlier chapter, and they are not included in this count), many spoke of the government's actions. There was a difference between the two cities, though not a huge one: half of the Seattle claims concerned hostility, in contrast to three quarters of the Spokane claims. Several of the hostile claims in Seattle regarded a story that I have discussed in previous chapters: the brouhaha that arose over a donation by a lesbian city council member to the local public school system for the purpose of buying gay-themed books for the school libraries. Several respondents were not at all pleased by the way the city handled the situation. Although in the end the librarians got the money, people thought that the donation was made into an inordinately large issue.

On the hospitable side, some Seattle respondents pointed to the many types of support available to gay and lesbian teens in the schools. One activist stated:

I have some experience working as an advisor to a youth group and knowing the kids in high schools here and how much is available to them, not only in support counselors but in support groups in many of the high schools. And what they have. I think it's OK. It's not perfect, but it's certainly better than a lot of places in this country.

My youngest respondent in Seattle was a college freshman, and he had some positive things to say about the level of support he received as an openly gay teen in high school:

> Like, my high school, there was definitely some teachers, it depends on the teacher, some teachers are definitely supportive about bringing up homosexuality in the classroom, and others are like, let's not talk about it. So it depends on the teacher. And I've come across a lot of teachers who have brought up homosexuality in the classroom and who have read from homosexual literature. (TL: And they knew you were gay?) Yes. (TL: Do you think they were bringing it up to make you feel more comfortable or, if you hadn't been in the classroom, do you think they would have been less likely to bring it up?) I don't think so. It's just a general part of their curriculum.

In contrast, my youngest gay respondent in Spokane (who was, unfortunately, a young man of few words), said, "It wasn't talked about when I was in school. It was never mentioned at all." There was some other evidence that people in the Spokane schools didn't want to talk about these issues. The gay president of the Spokane chapter of Parents and Friends of Lesbians and Gays expressed his frustration with a failed program:

> Last year in PFLAG I was trying to do a speakers bureau and we sent out *hundreds* of letters and did a few follow-up phone calls to the PTA groups trying to get PFLAG to come and talk in one of those PTA things. We got a lot of them back saying, "Take us off your list." We didn't get one single person that would have us come in. And we did high schools and junior highs, we didn't get one single offer.

A similar story that corroborates this attitude comes from an HIV/AIDS activist who had his own frustrations:

> (TL: What about teaching about gay and lesbian issues in school?) That's a real hot-button issue right now, and Spokane would be very hostile to

that. In fact, even in working in the HIV/AIDS arena, we still get districts that are specifically saying, "We want you to bring a speaker, but it *can't* be a gay man." So those lines are very, very clear.

Spokane gay respondents also brought up the equity director that some of the Christian conservative respondents mentioned. This topic elicited somewhat mixed feelings: it was seen as a sign of progress that she was hired, but the fact that she rather quickly left the job (to move to Seattle, no less) reiterated the hostile nature of the climate, as this activist suggests:

That would be a hot-spot issue here. It's a very hot, hot button, it has been and already is. (TL: Has been, through what?) The equity director for the school district has left, and I don't know whether the school district's going to continue that. (TL: What was the equity director?) It was a program, where they had a gal that would go into the schools and they would teach children not only about sexual identification, but they would talk to people about equity in race, and talk to them about how you don't call kids niggers and things like that. (TL: Are you talking about ____?) Yeah. Yeah, she's left, she moved to Seattle. (TL: And you think part of her moving was due to . . .) Yes, I think it was, there was a lot of flack about that program.

Even though the school district is making obvious efforts to improve the situation for gay students, there remains much resistance to it. The few respondents who were optimistic about progress tempered their optimism with skepticism. The first quote below comes from a primary-school teacher, the second from an activist:

Well, the district has the language written into our guidelines of what students are to know, and to understand and to practice. We're supposed to practice inclusive language, and they're not supposed to harass people, or be disrespectful to people in regard to race, religion, one of those things is sexual orientation. (TL: OK, that is written in . . .) Right, it *is* in there. This year we're going to find out if it's that they really mean it, because I'm going to read some books, to find out if their money is where their mouth is. And so I'm going to read some books that deal with gay families, because we have gay families in our classroom, and in, in this school, I know of. And so, in my classroom I talk about this, so I'll let you know [laughs]. (TL: OK. What book, what books do you plan on?) I don't know. Books like *Heather Has Two Mommies* or something like that. I have, I don't know, I have to read them and see if I think that they're appropriate, and believe me, I'm going to have it planned out how I do this.

That is included in District 81, which is the school district for the city. They include that in their diversity program, gay and lesbian issues are included. But there is some controversy. It depends on which high school you go to. Some high schools have started groups, like gay/straight alliances. I think there might be more supportive people for that. Because there's been a lot of education over the past few years in Spokane about the dangers that gay and lesbian youth are under. You know, a lot of research has been coming out. And that really concerns people here. Spokane people are not horrible closed-minded people, I really think that, you know, they might go, "Don't teach gay sex in school, don't talk about homosexuality, don't talk about condoms," that kind of thing. But when they see, you know, that gay and lesbian youth are four times more likely to experience violence at school, that's disturbing to most people. And that's becoming more and more known here, and educators are becoming more aware about it. And we have a great youth group here, luckily. And they've done some great education on that.

This is one of the areas where Seattle is simply a few years ahead of Spokane. The programs are in place in Spokane, but people there are still very much in the "testing the waters" phase. Progress is being made, but people are still unsure of how much the administration's actions are simply lip service.

A second major issue, and one that arose completely on its own, was elections. This theme was much more prevalent in Seattle than in Spokane, and it was the largest source of hospitable claims in Seattle: twelve hospitable claims, one hostile claim. Six of these hospitable claims were quite simple: Seattle had gay elected officials. Indicative of these claims is the following dialogue with one of the directors of the Lesbian Resource Center:

(TL: How would you characterize Seattle in terms of issues pertaining to gays and lesbians: hostile, hospitable, or both?) Well, I feel like, Seattle is, I feel like our issues are pretty well represented. And I feel like gay people are really setting a lot of the agendas. For example, Tina on the city council, and Levinson's the deputy mayor, and there's a whole bunch of high-level queer people, so that feels pretty hospitable. (TL: So just having those people in the upper echelons of governments?) Mmm-hmm. (TL: Has this changed over the past five years?) I think I haven't noticed a change. It seems that there's more people in now but it seems like we've always had, over the last five years, we've always had pretty good access to that stuff. (TL: When I say, "How does the city treat gays and lesbians?" you automatically look at political representation as a major way to feel this out?) Well, yeah, of course that's one way, and I actually have a lot of, sort of "but then" feelings, and that'll come up later, but just sort of a cursory glance at the city environment, the fact that there are people in the political establishment, it's a pretty remarkable indication.

Spokane respondents used this observation as a way to contrast their city with Seattle, to show how their city was less hospitable:

Over in Seattle there are people in prominent positions that are gay. And, like, here in Spokane, I can't think of anyone that's openly gay that's in a real prominent position. Probably in their own business, but not openly to the city in that sense that you find people running for the city council and that type of thing.

In addition to being able to elect officials from their own community, Seattle respondents spoke of non-gay politicians and how much clout the gay community had among them. The gay and lesbian community is a large enough—and well organized enough—segment of the voting population to garner attention from candidates:

The political part of the gay and lesbian community has been very active in putting our needs forward and in working within the power structure as it exists to make that part of the community be considered as important as any other ethnic community or neighborhood within the city of Seattle. And I think you can see that paying off now, if nothing else by how many people that are running for election tend to court the gay and lesbian community, try to attend the pride parade, and you know, with the SEAMEC [Seattle Municipal Elections Committee, which rates candidates on their standing on issues of concern to the gay community] ratings, that's another way that I think people try to put themselves forward and say, specifically, this is what I can do for you as a community, when they're running for election.

In addition to creating a feeling that the gay community needs to be courted, candidates realize it is *acceptable* to court it. In Seattle, this has occurred. A nonactivist explains:

(TL: How would you characterize Seattle in terms of issues pertaining to gays and lesbians: hostile, hospitable, or both?) I think in Seattle itself it's very hospitable. Certainly in terms of the city government, and there's I think only one openly gay person on the city council now, but the city council and the mayor have always been, I think, open to gay issues. I went to Gay Bingo a few days ago and one of the first callers of the letters was Paul Schell, who as you know is running for mayor, and will probably be the next mayor just as far as it looks, so, at least he seems very open to gay issues, and wasn't afraid to appear openly at a gay event. So, I'm sure not everybody in the city is so tolerant of gay people. I'm sure there's a lot of homophobia out there, but I think the level of intolerance is so low that any intolerance that's out there, it's sort of, it forces it to be a little bit more quiet.

The fact that Seattle has Gay Bingo—a monthly event that raises money for AIDS charities—is a hospitable sign in and of itself. But in addition, the city's leading mayoral candidate attends it reading numbers off ping-pong balls while sharing the stage with drag queens. This offers a perfect example of the increasing intersection of mainstream politics and gay culture in Seattle. The end of the excerpt above hints at another way the political establishment favors Seattle gay men and lesbians: not only can openly gay candidates get elected, but openly *anti*-gay candidates *cannot* get elected, such as this activist reaffirms:

We have very friendly city government, increasingly, and that's especially true at the top and through the workforce. I think at the department level it's increasing, so that we're having more support and services. For example, domestic violence victims that are in same-gender couples. So I feel like people that are anti-gay in Seattle, for example, will have a real tough time getting elected. So that's my barometer, that the voting crowd anyway is not likely to vote for someone who is a bigot into our local elected office. I think being pro-gay helps you.

Contrast the above to the following claim made by a longtime Spokane activist, and this difference between the two cities becomes clear:

But Spokane certainly has its share of politicians and stuff like that who see homophobia and fear of homosexuals and all that kind of stuff, as a method to gain power, and they use it. (TL: So they use homophobia in order to . . .) There are people who have made a career out of being homophobes in the legislature and they know better than to say the things that they say, but they say them because they think it wins them a certain part of the electorate, and they manage to get reelected, so they keep doing it, but they know better.

In the previous chapter, some Spokane gay respondents claimed that the public was no longer willing to put up with overt anti-gay behavior, such as gay bashing. But this respondent claims that savvy politicians still are able to engage in anti-gay speech without serious electoral repercussions. This is not true of Seattle.

Spokane respondents did have a number of positive things to say about their mayor. This theme is reminiscent of one of the themes regarding the general public: the embodiment of the climate within an individual. Just as only gay men and lesbians engaged in this reading of the public, they were also much more likely to do so with the local political structure than Christian conservatives. At the city level, such claims were more common among Spokane gay men and lesbians. A short time before I conducted my interviews there, a small coalition of gays and lesbians sent the mayor a letter in support of a human rights ordinance. Just the fact that he was willing to give the group an audience was a hospitable sign for several respondents. To some, the fact that this is possible is the most important aspect:

> As I recall, when Garrity was elected, I thought he ran really on a business platform, that he was going to be pro-business. And then he kind of became an advocate, somewhat, I don't know enough about it, but some friends of mine would say, no, he's not doing near enough . . . he even came to the Grethe Cammermeyer luncheon, spoke, and has written letters for our INBA directory, to be in there supporting the community. That blows me away. I don't think that would have happened ten years ago in Spokane. I think a mayor would have been worried about committing suicide doing that.

> We've had two mayors in succession who have been very supportive of the gay community, whereas the mayor before that and the councilpeople in

that period of time, if they were at all supportive of the gay community, they didn't want anybody to know. (TL: So now you can be a supportive politician, and it's OK?) Right. I mean, it's part of a general climate of acceptance and diversity and stuff like that.

This climate-perceiving strategy of focusing on leaders continued in the sections of the interview on the state and national levels. At the time I was conducting the interviews, Washingtonians were just getting to know their new governor, Gary Locke, who in 1996 defeated Ellen Craswell, the Christian conservative Republican candidate. Washington gay men and lesbians were somewhat optimistic about Locke, but doubted his ability to improve the climate given by the previous governor, Mike Lowry. They viewed Lowry as an advocate for gay rights, and some were sad to see him go. An activist in Spokane explained his feelings about both governors:

(TL: How supportive, do you think, is Washington State of gay and lesbian causes?) I don't have much to compare it to. But I think it's fairly supportive. I don't see it really as being even nonsupportive, I see it as supportive. Not neutral, but proactive. (TL: What makes you feel that way?) I think because of what I've seen in King County and Seattle or what's transpired in Olympia, the leadership of the governors in recent years. Mike Lowry always flew over to the Privacy Fund [a gay political organization] fund-raiser that we had here every two years, always showed up. Governor Locke, he campaigned with gays and lesbians here. He actually solicited our votes here in Spokane. That to me says, yeah.

At the national level, some respondents used Bill Clinton to characterize the climate. But his wishy-washy nature caused frustration for some:

We've all beat up on Bill Clinton so damn much, but I think he's kind of between a rock and a hard place. He's like, "Yeah, I'm sort of in favor of this," but what has he done? And I'm like, God, look at how things have changed in the last two terms, just him *saying* that has done something. Yeah, it would be different, and it may be better if we had the legislation probably, but, you know, lighten up, things have gotten better.

Verbal support, then, gets one only so far. For example, while politicians' letters in support of the gay community are symbolic of a hospitable climate, they really don't translate into support that will improve the lives of gay men and lesbians. The actual actions of legislators are just as important, if not more so. Gay men and lesbians in Seattle pointed to policies that are written proof of a hospitable climate. A lesbian nonactivist tells how she ended up in Seattle:

> My partner and I did kind of an extensive study of different areas; we used the book *The Hundred Best Places for Gays and Lesbians to Live,* did some research on each of the cities. Of course, living in the South, we had Atlanta to work with. We found that really hostile. So, we came out here for our fifteenth anniversary. And we fell in love with what we felt. While it's a humongous city, it has the friendliness that we were used to down South. A lot of it was how gays and lesbians were treated, and the laws that were in place to protect them in King County.

Other respondents spoke of the same policies, such as another nonactivist lesbian who, in response to the question, "Would you recommend this city to another gay person who is thinking of moving here?" replied:

> Yes, I would. There are things that don't exist in other places that I'd never heard of before I moved here, like domestic partnership. You know, that I'd never heard of until I moved to Seattle and that entices a lot of friends that have heard about it that live in other places.

In Spokane, at the time I conducted my interviews, members of the gay and lesbian community, as part of their outreach to the mayor and city council, were trying to get the politicians to consider legislation that would protect gays and lesbians from discrimination in housing and employment. Such an ordinance has since passed and has even withstood a citywide vote to rescind it. Before these events, the hopes for such a change were sign enough of an improving climate for Spokane gays and lesbians. Domestic partnership registration, though, seemed farther off, and several respondents spoke about why this was a sign of a hostile climate. The lesbian schoolteacher I interviewed explained it quite poignantly:

> (TL: What is it like to live in Spokane as a lesbian?) Well, I'm probably just learning that. Well, I think it's isolating, for most of us. I think that for most gay people period, whether you're in Spokane or not, I think it's hard because there isn't a lot of validation or support for who you are or,

supporting, supporting, say a partnership. If you're in a heterosexual relationship, everyone recognizes that as such, for example. And we don't
have that recognition. Sometimes we don't even recognize it within our
community the same way we would recognize a heterosexual partnership.
For example, when my partner and I try to do things like a married couple would, sometimes, legally we can't. For example, I'm trying to think of
an example, it happens all the time, just ownership of things, putting it in
both of our names and making sure that if one of us, if something happens to one of us, one of us dies, the other one gets it. I mean, there's rig-
marole that you have to go through, so that things'll be left to your partner. It doesn't have to happen if you're legally married, you know.

At the state level, policies were a common theme. The mixed track record at the state level made it difficult for respondents, such as this Seattle
activist, to definitively characterize the state climate:

(TL: How would you characterize Washington State in terms of issues
pertaining to gays and lesbians: hostile, hospitable, or both?) I would say
both. On the one hand, the gay and lesbian civil rights bill comes up every
year for the past twenty years and it doesn't have the votes, doesn't have
the votes, doesn't have the votes. At the same time, Craswell was defeated
soundly and she had really extreme views. It wasn't just because of her
views on gays and lesbians, but she was pretty far out there. The state
chose to fund protease inhibitors as part of its health plan and in Washington State I think that still 80–90 percent of AIDS cases are gay men. So,
it does things to support gay and lesbian issues, but there are limits, and it
hasn't gone all the way. I get the sense that the state legislature will not like
what UW [University of Washington] has done with domestic partnership issues. And I think the changes for state employees about domestic
partnership benefits will be a long time coming.

At the national level, the numerous policies on the minds of gays and
lesbians at the time also caused for a mixed reading of the climate. Gays in
the military and the Defense of Marriage Act were used to characterize a
hostile climate. The push for the Employment Non-Discrimination Act
and hate crimes legislation were used to characterize a hospitable climate. However, people often talked of all of these policies in the same
breath, and often ended up with quizzical looks on their faces because of

the difficulty in telling what direction the country was headed based on the mixed bag of policies before them. An activist in Seattle:

> And we have a political climate where, at the national level, the employment nondiscrimination act could come up for a vote in one of the houses of the legislature but it seemed like they were brought there screaming because of the defense of marriage bill so you have the two of them juxtaposed. You have the defense of marriage bill and then you have, and then you've got increased AIDS funding which has been a good thing. Certainly since Clinton has been president changes in that area have been somewhat positive. So you've got a little bit of both. (TL: So it's kind of hard to judge?) Right. Then you have gays in the military: a complete setback but at the same time it was an issue that came to the floor that people were talking about, that everyone was suddenly aware of in this country, and so that was progress even though it was terrible.

Often, as illustrated above, legislators won't create the desired laws. Sometimes, if you are living in the right place, you don't need legislators: you can forge your own laws. In a number of states, including Washington, one can make a proposed law an initiative, collect the required number of signatures, and place the initiative on the next statewide election ballot. The use of the statewide initiative has grown in popularity in recent years, with sometimes ridiculous results: citizens in some states vote on dozens of initiatives each year. In Washington, there were three initiatives about gay issues in the 1990s. In 1993, there were two initiatives, I-608 and I-610. Both of these initiatives sought to restrict the rights of gays and lesbians. Neither was able to collect enough signatures to appear on the ballot. In 1997, there was I-677, which sought to make discrimination against gays and lesbians illegal within the realm of housing, accommodations, and employment. Such protections already existed within Seattle and a few other municipalities, but the proposed law would apply statewide. Although the proponents of I-677 were able to collect enough signatures, the initiative was soundly defeated at the ballot by a 60-40 margin.

These initiatives were statewide, so many of the claims made about them were at the state level. However, many gay respondents in each city used their city's responses to the initiatives to assess the city climate. I conducted the majority of the interviews after I-677 had made it onto the ballot, but before the election. Respondents spoke of I-677's prospects quite hopefully and were anxious to use it as a litmus test for public support. An example from Spokane:

> (TL: How supportive of gay and lesbian causes is the general population of Spokane?) That's hard to gauge. The conventional wisdom, which really has never been tested, is that Spokane is not. And it will be interesting to see, for instance, how well the ballot initiative does, because Spokane has never really had to, you know, present a political view on the issues. We certainly have had minority views which can be very loud, and give the impression that Spokane is this way or that way, but I think it all comes back to basically Spokane is a place where people are more or less willing to live and let live.

Unfortunately, I conducted only a few interviews after the initiative failed at the polls. But based on those few interviews, people were assessing the loss in interesting ways, such as this Seattle activist:

> I was thinking about that on my way down here this morning that, with Initiative 677 going down at the ballot, I think that I am annoyed that some people, I think this is mostly turf, have been outraged that Hands Off Washington actually put in on the ballot and so on without consulting them. I read all these letters, and I believe that whatever we can do to forward the good of our people, we should do. I think that it was a good thing. In any case, I think that part of the reason that that failed is because people are really complacent because, I think at least in Seattle, I think life is pretty good.

Interestingly, a number of respondents *appreciated* the anti-gay initiatives because they created solidarity among the gay community. A Spokane activist said: "It created an awareness and it made the gay community and supportive people get together and form the coalitions and be prepared." In contrast, some respondents, such as the following Seattle activist, did not like the idea of a *pro*-gay initiative and expected negative consequences out of it:

> But I still don't want to see a statewide vote on nondiscrimination. I'm not psyched about that. (TL: If it didn't pass, what ramifications would that have?) I think it would give more conservative legislators and school

districts and other things evidence to retreat on some of the advances they've made for gay rights. I think that there would be a sense of, "Well, obviously people don't support this, and so we shouldn't be passing laws that people don't support." It might also fuel statewide anti-gay initiatives. We have successfully kept those off the ballot, and if a gay rights initiative goes on the ballot and fails, that's just begging to rekindle that fire, which is essentially doused. I see it as an excuse for increased hostility, legislative and otherwise.

While political scientists are interested in the initiative process, they primarily concentrate on the legislative effects of such initiatives, or the public opinion surrounding such initiatives (Gamble 1997). The presence of voter initiatives, even if they don't make it to the ballot, is watched carefully by gay men and lesbians, as such initiatives can push the climate in a new direction. Because the prominence of ballot initiatives is an increasingly common phenomenon, more research needs to be conducted in order to assess how ballot initiatives affect people's perceptions of the political climates they face.

Conclusion

From looking at only the direction of the claims, it seems that gay men and lesbians face a more hospitable political climate than Christian conservatives. But when one looks at the way the two groups talk about the role of the government, an important difference comes to light. Christian conservatives tend to focus on the permissible actions of their *own* members within the political sphere: the political climate determines what Christian conservatives can and cannot do. Gay men and lesbians dwell on the permissible actions of *others*. They see this as a major signifier of their standing within the political sphere: the political climate determines what others can and cannot do to them. For example, while both groups are concerned with school issues, Christians look at what their children can and can't do. Can they pray? Can they evangelize? Gays and lesbians look for programs that will prevent other students from harassing gay youth. While both groups seek voice at city meetings, Christians focus on achieving this voice as an end in itself. Gays and lesbians see this voice as a means to achieve policies that will forbid others from discriminating against them.

The two groups, then, have different ways of looking at the role of the state. Christian conservatives view the state as an actor who infringes on their rights; they seek less state intervention. Gays and lesbians view the state as a protector; they seek greater state intervention. Although gays and lesbians may perceive an increasingly hospitable political climate because they have, in some respects, achieved their goals (Campbell and Davidson 2000), the fact that they require such intervention can be interpreted as the persistence of a hostile climate. As Lehring (1997, 193) argues: "The fact that they seek state protection is evidence of their present social and political inferiority however unjust the discrimination they face."

This trend is not without exceptions. But overall with regard to the political sphere, gays and lesbians are more concerned than Christian conservatives with the possibility that people could do things *to* them. They see themselves as objects: of people's derision, harassment, and discrimination. Christians don't think in this way as often, and are more likely to see themselves as active subjects. The next chapter examines in much greater depth how these two groups think about themselves and the extent to which their identities are the objects of scrutiny within the context of their daily lives.

5

Being in the Communities

Up to this point of the book, the elements of climate I have discussed were connected to major institutions in American society: the media, public opinion, and the government. This chapter focuses more on the personal and examines what it is like to actually *exist* in these cities as a Christian conservative or a gay man or lesbian. The ideas in this chapter revolve around two themes: identity and community. Regarding the first theme, I use the interview data to assess what it is like to carry around one of these two identities in Seattle or Spokane: Are they a burden or a blessing? Is it acceptable to display the identity, or does such a move carry with it various types of risk? Regarding the second theme, I address the ways various aspects of the Christian or gay community in each city make life harder or easier for the individual members. At the end of the chapter, I explore the connection between these two themes.

In the introductory chapter, I suggested that both Christian conservatives and gay men and lesbians must deal with identity-related issues. Members of both groups hold identities that are, by some, considered marginalized. Displaying these identities in some situations may pose considerable risk to these individuals: they could face ostracism, lose their jobs, or face physical danger. Members of both groups can choose, to some extent, to whom and in what situations to disclose their identities.

However, once I started collecting the interview data, a pattern quickly became evident to me. In assessing the political climates in the two cities, gay men and lesbians were *far* more likely to discuss the relationship between identity and risk than were Christian conservatives. The ability to disclose a gay identity is a major way by which gays and lesbians characterize their climate. The rhetoric of the closet—being in it, being out of it—is alive and well in gay discourse. For many gay Americans, the nature of the closet has changed such that it is not the all-encompassing phenomenon it once was (Seidman 2002). But to many of the gay men and lesbians I interviewed, the very definition of a hostile climate is one in which one cannot be out of the closet, whereas a hospitable climate allows one to display gay identities with little fear of repercussions. Although Christian conservatives consider themselves under siege in a number of ways, similar rhetoric that connects identity to risk is far less prevalent in their assessments of climates.

Before I discuss the qualitative nature of these claims, here is a cursory quantitative overview that summarizes this difference between the two groups. In the forty-three gay and lesbian interviews, 276 references were related to identity and risk. In the forty-one Christian conservative interviews, there were only sixty-seven such references. Of these sixty-seven, 61 percent were prompted by my specific questions about this topic. Of the 276 gay and lesbian references, only 31 percent were prompted by my questions. Throughout the interviews, in response to a wide variety of questions, the gay and lesbian respondents made it clear that their ability to let their identities be known was of paramount importance in their climate perceptions. Because this theme was raised much more often in the gay and lesbian interviews, I will break from the structure of previous chapters and discuss these interviews first, followed by the Christian conservative interviews.

Risk and Identity among Gay Men and Lesbians

One of the starkest differences between the cities is the ability to express one's identity as gay or lesbian, either by outright telling people or by engaging in behaviors (i.e., holding hands, wearing identifying symbols) that might reveal one's gay identity. In Spokane, revealing one's identity remains so difficult that many respondents used this fact as an initial way to characterize their city. In Seattle, while identity revelation is a conscious endeavor for many gays and lesbians, there is much less angst and fewer ominous expectations surrounding it. Although Spokane has a significant gay and lesbian population, many members of this community feel that they must hide their homosexuality, making the population seem smaller than it actually is. The decision to be out of the closet in various aspects of one's life is a very conscious one in Spokane—one of the very first things brought up by many respondents in the interview. For example, when I asked a director of a gay youth group how she would describe Spokane to someone unfamiliar with it—a question that came up in the first section of the interview—she responded:

I would certainly warn somebody, depending on what they were accus- toed to, as far as if they're, for example, somebody who's used to being very out. I would warn them a little bit about survival in Spokane. It would be more difficult to be out here. I might even, depending on what their circumstances were, advise them not to be out here.

The rhetoric of being "out of the closet" or "in the closet" was more prominent in Spokane than in Seattle. The majority of the Spokane re- spondents claimed that there was at least some difficulty involved in living one's life completely out of the closet. This is especially true in a relative sense. References to more hospitable cities, such as Seattle or San Fran- cisco, were quite common, such as this response from a nonactivist gay man. When I asked him if he would recommend Spokane to another gay person who's thinking of moving there, he responded:

Well, not if they want to be out and open. (TL: So that's not a possibility here?) Well, to a limited degree, I mean, obviously in your circle of friends. I don't know, I guess that's about all that anyone wants wherever they live. So, I don't know, I just have several friends who live in San Fran- cisco, and, you know, I go down there quite a bit, you know, it's just a whole 'nother world. So . . . (TL: So, as long as they were willing to not be as out as they would be in San Francisco, it would be an OK place to live?) Yeah, if they're willing to give up a degree of being out, it's fine.

But being out among one's friends is simply not enough for some gays and lesbians, and the inability to talk about certain aspects of their lives is a source of frustration and a sign that Spokane is not hospitable toward them. This frustration often leads people to define hostility within certain environments: one can measure the level of hostility by one's ability to dis- close. A nonactivist lesbian put it this way:

And just my experiences from different places of work and my friends' places where they work and it just seems kind of hostile in a lot of ways, in general, it seems that way. (TL: Individual people are hostile, or?) I think the places I work, I mean, if I were to ask, and I have, and we've talked about, like, half a dozen friends, and say, "OK now, the places that you work, tell me what those environments are like." I think that all of them would say at one time or another it's been pretty hostile. I can't think of that many friends who have gay-friendly environments per se, or places where they can feel comfortable talking about their lover or their dates or their lives.

In Spokane, there are gays and lesbians who do engage in such behaviors, but they do so in a very measured, very conscious way. As a gay activist suggests, "You need to know the geography. You need to know things about whether you can or cannot hold hands, where you can give, not so much give a hug, but give a kiss, and I don't mean a romantic kiss, but just a kiss of hello or farewell, even, to another man." Spokane gay men and lesbians are constantly sorting through places and people, in every situation keeping track of what they can and cannot do.

And it's not only whether or not one can be out. It's also *how* one goes about being out. A theme that came up in fifteen instances in Spokane but only once in Seattle is what I call the "in-your-face" theme, so named because many Spokane respondents used these very words. In Spokane, one can be gay or lesbian and be open about it. What one must not do is carelessly flaunt one's homosexuality in front of people. Gay respondents characterized Spokane as having remnants of a frontier mentality, including a "live and let live" attitude in going about one's daily affairs. Such libertarianism implies a double-edged sword, though, as it potentially divides gays into good and bad camps, with the "bad" gays being those who flaunt it. Non-gay Spokane is willing to have homosexuals living there, but only if they are not identified as such on a regular basis. The definition of in-your-face behavior varies from respondent to respondent. Here are three examples of this theme:

> I think there's definitely messages that there are boundaries, that if you're a good gay or lesbian individual and you respect those boundaries, then your life will be OK. And if you have problems, they are generally brought on by you. (TL: Can you illustrate this with any stories or incidents?) In my job situation, there's an individual in one of the seven counties where he was living in a partnership and his partner was [HIV] positive and the partner went out and partied and got drunk and so the police ended up picking him up and taking him home. And he made the judgment error of coming out to the police individuals, and so consequently his partner was fired by the school district he taught for shortly thereafter and one of them was taken out and beaten severely, and so, again, that communicates a justification that they were in their face about it, and really, when push comes to shove in eastern Washington if it's not confirmed, they feel

justified in letting it slip. But if it's brought to the community's awareness, then it's very clear that punitive actions have to be taken. It's that Wild West mentality.

You never know when someone's going to come driving down the street shooting. Nowadays, they shoot at you for nothing. That is, that's to me, still a little scary for me to be doing, in public. (TL: What, like, holding hands, or?) Yeah, holding hands in public, or kissing in public. I actually did see that once in Spokane. (TL: So you did see that once in Spokane?) I've only seen that happen once, I mean, like broad daylight downtown, you know. (TL: And what was your reaction to that?) Oh, I loved it, it was funny. Actually, I thought it was kind of funny. But I think they did it on purpose, but it shocked a few people. Makes people's heads turn and they just sit there and talk and whisper. (TL: So you think that that kind of stuff is too risky?) Yeah, I do. We still kind of live, everybody seems to be moving here, all those hate groups for some reason, in Montana, and here. It's still, I'm still kind of afraid of doing that. (TL: So you actually don't do it because you think it's just, you think it's just . . .) I think it's just pushing it in people's faces, and I don't think we should be doing that.

You don't want to really put DYKE, I guess I'm not secure enough in Spokane to put a big bumper sticker that says DYKE on it on the back of my big old 4x4 pickup. Probably, you know, that's so in-your-face, and people are NOT confrontational and NOT in-your-face in Spokane.

While obviously there was some variation in what Spokane respondents meant by this phrase, the underlying idea is that in many situations within Spokane public life, it is best to keep your gay identity to yourself.

In Seattle, the exact opposite theme was dominant. Many Seattle respondents started talking about their city by saying how free it felt to let their gay identities be known. They were thankful for this aspect of the environment in which they lived. One nonactivist respondent lamented about her impending move away from Seattle. She was returning to Houston to be near her family, and although Houston is a large urban area, she spoke about all the aspects of her life that were about to change:

It's about where you feel safe and where you feel you don't have to lie to live your life. I have really big fears about going back to Houston, after living here in Seattle and being so out whenever I want to. You know, I can tell people at my job, "Oh my God, I'm thinking about asking this girl out, I don't know, she may turn me down." I'd never do that in Houston for fear that I would lose my job. And I don't know how well I'll be able to adjust that down to a life in the closet. Cause that's what it's going to be basically when I go back to Houston. But I want to live back home where I grew up, so it's like giving up these things in order to live where I want to live. (TL: You do see yourself changing your behavior when you go back?) Oh definitely, definitely. I mean, there's no way, I mean, I walk down the street holding hands with someone here. I've bought flowers in places and had them sent to a woman with a note and that would never happen in Houston unless it was in Montrose [the gay district in Houston], you know, maybe it would happen, but my behavior will change drastically. I have friends there who are really defensive when I say that I don't know that I'm ready to do that, to make that change, you know, [they say], "Well life is fine, I don't need to French kiss my boyfriend on Montrose Boulevard," and I was like, that's not what I'm saying, I'm saying that there are other things. You won't go shopping together outside of a certain area like a couple would. You wouldn't go to Humboldt, Texas, which is right outside of Houston, and go to the Safeway there and hold hands in the market or act like a couple not even holding hands and think it was okay. You just wouldn't. (TL: Saying, like, "We need this" or . . .) And "Honey what about this and oooh, what about that," you just wouldn't. You go in, you walk a mile from each other, and you say, "What about that, Bill," and here I think people are a little bit freer and they have a lot more space to breathe in that and it's everyday life, you know. And there it's not, it's not everyday life.

Several times, Seattle respondents expressed this same type of frustration with Spokane. If Seattle respondents did visit Spokane, they would carry themselves quite differently than they would in Seattle, such as this example from a Seattle activist:

It's a sense of being really safe on my little square. But not really wanting to go to any of the other little squares. Because Seattle really is a haven in a general area which is a little less tolerant, in a statewide environment which I perceive of as being much less tolerant. So, I'm glad I'm here, and I'm glad I've got it good, but I won't go traipsing through Spokane any time soon. I may *walk* through Spokane, I may visit Spokane, but I certainly won't traipse.

Whereas living openly in Spokane is possible, albeit difficult, being out in Seattle was repeatedly described as easy. A nonactivist doctor describes his life in Seattle:

(TL: What is it like to live in Seattle as a gay man?) I think it's very good, I think it's very easy to be open here. . . . Certainly I feel comfortable about being open about my sexuality everywhere I go, you know, I live with my partner and, you know, we walk around, at least Capitol Hill, holding hands, and we'll do it . . . we kiss openly downtown or in the University District or at the airport and I don't really care. I mean, I think if we went outside the city into the suburbs we probably wouldn't be as open about it.

Disclosure, then, is a very situational phenomenon that gays and lesbians must negotiate on a daily basis. One is never just "out for good." Inside Seattle, the respondents felt free to disclose; outside of Seattle, they immediately modified their behavior.

There were even a few places within Seattle where a number of respondents were significantly more wary. What all these places had in common was that they tended to attract a more working-class crowd. It is a generally accepted social science finding that more education brings more liberal attitudes on a variety of issues, including homosexuality (Loftus 2001). In working-class environments, odds are good that the average level of education is somewhat lower, and gays and lesbians are sensitive to this. Working-class pastimes that came up repeatedly were baseball, bowling, and going to shopping malls. Here are a couple of examples of this, the first from a nonactivist woman, the second from an activist man:

We are probably a little more cautious when we go to a Mariners game. We love baseball, but it's just a different crowd of people. I find myself sometimes wanting to be closeted at a Mariners game. Because when people get a lot of beer in them, they tend to expose their real selves.

Just last night, my partner and I were walking at Alki Beach in West Seattle and I've always loved West Seattle—the beach—because it just feels so far away and I love the water and the feeling I have when I watch the sunset and all that. But the thing that I noted was that the community there, just the sense of it, hasn't changed really, maybe changed somewhat, but over the years has felt very white, very heterosexual, rather young, perhaps even predominantly working class, and for whatever reason that seems to be less hospitable to the open display of people walking down the street arm and arm or whatever. And there's a feeling, just this sense, that it's not quite as comfortable to be in that spot.

So, it is incorrect to assume that Seattle is *so* hospitable that gay men and lesbians don't have to think about disclosure at all. They do. Shortly after the gay activist made the above statement about the beach, he added:

The thing that I feel is a shame about being gay is that when you choose, when I choose to touch or do something like that publicly, there seems to always be a little of me thinking about it. There's a consciousness about, OK, so here you go. It's just that awareness. I'd like to imagine—I don't know if I can imagine—that it doesn't happen for someone as part of the heterosexual majority. I imagine they just do what they're doing and don't think about it. (TL: So there's a little bit of you that's always conscious?) Yeah. And I wish that wasn't there.

As much as I like this last statement, it seems a little trite to me when I consider the consequences of being out of the closet in Spokane. A significant number of Spokane respondents had stories of people who had faced unpleasant consequences for disclosing their sexual orientation. Most of these consequences fall into two categories: physical violence and employment. Part of the reason why the Spokane respondents felt they could not reveal their sexual identities is the prevalence of hate crimes in the Spokane area. With the death of Matthew Shepard, hate crimes against gays and lesbians moved into the national spotlight. However, the threat of hate crimes directed at gay men and lesbians has been long-standing, especially in Spokane. While only four Seattle respondents made climate claims relating to hate crimes, eleven Spokane respondents did so. Around half of these references were to specific incidents that had happened to them personally, while the other half concerned crimes directed at the community in general. The personal incidents ranged from bothersome to bone chilling. From the bothersome side came a gay activist's account of an incident from six months earlier:

Well, I did get slugged one night by somebody who knew that I was, found out I was gay, and . . . I never reported it or anything. (TL: This person was somebody you knew?) No, no it was kind of a stranger, and it was in a conversation, and it was outside, and just talking, and I made a comment about it, and actually I'd given him a ride, and we got the point . . . (TL: Gave him a ride to his place?) Yeah, and got to the point where I let him off, and he turned around and hit me. In fact, hit me three times and stole my garage door opener. (TL: So, you told him, you gave him a ride . . .) Yeah, and he'd asked some pointed questions, so he must have sensed that something was going on, and so when I said, "Yeah, I'm gay," and all, and he just says, "Hmm, well I don't think very much of that," and just had some general conversation, and then when I went to let him out. . . . So it's, it's an unreported . . . (TL: Why didn't you report it? It's not your style, or?) Well, I didn't get hurt, to any extent, and . . . I thought, well, I don't want to go through the issue of having it publicized in the paper perhaps, I'm a businessman, I don't need to have my name in the paper for something like that, and have it be labeled as gay-bashing.

On the bone-chilling side comes a story from a nonactivist woman, who, when asked, "What is it like to live in Spokane as a lesbian?" immediately responded:

It's all right. I feel like I do OK. I don't, you don't do public displays of affection unless we're, like, in a gay bar, or in the gay church or at a group of friends' houses. We just don't do it. [My partner] and I had a bad experience: we got beat up in a bar. In a gay bar by some straight people that basically just came in to beat up on some lesbians. At one point in that altercation, I thought I was just going to die. I was laying there on the ground, this guy was on my back. I had really long hair at that time and his hands were just kind of wrapped up in my hair, and he just kept punching me in the face, and I was thinking to myself: I'm going to die here. I'm going to die. Probably the fear of something like that happening again is probably why I don't, and why she doesn't, kiss in public. We just don't.

This was by far the most serious crime recounted in the interviews. Although the police were rather unhelpful and the perpetrators went unpunished, the victim has since shared her story with the city council as part of an effort to raise awareness of gay and lesbian issues in Spokane. While the official telling of such stories may make the arguments for legislation stronger, the circulation of the stories within the Spokane gay and lesbian community reaffirms that this kind of nightmare is a possibility.

The fact that the incident occurred within one of the few purportedly safe havens (the gay bars) in Spokane adds resonance to the risk.

Other Spokane stories about hate crimes were of a more general "this kind of thing happens" nature. A nonactivist man responded to my question, "What is it like to live in Spokane as a gay man?" with the following short reply:

> Scary. (TL: Can you illustrate this with any stories or incidents?) Oh, you know, people, like these young kids who go by the bars screaming at you "Fag!" You know, when you're going up and down the sidewalk. (TL: Is this a regular occurrence?) Yeah, kind of. I mean, it's no big thing. I've never had someone say that to me personally. (TL: But you've heard of it happening?) Yeah. You know, they're kind of just shouting at the crowd in general.

Such an excerpt offers evidence that small-scale events are important. Although getting called names outside of a bar is in no way as serious as being beat to a pulp inside the bar, both of these types of stories become common knowledge to gay men and lesbians, and they use both in similar ways to characterize the hostile climate around them. A final type of crime story that arose several times in the Spokane interviews was the smashing of the office windows of the Peace and Justice League, which houses the fledgling Rainbow Regional Community Center for the gay community. Although uncertainty remains regarding whether this crime was specifically directed at the gay community, its occurrence right around the week of gay pride activities makes this interpretation that much more plausible. Spokane is a city where hate crimes can happen, both to individuals and to the gay community as a whole.

The references to hate crimes in Seattle, although infrequent, were also equally divided between the personal and the general. Of the few personal occasions, one person was yelled at and pursued by a group of young people, another briefly recounted getting beat up outside of a lesbian bar around 1980. Of the few general events, one person claimed there had been an increase in the prevalence of straight men raping gay men, another said that kids are spat upon in schools when engaging in gay activism. Interestingly, some Seattlites' reactions to verbal hate crimes are indicative of how hospitable Seattle is. Below are two examples of this, the first from a lesbian activist who had lived in the city only a year, the second from a gay activist:

(TL: Do you like the city?) Uh-huh. I like it a lot. (TL: What do you like about it?) I like that the gay community is integrated. Like you can go anywhere. I can go anywhere and hold hands with my lover and it's not been an issue. I was here five months before someone called me dyke from a moving car, and I didn't understand what they were saying at first. And I took that as a good sign.

And there was a time about two years ago when a couple of my friends were walking down the street and they were walking across the street at the intersection and the car that was stopped there, it was like a pickup truck with these two guys, and they yelled "Fag!" out the window, and the two friends looked at each other and decided to do a big kiss right there in front of the car, sort of a mini-action. And they did that on Broadway without fear of these guys getting out and shooting them or hurting them or anything like that. I think in Seattle there is a real sense of safety. I guess that qualifies as harassment, but at the same time . . .

These two excerpts are striking because they involve behavior that in Spokane was treated as a significant sign of hostility. In Seattle, though, such catcalls are treated with much less seriousness. What accounts for these different interpretations? In Seattle, because of the relative infrequency of such incidents, bigotry can be treated as an oddity, something at which to poke fun. In Spokane, it occurs more often. Combined with other aspects of the hostile climate, it becomes something that gay men and lesbians have to process and deal with. It is harder to consider the bigots as freaks (Gamson 1998) when there are a sizable number of them.

Although Seattle respondents made far fewer references to hate crimes, both groups are concerned about the possibility of such crimes. When I asked the respondents, at the end of the scenario section of the interview, "Is there anything else you can think of which would affect your perceptions of how hospitable your environment is toward gays and lesbians?" the most common response for gay men and lesbians in both cities was hate crimes. In Seattle, of the fifteen people who had an answer to this question, seven referred to hate crimes. In Spokane, of the fourteen people with a response, ten mentioned hate crimes. Some mentioned that it would take only one serious gay bashing in the community to affect their feelings about the environment in general. While frequency is obviously important, the mere possibility of a hate crime is enough to affect people's beliefs about their city.

The other major concern regarding the consequences of being out related to employment. Around half the Spokane respondents spoke of the fear of getting fired because of their sexuality. At the time of the interviews, Spokane was not covered by any employment discrimination legislation (the city council passed such legislation shortly after I finished conducting interviews). In contrast to the Houston-bound Seattle woman who could talk at work about her quest for a girlfriend, a number of Spokane respondents told specific stories of the consequences of being too open at their jobs. My youngest respondent in Spokane claims to have been fired for such a reason:

> When I opened up to my job, I lost my job. . . . I was working at [a local hotel], and I had been working there for, like, a week. And I asked my boss if I could have three days off to go to Seattle. And he goes, "Well, what do you need to go to Seattle for?" I go, "Because I want to go to a parade." And he goes, "What kind of parade?" I said, "Well, it's a gay and lesbian parade." And the next day I came in to look at the schedule, and I was marked off the schedule.

I wondered whether asking for a vacation after only a week on the job might have been his undoing, but I did not share this thought with him. It seemed that he had told this story numerous times before, perhaps to the members of his gay youth group. One does not need to hear too many of these stories before deciding that in Spokane, it is better to stay closeted at the job. An employee's fear of firing also affects those close to her, such as this lesbian respondent speaking about her partner, who works at a local lumber mill:

> My honey could not become a Lesbian Avenger [laughs] and take her shirt off because it would be on the news and that wouldn't be fun. You know, we had a problem one year because she was very worried about her job, as far as being in the parade and I said, "Fine," I said, "That's OK, but realize that I'm not going to *not* do it because you can't. I will still do it." And I said the other thing is that remember there aren't just gays and lesbians and bisexuals and transgenders in this parade, there are heterosexuals too. And I said, you know, just because you're in the parade doesn't mean you're gay, you know, it didn't, it's not an obvious conclusion. So there are those kind of things.

In Seattle, there was concern over employment, but such concern was notably more abstract and hypothetical ("this could happen") than in Spokane. Many people spoke about how supportive their workplaces were. One of the things that makes being out easy in Seattle is the relative lack of consequences. The chance of something negative happening exists, but it is small. To many in Seattle, the chance is too small to affect their behavior, and they therefore live their lives out in the open. In Spokane, the probability of negative consequences is high enough to still weigh heavily on the minds of Spokane gays and lesbians.

In addition to talking about the individual implications of being out of the closet, activists in Spokane had much to say about the effects that the closeted nature of the community has on prospects for social change. Identity disclosure is important not only to individuals' personal progress, but also to the goals of the local gay and lesbian rights movement. In discussing the tenuous relationship the gay community has had with the Spokane police, an activist implies that the continuing problem with the police is related to the closeted nature of the gay and lesbian community:

> Part of the problem in this town is getting anyone to come forward, especially if the police have harassed them, you've got to be careful, because a complaint to the Human Rights Commission is public and goes right to the police, and they've been known to come back and harass and silence people. So people say, "Why bother to step forward?" Well, you can get a lawyer. Or we can take an unwritten complaint. Keep it public, but say that the person refused to file an official complaint because, blah, blah, blah, or the family's in town and they don't want it to hit the paper, so there's all sorts of problems in getting folks to come forward, but the stories [of police harassment] are there. And there's too many of them to discount all of them as fabrications.

The earlier story about the man who got slugged in his car is a perfect example of what this activist is saying. Another example of this effect on social change comes from an AIDS activist. When asked why some people don't get involved in activism, he replied: "Some people don't want to do it because they're, I mean, we've got people who have wanted to help more, but [whispers] they don't want to be seen." Spokane gay men and lesbians are trapped in a Catch-22: to improve a hostile environment, they need to step forward, but many will not step forward until the environment improves. This makes for slow progress. A gay PFLAG (Parents and Friends of Lesbians and Gays) activist sums up the problem in the following contrast to the civil rights movement. He was discussing the prospects for gay marriage:

> I don't think that it's going to be real soon. I kind of think that we're in the same boat as maybe the blacks were in the '60s. And the problem there is that the blacks had an advantage in that if you were black, you know it. It's quite obvious. With gay people, you've got to make the decision, are you going to be out or not, are you going to let people know you're gay or not, and there's a real fear factor. If black people were able to say, "Gee, I'm not going to tell anybody I'm black," and have it be true, then I don't think there would have been the same amount of progress.

In speaking of the high level of fear that they perceived among nonactivists, Spokane gay activists were noticeably frustrated. Several key community leaders claimed that such fear is unfounded. They based this perception on their wide array of experiences. They have compared what it is like to be out in Spokane with what it is like to be closeted, and have decided that the former is preferable. Their frustration comes from their inability to convince others that it is better to be out. Thus, what we have here, according to the activists, is a pervasive *mis*perception of the climate in Spokane. I offer three examples of this key point, from three different activists:

> (TL: There are many reasons people have for not being an activist. What do you think some of these reasons are?) Fear. Bottom line. And I'm very direct about that and that's why I can piss people off here. They will give you a lot of excuses. They'll say, you know, "Oh, I'm not a political person," or whatever. They don't realize, to me, activism is an expression, is an extension of your everyday life. It's where you shop for groceries, it's whether or not you come out to your folks, I mean it's so many basic components. But people are just scared out of their gourds and a lot of times, my experiences are all I can speak from, 90 percent of the fears that I had never materialized. They were things that I created and rationalizations for hugging on to that closet so strong. But I've had so few repercussions, and as a white middle-class male, that may be part of it. But folks respect the integrity, and they really do respect folks who put themselves out there, and whether or not they get it, I've never been bullied, I've never been intimidated, I've never been harassed, in four and a half years, ever.

(TL: What is it like to live in Spokane as a gay man?) Well, Spokane has this sort of live and let live atmosphere and people don't really concern themselves really that much with what other people are doing. So I think that that makes it easier than a lot of people think. I think there are a lot of people in Spokane who are really afraid that they're going to lose their job or whatever, and I think a lot of that is expectation that they would discover isn't really true. Because I think that . . . there certainly are, you know, we have our share of people who are homophobic and go around demonstrating that for anyone who cares to see, but I think that the large percentage of people in Spokane, they may not necessarily be supportive in the sort of general realm of, you know, they're going to vote for this or they're going to vote for people who vote this way, but I think that in personal interactions, it's not an issue for most people in Spokane.

I think there are truly some founded fears, I'm not for outing, and I believe you have to do it in your own process. But I see too many people around that are just goofy about it. I think that they have unfounded fears. I think if they did some of this stuff, they would find that nothing would happen. I think that's true for a lot of people. A lot of situations. People are just giving themselves an incredible amount of stress doing stupid deceit things. They are very very out to everybody, except their Mom and Dad, who live here. And they're having to lie about everything they do. They have to invent a whole life, because everything they do is gay and lesbian oriented. They have to. What church do they go to? They can't say MCC [the gay church]. But their parents will say, "Are you going to church?" And so it's like, do you say no, or do you say, "Yes, I am, and I go to a gay church"? And I know, because I never did it to this extent. But the extent I did it to was about enough to drive me nuts. I was spending so much energy on that, that I didn't have energy for other things that were more positive or constructive.

The Spokane respondents made a number of references to ways in which the climate was improving, specifically with regard to the level of disclosure that was possible. These references were evenly divided among activists and nonactivists. However, it was only the activists who made the connection between the improvement of the climate in this respect and the prospects it brought for future social change. Activists in Spokane saw a good deal of momentum building in their city, but they had yet to concoct an appropriate strategy to turn this momentum into mobilization. The fight for social change is partly a perceptual one: many people need to feel that change is possible, or that a good deal of change has already occurred, before they will join the cause.

Risk and Identity among Christian Conservatives

This section is shorter than the last for a very simple reason: there is substantially less to discuss. The most notable aspect of Christian conservative views on risk and identity is the paucity of references to this topic in the interviews. Just in terms of the raw numbers of references to the topic, Christian conservatives were overall four times less likely than gay men and lesbians to talk about issues related to risk and identity. And since a majority of these claims were prompted by my specific interview questions, some Christians may not have broached the topic had they been left to their own devices.

While the major topics I have discussed thus far—the media, the public, the government—seem to be of roughly equal importance to the two groups in the study, more personal issues relating to identity and risk are simply not as important to Christian conservatives as they are to gay men and lesbians. When asked to characterize the climates they experience, the vast majority of the Christian conservative respondents do not think about whether or not they can freely display their identities to those around them. While Christian conservative identities may be highly salient aspects of individuals' overall conceptions of their personhood, and while Christian conservatives feel that they are stigmatized by society on numerous fronts, this stigma is not wrapped up in risk to the same extent that gay and lesbian identities are. Below I discuss a few important themes that arose out of the Christian interviews, in roughly the same order as the gay themes. But keep in mind that the examples I offer are representative of far fewer claims than the examples I used in the gay and lesbian section above.

There were a number of Christian conservatives (four in Spokane, six in Seattle) who said that at certain times, they refrain from displaying their Christian identities, or at least temper the amount they weave their Christianity into interactions with non-Christians. An activist in Seattle offers a good example of this type of thought process:

In conversation, let's say with a Christian friend, the conversation is not necessarily, I mean, we're not down on our knees, you know, all the time, but it kind of flows in and out of your conversation, about faith, or about prayer, or about the Lord or whatever, and if I'm talking to my non-Christian friends, the only time it does is if I bring it up, about some issue, and then it's usually responded to a little bit, with a little bit of discomfort. So in that respect I do see a difference maybe in how much freer I am to be myself with Christian friends. I'm a little more cautious because I don't want to, you know, shove anything down someone's throat. However I want them to know, so I'm open in that respect. (TL: So it's hard to find the right balance?) A little bit, yeah, a little bit, and I'm sure there are people, I know there are people who it's uncomfortable for them to maybe be around me, not many, because, for example, and this is confidential, one of my family members who I love dearly, I just love her to death, is not a Christian, and so, you know, we accept each other totally for where we are, tell each other we love each other, but yet there's that difference that's there. I'll spend some time visiting with her, and enjoy it, we talk about kids, family. But to me, it's sort of more surface conversation, there's not a lot of depth because, if you get in depth, I have to go there, because that's, for me, where it is.

Among the Christians who talked about this topic, there seemed to be a healthy amount of concern over the comfort level of those around them. They understood that certain aspects of Christian culture might make their non-Christian friends uncomfortable, possibly driving them away. They alter their actions not out of fear, but out of concern over offending those around them. A nonactivist from Seattle related:

If I'm at a lunch with all these people—none of them are Christian, say, at work or something—and they're chatting and talking, I wouldn't say, "OK everyone, let's stop and pray." I don't do that. I don't do things to make their lunch uncomfortable. I pray only to myself. I won't go into a big long thing, or say it out loud or anything. But not because I'm worried, I just don't want . . . (TL: That would be pushy?) Yeah, I think that would be really pushy and they would think I was doing it, too, just to make them uncomfortable.

The concern here reiterates themes that arose in earlier chapters. Christian conservatives are sensitive about their public image. Therefore, in interactions with the public, they are careful to enact their identities in non-offensive ways.

I turn now to the consequences of identity revelation, dealing with the two themes I discussed above for the gay and lesbian respondents: violence and employment. Nine Christian respondents mentioned hate crimes. What is interesting about these references is that most of their statements use the conditional tense, with words such as "might" or "could." For example, an evangelical pastor and a nonactivist in Spokane were both responding to the same question: "How 'risky' do you feel these actions are? That is, in doing these actions, do you ever feel that there could be negative consequences?"

Yes, I do. Well, in the community here, you've got all different kinds of groups: militant groups, hate groups, things of this nature. If you display it, you are an easy target. Whereas, if I'm driving my van, and I don't have the emblem [of his church] on the side, I might pass right by them and they'd never notice. They might want to do me evil and do me harm. So it's to my advantage, because they didn't recognize me.

I guess there could be, but I don't fear that. I'm sure that, like, driving downtown at night by myself, if somebody who was really against Christians saw my little symbols on the car, I guess they could be mean toward me if they wanted, but I don't really think about that, I don't have any fear toward that.

The two instances of actual hate crimes in the Christian interviews involved cars as well. The first comes from a Spokane activist who was visiting Seattle at the time of the incident, the second comes from a Spokane nonactivist:

I had a fish on my car, and it started right to the fish and it keyed my car across the fish so I knew that's why they did it. And then they keyed all the way across the car. So I know it can happen. So that's the only thing I've ever had that I know of.

I have been flipped-off for having a Christian thing on my car before. (TL: You've been flipped off?) Yeah [laughs]. (TL: How long ago was this?) Quite a number of years. (TL: How do you know it was connected to . . .) There wasn't anything else I was doing [laughs]. It said on the back of my car, it was just kind of a beautiful kind of a sunrise and it just said "Jesus Cares" and yeah, I think that caused a problem for that particular person [still laughing].

Compared to the lesbian who thought she was going to die while getting beat up in the gay bar, these two incidents pale in comparison. Another sign of Christian conservatives' relative lack of concern over hate crimes comes from the end of the scenario section of the interviews. As I described above, a large number of gay and lesbian respondents mentioned hate crimes when I asked what else would affect their perceptions of the climate. No Christian conservatives gave such an answer to this question. I am not arguing that hate crimes do not happen to Christians. In fact, of the 8,759 hate crimes reported to the FBI in 1996, more of them related to religion than to sexual orientation: 1,401 compared to 1,016 (Leung 1998).[1] But when it comes to characterizing the climate around them, Christian conservatives hardly take hate crimes into consideration. They do not fear for their personal safety to the same extent that many gays and lesbians do.

A number of Christian respondents did have employment concerns. Again, not as many as the gay and lesbian respondents did, but there were some references (five from Spokane respondents, two from Seattle respondents). The most egregious example comes from an activist in Spokane:

I was talking to a businessman that said when he sees anything that's referred to as a Christian, on an application, for instance, he won't even, he throws that in the garbage as soon as they're gone because they are the worst workers, he told me, and they make their faith, they use it as an excuse to either be gone on Sunday . . . and he listed a whole list of things.

A nonactivist woman in Spokane expressed concern for her husband's career, even going so far as to alter her behavior over it: "I have been a little reluctant to [write letters to the editor] because of my husband's position in this city. And because our name is so unusual. So I would have to be careful with that, because I wouldn't want to affect his business standing in the community." There *are* examples of Christians concerned about the implications of being out as Christians in their communities. But overall, in contrast to gays and lesbians, such concerns came up markedly less frequently. Also, the obvious difference between the climates toward gays in Seattle and Spokane is not present when contrasting Seattle and Spokane Christian conservatives.

As in previous chapters, Christians made references to homosexuality. Some of the Seattle references of this type regarded being an "out" Christian on Capitol Hill, the gay and lesbian neighborhood in Seattle. For example, I was discussing risk with a Seattle activist:

(TL: Earlier we talked about how different areas of the city might be thought of as more hostile or hospitable. Do such characteristics of an area determine where you go in the city?) Sure, yeah. Like I don't frequent Capitol Hill much. (TL: So you don't frequent Capitol Hill because you do feel that hostility there?) I don't go there for any outward thing. I will go there and go for a movie, but I'm not going to wear any of my stuff [laughs]. (TL: You wouldn't change how you act?) No. (TL: But you would not wear the pin?) I wouldn't wear a flag: "Hi, I'm a Christian [laughs]. Come and get me! [laughs]." You've seen the cartoon with the bears, from *The Far Side*: "Bummer of a birthmark!" (TL: And you would feel like that up on Capitol Hill?) Yeah, I would. I'm not comfortable in that environment.

The equation for this woman is clear: as the number of gays and lesbians in a neighborhood rises, the likelihood that she will face hostility rises as well. Risk-free places are where homosexuals are not.

Christians were also concerned about the consequences of battling homosexuality. Doing so makes one an easy target. An evangelical pastor in Spokane explains:

(TL: With regard to the answers from the previous question: how risky do you feel these actions are? That is, in doing these actions, do you ever feel that there could be negative consequences?) Yes, I do. And the negative consequences, I don't always feel that way, so far the environment has been pretty tolerant and accepting, but I think that it's changing and I think that the negative consequences could be with my children. I think they could be, people could treat them differently because of stands that I take publicly. I think they could be harassed at times because of that, so. . . . But I don't feel like I'm inhibited in any way at the present. I lived in Portland ten years ago and was in a church down there and, I don't mean to be coming back to this issue because it's not the core issue that it's made out to be, but the gay community is very militant as well, and they will not tolerate any type of idea that homosexuality is a choice, that it is, quote, curable, or any of that. And I was in a church down there that took a very low profile on the thing. But they had a man who had a ministry there, he had been gay and had come out of the gay lifestyle, he now had a ministry *to* gays and trying to free them from that bondage, and the church was picketed on a Sunday, and they were harassed in the service, and I would expect that to happen here someday. I would expect to show up on a Sunday morning and have pickets at the front door because of our position on pro-life issues or, or the gay movement issues, and I would expect it to disrupt the church service sometime. It's happened all over the country, it's going to happen here. Hasn't happened here yet, but someday it will.

This is yet another way that Christian conservatives use gay progress as a signal of an increasingly hostile climate toward themselves. But as with every other risk-related theme, Christians didn't speak of this terribly often. Their decisions to refrain from actions that would reveal their identity are motivated by other factors, such as prospects for evangelism. Whereas gay men and lesbians in a hostile climate are sometimes scared of what other people might do to them, Christian conservatives simply don't want to scare other people away.

Aspects of Healthy Communities

Living as a Christian conservative or gay individual can be made harder or easier by the level of community one feels. If living in the city is a hostile experience, a sense of community within your group can act as a safe haven from this hostility. In this section, I examine how respondents perceive the health of their "minority" communities. While both of these groups have incredible diversity within them, making it difficult to speak of a single community, respondents often spoke of their communities as singular entities: "*the* gay community," "*the* Christian community." Although I appreciate the possible differences between the climate perceptions of specific constituents of the communities (i.e., a drag queen and a gay Republican probably have different perceptions), here I am interested in these overall perceptions.

While the raw size of the community matters (i.e., it may be quite unpleasant to be the sole lesbian in a small town), I argue that two other factors are important. First, a community's health is connected to its organizational capabilities. Social movement theorists have long viewed a community's ability to organize as an important variable in the likelihood of social change (McCarthy and Zald 1977; Piven and Cloward 1977). Second is the extent to which these organizations are linked in a network. People don't perceive community health through merely the number of individuals in the community, or the number of organizations. They also assess the cohesiveness of the community. Two related questions from the interviews were particularly useful to analyze these themes: "Are there any (Christian, gay and lesbian) elements that are not represented in _____ that you would like to see represented?" and "Are there any (Christian, gay and lesbian) elements that *are* represented in _____ that you would prefer to *not* see represented?"

Gay and Lesbian Communities

There is no getting around this fact: there are more gay men and lesbians in Seattle than there are in Spokane. It is estimated that Seattle has the fourth largest population of gays and lesbians in the United States (Singer and Deschamps 1994). I have already discussed some of the effects of this plethora of gay people: the media pay attention to them, the public knows they are there, politicians court them. Another effect is the number of organizations that the community can support. Each city's organizational capacity is mentioned as a source of hospitableness in both the Seattle and Spokane interviews, albeit slightly more frequently in Seattle. The specific way in which this theme manifests itself in the two cities provides an interesting contrast. In Seattle, a common sentiment was appreciation for the wide array of groups within the gay and lesbian community. The lesbian activist who had moved to Seattle a year ago expresses this: "There is so much here that I never saw before, I don't know. Like, they have a group for fat women, I mean, a pool party every month. I *know* we didn't have that in California." Echoing this is a middle-aged lesbian who recently came out of the closet: "I feel like a little kid sometimes. I mean, I feel like there are a million different avenues that I can take, and since I have been a homebody for so many years, this is a bit difficult for me." Others commented on the prospect of being able to get everything one could possibly need from the community. This is illustrated by a nonactivist woman:

> Well, to illustrate the goodness I think would be Capitol Hill and the large number of businesses, many things that people need, they can go to

a gay-friendly business and give them their money and get what they need, be it a post office box or clothes or whatever. Other examples, I guess just that there is a choice and a variety. There is two lesbian bars. Many cities just have just one, both gay and lesbian bar, if they have that. It's not that I am all for segregation or something, but it's just very nice to have the choice of just a woman's bar. Restaurants even. Both The Easy and The Rose [two Seattle lesbian bars] have food. That is one of the biggest examples, as well as if anything negative or whatever were to happen I think there is support here for me. The Lesbian Resource Center and there are crisis lines and departments to help fight for my human rights.

If one takes a look through the business directory put out by members of the gay and lesbian community, it's easy to see that this woman is correct: virtually every possible need one has could be fulfilled within the gay and lesbian community.

While such a life is not possible in Spokane, there were eight respondents who saw a hospitable climate in the presence of organizations. Rather than amazement over the array of organizations, the tone was more of a thankfulness that a number of resources were available, and that such organizations could survive. Also, the organizations that do exist in Spokane are more reliant on structures within the general community, such as churches and bookstores. These themes are illustrated by the following three excerpts, the first two from activists, the last from a nonactivist:

Right now Spokane has a couple of really good starts. We have a fairly popular gay newspaper. We have the Rainbow Regional [Community Center]. We have two or three churches in the area which have organizations.

(TL: Would you recommend this city to another gay person who is thinking of moving here?) Yes, qualified. I would say, well, what do you look for in a gay community? Is that important to you? If it's really important that they have a lot of gay and lesbian resources, I would say, you're not going to be happy in Spokane. If they really like more of a home life, more of an outdoor life, and are okay with some gay and lesbian resources, then you're okay in Spokane. Because there are some. There's not tons, but they are here.

Well, certainly there's got to be some support in Spokane because there's places for PFLAG to meet; churches make space for PFLAG, the university at times, Gonzaga [University] puts on special programs, there's the gay and lesbian business owners association, and they publish the Yellow Pages, which is carried in several bookstores, so certainly there's community support there.

Spokane does not have the gay and lesbian population base to establish a community that is completely self-reliant. However, it has a large enough gay and lesbian population, and enough committed activists, to support a limited number of organizations. Some of these organizations do need to rely on support from the larger community, but as long as such support exists, they will continue. In contrast to other places, in Spokane there is a greater need for individual self-reliance, as this nonactivist suggests: "It's OK if you're the kind of dyke that wants to settle down and have the dogs in the backyard and, you know, take out the *This Old House* handbook, and go camping on the weekends. If you want to go to big lesbianfests . . . then it's probably not the greatest place." Gay-oriented physical spaces, organizations, and activities are important, not only to individual gay men and lesbians, but also to the movement. In such spaces, people can gather information about the movement and "try on" gay or lesbian activist identities (Taylor and Whittier 1992), and this is where much mobilization begins. In Spokane, the only gay-oriented spaces are the gay bars, and even those are not always safe spaces.

Another way gay respondents judged the health of the gay community was by focusing on intracommunity conflict. A healthy community is one where the members of the community work well together, and one in which it is easy to get people involved. These two themes popped up in both cities, although they seem to result from different factors in each: in Seattle, they result from a hospitable climate; in Spokane, the cause is a hostile climate. For example, in Seattle an intracommunity theme was infighting, illustrated by two activists:

I still think that we put each other down a lot, and I'm guilty of this too. I mean, earlier I was complaining about HandsOff [a gay rights organization]. And it does pain me that I feel that HandsOff is a badly run organization, but it also pains me that I should be attacking HandsOff. I mean, they're not the enemy. They're part of the community, you know what I mean? We're all working in the same direction, you know, and I guess I think that there's still a lot of infighting that's unfortunate. And it's interesting because I think this situation is because we're big enough to infight. We now have enough diversity in the community, in a place like Seattle.

(TL: What is it like to live in Seattle as a lesbian?) On a certain level there is a lot of resources for us, but in the lesbian community there's a lot of division and that's grown more so over the past five years, I'd say, because the community has gotten larger. You know, when I came out, everybody knew everybody. It was very small, and not to say that we didn't have fights or problems or whatever, but we all knew who we were and had a network and there's a lot more class divisions now and there's a lot more political divisions within the lesbian community than there used to be. And that's just maybe part of getting to be a larger community, but for people like myself, and there are more people like me that travel in and out of various parts of communities, it makes it hard, because a lot of people don't recognize how broad the community is. I think we're a lot more segmented than we used to be.

The source of the problem in these examples is the perceived size and strength of the gay and lesbian community. They imply that if the community were smaller and more besieged, these problems would go away. In Spokane, where a lack of activism was the most common intracommunity complaint, the source of this problem was the hostile climate. Activists were frustrated by this:

When it comes to money, it's tough. It's hard to pry good money loose. As a financial advisor these past few years, I'm used to moving tens and hundreds of thousands of dollars around for people, so when it's tough for the Pride Committee to get $4,000, I think "What's wrong here?" When Spokane AIDS Network is operating on a very slim survival budget because nobody's giving money, I wonder. Some of these deeply closeted men and women take huge cruises, expensive cruises, all over the world, build palatial homes, and they don't put any money into the cause, you wonder: how supportive are people? Twenty percent of the people do 80 percent of the work. That's a fair assessment.

I think there's probably a general atmosphere that you can't change things. I think people in larger areas feel, largely, much more empowered.

You know, this is something I don't like and there's something I can do to affect that. And I think that's particularly true of the gay community here.

Both cities' respondents reveal that having a good-sized community is not enough. In fact, growth (as measured in terms of the number of people) can hurt the community if it is not handled in an appropriate manner. A healthy gay and lesbian community is one that has a significant number of organizations that are well networked and are willing to work together for social change. A smaller community could feasibly be more effective than a larger one if it is better organized to serve the needs of its members.

Christian Conservative Communities

Some of these same themes arose during the Christian conservative interviews. Typical of the pattern shown in previous chapters, Christian conservatives in Spokane were more optimistic about the state of their community than were Seattlites. For example, Spokane Christian conservatives were happy not only with the number of organizations and churches available to them, they were also excited about the extent to which these organizations worked in concert to form a real community. They were proud that their leaders had managed to overcome the often divisive denominational differences that plague other communities. The Greater Spokane Association of Evangelicals, the local version of the National Association of Evangelicals, has several characteristics of a successful movement organization: it has a membership list, it meets regularly, and it has a hierarchical structure (Gamson 1990).

In addition to organizations, the respondents had several things they could point to as examples of how cohesive the community was. An activity about which Spokane Christian conservatives were particularly excited was called Sunday in the Park. Held in the summertime (during which I conducted the majority of my Spokane interviews), members of many different churches would meet for prayer and song in Spokane's scenic Riverfront Park, which is located in the center of the city. Christian respondents again and again brought up this event. For examples, a pastor and a nonactivist had this to say:

The churches work together, cooperate with one another, encourage one another, a lot of more joint things that are done. (TL: Can you illustrate this with any stories or incidents?) Well, just like for this summer now, for the next nine Sunday nights, fifty-two churches are cooperating together in the Sunday Nights in the Park.

I mean, you've got the black churches with the white churches for the first time ever, and they're working together for positive results. And Sunday Night in the Park, we went Sunday, and they had all kinds of people there, so, I think within the churches themselves, there's a really strong growth towards reconciling, everybody becoming brothers, and everybody's together.

This event also serves as an example of Christians using public space (in the symbolic center of the city, at that), which proved to be important with the issues in chapter 4. This organizational theme overshadows a related theme: the number of Christians. While four Spokane respondents perceived a hospitable climate through the large number of Christians present in Spokane, nearly three times that number perceived hospitableness through the number of Christian organizations and how well networked these organizations were.

Perceiving hospitableness through the presence and cohesion of organizations was much less common among the Seattle respondents. On the hospitable side, the Seattle area is home to headquarters of several large national and international charity organizations, which one of the Seattle Christian activists immediately listed when I asked her if she would recommend Seattle to another Christian thinking of moving there: "Yeah, I would. We've got a lot of things going on here. You've got Christa, Worldvision down there in Federal Way, you've got World Concerns, this is their headquarters." But unlike Spokane, Seattle's Christian Conservative community is not well networked. This claim is part personal perception: while I had little trouble setting up the Spokane interviews, due to the well-developed network I had tapped, setting up the Seattle interviews was significantly more difficult. Among the Seattle respondents, there weren't any hospitable mentions of the Christian community working together. In fact, Seattle Christian conservatives perceived a void. When I asked an activist who is formerly from Minnesota, "Are there any Christian elements that are not represented in Seattle that you would like to see represented?" he replied:

Well, I think what is missing is a united front of the Christian community. In Minneapolis, the National Association of Evangelicals had a local chapter and it would have a monthly meeting and there would be 130 to 140 pastors and out of that comes committees and then social concerns and then you do things. The Association, the National Association of Evangelicals chapter in Seattle, has about twelve members.

At a loss to explain this situation, he took a guess that the geographical design of Seattle (with its bodies of water, bridges, and subsequent bad traffic) might be what is preventing the formation of a cohesive community. In a city the size of Seattle, even though church attendance is low, there are many Christian conservatives. Large numbers hold little efficacy if the community of which they are a part is not networked properly. A networked community, like the one in Spokane, has a greater chance of having an impact in the larger society, as this Spokane pastor suggests:

> Something that I've noticed happening is that local churches are coming together, primarily around their common commitment to Jesus Christ, and then from that there is a certain amount of reconciliation with different races. There is a networking of resources. This has been a positive shift. There's been a real historical revival among the churches for their people to not just do their own stuff, but also to go out into the larger society.

The presence of community-oriented media could help facilitate this networking. One element four Christian respondents brought up (three in Spokane, one in Seattle) that was absent from the gay interviews was the presence of radio stations. Several spoke of the existence of Christian radio stations and the pleasure they get from listening to them, but no one mentioned that the stations have the ability to make the Christian community more cohesive. It was simply an amenity that any good Christian community should have.

Conclusion

Overall, as with the identity references, there were fewer mentions of the importance of community in the Christian interviews (52 references) than there were in the gay and lesbian interviews (138 references). It is understandable that identity would be more important to gay men and lesbians, with the rite of passage of coming out playing a major role in gay life, as well as the additional risks involved in coming out that I described above. But why do gays and lesbians talk more about community than Christian conservatives? I suggest that the two themes are in some way connected: the identity-related problems that the gay community has historically experienced have caused gays and lesbians to place more emphasis on community as well. Christian conservatives, historically less ostracized, have had less need for consciously creating Christian communities that protect their members. Christian conservatives *do* form communities. But community organizing among gays and lesbians happens on a grander scale. A relevant contrast of the two groups comes from a former president of the Greater Seattle Business Association, an alliance of gay organizations and gay-owned or gay-friendly businesses:

> Just recently, Michael Medved—you know who he is, he's a conservative host at KVI from noon until three—he took the first hour on his program a couple of weeks ago and he had gotten a copy of the GSBA guide and directory. It was kind of a funny story how he got it, but kind of a long story so I won't, anyway, he went through it with a fine-toothed comb and he spent an hour saying how outrageous this is and saying, "Look how organized these people are," and reading my president's message over the air, and saying "Look at these people, they're buying from each other," saying this is the way we could become strong, and "Look, they've got a scholarship program, and encouraging young people to come out as gay and lesbians in high school by offering scholarships," and so of course we were kind of stunned by it and got copies of the tape and listened carefully to what he said and, we just said, oh well, there's that segment. You're not going to change their minds. We decided just to write a letter to the station and say, to correct some of the things that he said that we felt were factually incorrect, that he said, and not get all bent out of shape about it, and I guess my feeling is that's what I would expect to be on KVI, it seemed like he was pandering to his listeners. It seemed like he was probably more intelligent than his listeners and knew that he was, and just kind of trying to make a big issue. It seemed like he was having a hard time telling what was his issue. Basically, what it seemed like it boiled down to is why aren't what is called pro-family, why aren't we as organized, why don't we have a guide? And he got some listeners to call in and say, "Oh yeah, let's start one, and let's have a family day parade on the same day as the gay and lesbian parade."

In this excerpt, one can see the connection between identity and community. One of the primary functions of community is to shelter the vulnerable within the community from risk. In the gay and lesbian interviews, several people claimed that those who face the greatest risks in the communities are the kids who are trying to come out in the schools. Because of the high level of risk in this situation, members of the community create new structures, such as the GSBA scholarship program. Gay men and lesbians in both cities have created elaborate community-level defense mechanisms to deal with hostility. In Seattle, a lot of the energy revolves around school issues, as that is where the hostility is perceived as greatest these days. In Spokane, a majority of the gay organizations serve primarily as social support mechanisms to help those within the gay community cope with the stress involved in living lives in a hostile climate.

In contrast, Christian conservative community organizations are much more outwardly focused. Many of them are charity oriented. They seek to provide services not to members of their own Christian community, but to the needy of the larger community. True, sometimes these services are combined with evangelism, which could be perceived as an effort to enlarge the Christian community. And there is an effort among some Christians to patronize Christian-owned businesses (many Yellow Page ads feature the Christian fish symbol). But within the Christian communities there are fewer support-oriented organizations designed to help Christians deal with the fact that they are Christian. For example, in the communities, there are no "Parents and Friends of Christians" groups.

There are exceptions to this rule, though. As the last excerpt illustrates, some Christians want to create structures modeled on those within the gay community. They perceive hostility from gay and lesbian organizing and want to respond to this hostility with similar efforts. Christian children form prayer groups at public schools—environments where, as we have seen in previous chapters, Christians perceive much hostility. It is possible that the high levels of hostility that Christian conservatives perceive in these two communities will cause further community building in the future.

6

Reflecting on the Other

In previous chapters, I discussed Christian conservatives' concerns about homosexuality as they related to the more general topics of the media, the public, the government, and identity. Because of the extent to which Christian conservatives use gays and lesbians as a means to characterize the political climates toward themselves, I will now give this topic a more thorough examination by pulling all of these claims together and giving them an analysis of their own. I also address the logical counterquestion: What do gay men and lesbians think about Christian conservatives? This is a question I have hardly considered up to this point because other themes dominated gay and lesbian characterizations of the political climates.

In fact, this difference is an important initial finding related to this topic: in the interviews, when characterizing climates, gays and lesbians talk about Christian conservatives *less* than Christian conservatives talk about gays and lesbians. In the gay and lesbian interviews, there were fifty-two unprompted claims about Christian conservatives (twenty-six in each city). In the Christian conservative interviews, there were ninety unprompted claims about gays and lesbians (forty in Spokane, fifty in Seattle). While this numerical difference is significant, so are the variations in the ways the two groups think about each other. How people talk about the other group is just as important as how much they say.

In conjunction with making sense of these unprompted references, I also analyze the responses to two of the scenarios from the interviews. One was a political scenario, designed to see how a negative political occurrence for one group was interpreted by the other group. For Christian conservatives, the scenario read: "The Washington State legislature passes a bill forbidding gay marriages." This scenario was hypothetical at the time of the interviews, but has since become a reality. For gay and lesbian respondents, the scenario was: "Ellen Craswell, outspoken Christian conservative, loses the gubernatorial race by a 60%/40% margin." This was in reference to the actual 1996 election and happened the year before I conducted most of the interviews.

The other scenario was an everyday scenario, designed to see how individuals' actions that displayed the identity of one group were interpreted by members of the other group. For Christian conservative respondents, the scenario read: "At a local restaurant, you see a male couple holding hands across the table." For gay men and lesbians, the scenario was: "At a local restaurant, you see a family saying grace before they start to eat." Although these two scenarios are not perfectly parallel, the comparisons of the corresponding reactions yield interesting results.

Seven Ways Christian Conservatives Think about Gay Men and Lesbians

While conducting and analyzing the interviews, it became clear to me that homosexuality represents many different things to Christian conservatives. To various Christians at various times, gay men and lesbians are

- a source of direct hostility
- an antithetical benchmark to judge how Christians are treated in society
- an example of government liberality
- a symbol of declining morality
- a contagiously diseased group from which they shelter their children
- a target to which they react poorly, resulting in a negative image
- a moral quandary with which they grapple.

Examining all of these different meanings makes it easier to see why homosexuality has become one of the most (if not *the* most) important social issues that draw Christian conservative attention at the dawn of the new century. Below, I examine each of these themes, offering examples and pointing out nuances along the way. If at times the reader gets a sense of déjà vu, this is because some of these themes have appeared in the earlier chapters. In order to understand the overall picture, it is necessary to return to these themes anew.

Gay Men and Lesbians as a Source of Direct Hostility

The most basic way that an opposing group creates a harsher climate for one's own group is through direct hostility. A number of Christian respondents claimed that gays and lesbians, sometimes by their mere (but growing) presence, created hostility toward Christians. For example, many Christian conservatives assume that gays and lesbians are against Christianity. Therefore, the more gays and lesbians, the more hostility. A pastor and a nonactivist, both from Spokane, expressed this feeling as follows:

> I think there was probably a little more hostility down in the San Francisco Bay Area towards Christians and I think that was due to the added population of gay people in that area. When it seems that the homosexual population are more hostile towards Christians than, well not more, but it comes out, I think, in the gay population. (TL: So they are more vocal?) More vocal, more hostile, more anti-old-line, denominational. A lot of denominations are saying that homosexuality is wrong. Which I believe that because I think that is what the Bible says. But, they are people too and we need to not be hostile towards that community. We need to not necessarily accept what they do, but accept them as people.

> I think there are hostile pockets. (TL: Like geographic pockets, or?) No, not necessarily. (TL: What are those pockets?) Social pockets. (TL: Social pockets?) Yeah, perhaps, oh, little groups, "I hate Christian" types, or "Disrespect my agenda and I'm going to push it," whether they be gays or, you know, certain little groups.

The same theme was present across the state in Seattle but with additional nuances. An activist and a nonactivist explain:

> Well, I would say the homosexual community is very antagonistic. But then, let's face it, a lot of Christians, at least professing Christians, have been very antagonistic toward homosexuals. Now, I don't compromise on the biblical position of homosexuality, but I have friends, and one of my best friends became a homosexual when I was in California. I still love him. I confronted him with it, and he said he knew I was right, but that's the way he chose to go. We have friends whose kids are homosexual, and we still love them, and we're not there beating on them, but they know where we would stand. But I think that what happens is that it's not homosexuals so much as the "in-your-face" militant homosexual approach that I think a lot of Christians take issue with. That's probably what I would take issue with more than anything else.

(TL: Any other changes you have seen in the past five or ten years? How has Seattle changed?) Well, for one thing . . . the homosexual community has involved themselves to a much greater degree and really have intimidated a lot of people just simply because of their coming out and then kind of bonding together and becoming almost strident in their wanting to call attention to themselves and as a result of that they tend to do a lot of intimidating, I think, to a lot of people.

These Seattle references point to a type of homosexuality that is perceived as particularly hostile. For them, "the love that dare not speak its name" has not only started speaking; it now refuses to be quiet. In the past generation, as the movement for gay and lesbian rights has grown, Christian conservatives have witnessed the evolution of homosexuality from existing in clandestine trysts and furtive glances to being a "lifestyle" that is lived openly and whose advocates are demanding recognition in multiple arenas of society. The separation of gays into strident and nonstrident types, into militant and nonmilitant camps, is an intriguing strategy. One maintains the ability to define stridency as one sees fit. As I showed in an earlier chapter, what it means to be "in your face" is completely subjective. For example, many Spokane gays and lesbians thought that public displays of affection crossed that line.

To see if the Christian respondents thought that a gay public display of affection was too "in your face," I offered them the hand-holding scenario. Does the obvious presence of homosexuals in everyday life create hostility for Christian conservatives? Some found the prospect unsettling: "I find that kind of offensive; I don't like to see it," "It would disgust me," "Mmmmm, disturbing." More surprising was a reaction from several respondents that is quite inventive. If the presence of gays and lesbians disturbs you, they say, simply deny that they are there:

I guess that doesn't bother me. And the reason I say that is because the assumption is that they are homosexual. And I grew up in a community where there were people who had come from Europe and it was very common to see men embrace, to see men hold hands, and so right away I guess because of the climate that we live in, we just make the automatic assumption, and so I guess for me I wouldn't react that way right away, because the person wouldn't react that way thinking that two girls holding hands were both lesbians. So it's a mindset that we get into.

I'd probably really question in my own mind, or if I was having dinner with my wife, about returning to the restaurant. It depends. That kind behavior I just don't think is appropriate. I think of my own son, both of my sons, who are single. I mean, I think of them going out to dinner with one of their buddies. Automatically you see two guys together having dinner and I think it's a crime to jump to the conclusion that those guys must be gay. Why can't two good friends go out and have a meal?

I would figure that they are probably saying a prayer. (TL: Would that affect how you felt about Spokane, if something like that happened?) Last week, we went to a restaurant north of town. I had some family members in town. We sat down to have dinner. And it was a smorgasbord place, so everyone sat around the table, we stopped and had prayer, and then we got our plates. Afterwards, the people from the restaurant came over and said, "We noticed you when you sat down. We wanted to say how proud we were because you stopped and had prayer." So, it enhances the Christian environment.

For these respondents, accepting the existence of the gay couple may be too close to accepting homosexuality itself.

While a good number of Christian conservative respondents felt threatened by the presence of gays and lesbians, none of these excerpts really makes a connection showing *why* the presence of homosexuality causes greater hostility. There were very few specific examples of the ways in which the gay movement itself caused Christian conservatives harm. Below is one of these examples from a Seattle pastor who was describing the problems that his church had as they were trying to construct a new building in response to their growing congregation:

Well, we found out what the real issue was there. And the real issue was that we were a fundamental Bible-believing church who, because of our convictions and the word of God, believe that homosexuality is sin. We also believe that abortion is sin. And these are issues that are perceived as social by the community. And they thought that we shouldn't be saying anything about those things. And so the community rose up against us, basically because of our convictions. Had we said that we were going to erect a monument to all of the gays in the county, they would have probably given us donations. But, because of that, we found out that the real battle was spiritual warfare that was going on with the people, not that they didn't want a big building going up in their city.

But even in this excerpt, as with other excerpts from previous chapters (the homosexual on the cross cartoon from chapter 2, the pro-gay school program example from chapter 4), the gay and lesbian rights movement is not the *originator* of the action. Rather, the actor in most of these situations comes from the larger culture (the city government, the newspaper, the school system). Occasionally, as with the example in chapter 5 in which the Portland pastor's church was picketed, the gay community *is* the source of the action. And it might be inferred that gays and lesbians are behind all of these maneuvers (as part of the ubiquitous "gay agenda"), but few Christian respondents came right out and said so. It seems that the biggest direct threat to Christian conservatives is the growing, obvious existence of gay men and lesbians and all of the connected cultural changes this has put into motion. Gay men and lesbians create additional hostility for Christians just by existing more openly.

Gay Men and Lesbians as an Antithetical Benchmark

In chapters 2 through 4, I showed that a common Christian conservative strategy was to compare how various elements of society treated both Christians and gays and lesbians. In most of the stories Christians told, their group was treated more poorly than gays and lesbians. Some involved a neutral contrast, stating that both groups engage in the same types of activities. What is interesting about these references is the matter-of-fact nature whereby Christians assume that gays and lesbians are their natural antithesis. Here are two additional examples of this:

(TL: What about prayer in schools. How supportive is Washington State?) I know just at the community college there's not a problem. They have Christian groups that meet. But then again, they also have gay and lesbian groups that meet, so, you know [laughs], you can look at that whatever way you want, really.

(TL: What about conservative Christian politicians? Are they given a fair shake?) I'm not one of them so I don't know but I guess my, I don't know if they're given any more of a fair shake than someone who's liberal or

158 | *Reflecting on the Other*

maybe homosexual in the Congress. I think they have a real uphill battle
to fight, but I don't know if it's any more of an uphill battle than someone
else coming from the other side.

One might think that the "opposite" of the Christian conservative movement would involve secular humanists or atheists or pagans. While these
groups are mentioned in the interviews, such references are few and far
between. For a good number of Christian respondents the embodiment of
"anti-Christianity" is the gay and lesbian rights movement. Partly because
they are one of the most consistently visible social groups, gays and lesbians have become for Christian conservatives the logical antithesis to
themselves. If a group does develop what they perceive as an antithetical
group, it is only natural to compare how the two groups are treated by
similar entities. Does your antithesis garner more media attention than
your group? Does the public look more favorably on your antithesis, at
your expense? Is your antithesis treated better by the state and its authori-
ties than you are treated? To all of these questions, as we have seen before
many times, Christian conservatives answer yes, yes, and yes.

Gay Men and Lesbians as an Example of Government Liberality

This next theme has some similarities to the last theme, but focuses on
an additional way that Christian conservatives think about the government in particular. It is important for Christian conservatives to be able to
assess where their government—local, state, or national—stands on the
liberal/conservative continuum. One of the ways Christians gauge this
placement on the continuum is to observe the government's treatment of
gay and lesbian issues. If the government makes a decision in favor of gays
and lesbians, this signifies that they are on the liberal end of the continuum. If they make a decision against gays, this is a sign that they are on
the more conservative end of the continuum. The government, at these
various levels, may only infrequently make decisions that directly affect
Christian conservatives (for example, statewide decisions about prayer in
school may be few and far between). But Christians remain able to keep a
read on the overall liberal-conservative continuum by watching the relatively more frequent legislation about gay men and lesbians. Below are two
examples of this theme. Both are unsolicited examples from Spokane
community leaders:

(TL: Has the climate in Washington State changed over the past five years?) I think it's gotten more in the liberal direction. Oregon passed its assisted suicide law, that's a clear step in that direction. The fact that we have had a, we currently have a mayor in this city and we currently have a governor who is in favor of partnership rights for homosexuals and lesbians. Those are *new* things that we have not seen until the last few years. They're becoming issues and they're becoming issues that they're wanting to put into law. And it's no longer at the stage of "We're just going to disagree about this," it's: "We're going to take steps to make this law."

I would say from the standpoint of our mayors and our elected leaders locally, no, we're not real conservative. Compared to Seattle, yes, but not anymore. We have a mayor now who's promoting and outspoken now about the homosexual agenda. Now, did he do that at election time? No. Would he be elected if he turned around and made that an issue? That's a good question. That would answer the question that you just asked me. I'd like to think he wouldn't be, but something inside of me says that he'd still be elected.

The "legislation against gay marriage" scenario produced similar statements. A pastor in Seattle responded: "I think that would give me encouragement, to think that they are moving in a good direction that stands for decency and honor, and time-honored tradition. I think that would give me hope that other legislation would be passed." A nonactivist in Spokane replied: "Oh, I'd like that. I think that I would probably let them know that I was in support of that, and it would make me feel happier living here, just knowing that Congress supports something that I believe in." Christian conservatives connect gay-related legislation to a broader array of political issues. If the state legislature is conservative enough to ban gay marriage, then they may also be conservative enough to pass other laws that Christians would also favor. If they are liberal enough to pass an antidiscrimination law, then they may take the state in other liberal directions. Watching legislative action toward gays is a kind of perceptual shortcut that helps some Christians quickly characterize how liberal or conservative the government really is.

Gay Men and Lesbians as a Symbol of Declining Morality

Just as Christian conservatives connect homosexuality to a larger political continuum, they also see it as part of a larger moral system. Christian conservatives see this moral system moving in a linear downward progression. Society is headed inexorably in the wrong direction. This philosophy is linked to endtime scenarios popular among some Christians (Harding 2000; Herman 1997). Taking quite seriously the Book of Revelations, some Christians believe that the end of the world is drawing near. This ultimate battle between good and evil will be preceded by a number of prophesied developments, one of which is the acceptance of previously deviant behaviors. If society begins to accept homosexuality, Christians take this as a symbol of a culture in a downward spiral, such as this evangelical leader in Spokane:

> I think as a nation we've slowly become callous to things that we said a few years back were clearly wrong. The whole philosophy that is being taught, prevalent, throughout our educational system that, humanism, you do whatever is right for you, whatever is right, so there are no absolutes, there's no right or wrong. Now we are being challenged in some of the extremes of that, things that for years was never even questioned, you know, and now all of a sudden we are being challenged and I think homosexuality is one of those issues.

The progression is easy to see: before there was no discussion of homosexuality; now, it is discussed constantly. With the steady progress of the gay and lesbian rights movement over the past thirty years, one can see how Christian conservatives would perceive it as a steady sign of a culture in decline. In response to the possibility of the legislature passing a bill forbidding gay marriages, an activist in Seattle who prides himself on being a strict biblical literalist replied:

> I'd be in favor of that. Because I think that marriage is an institution created by God between Adam and Eve and a husband and his wife, and the Scripture says that a man will cleave to his wife. Now, what two people do on their own we can't have any control over. But I would think that if society came to the place where it began to, well, the Scripture says that just as it was in the days of Noah, that's the way it will be when the son of man returns, when Christ returns. He prophesied that sin and that aversion to truth and to the word would increase in the last days. Daniel says that many will run to and fro and knowledge will be increased in the last days, and that if we recognize and see the signs of the times, we will expect that those who call good evil and evil good are going to increase in the last

days. While I say I love homosexual people, and I would expect eventually they'll win their point and they'll win their case and they'll probably have homosexual marriages and they'll have all of the special privileges and everything they're looking for, but it still breaks my heart to see it happen, because I can see where society is going, and I can see it marching inexorably toward a coming judgment from God that it can't avoid. When the Lord returns he's going to set things in order. Now, a lot of people don't believe that Christ is alive and that He's at the right hand of the Father, but I can tell you He is and He is coming back, because everything He prophesied in His word, everything is coming to pass, exactly as He said it would. Now in that case, we expect that society would become more and more like it was when he judged it with the flood, so I expect those things will happen. So if they pass a measure forbidding it, I would rejoice, and if they pass a measure approving homosexual marriage, I would not rejoice, but I can still be joyful, because I know the Lord said when you see these things start to happen, lift up your head because your redemption is drawing near. That means I'm coming back. When you see these things happening, lift up your head, because I'm coming back.

This leads to an interesting, counterintuitive strategy: it may be in Christians' best interests to surrender to a society in favor of homosexuality, because this gets one that much closer to judgment day. In some of the Christian responses to the hand-holding scenario, there was such a feeling of resignation. Morality is going to continue to slide downward, and there's not a lot anyone can do about it. This was especially true in Seattle, where the Christian respondents were faced with this scenario on a regular basis. An African American pastor in Seattle had this attitude:

Probably there's some times I would be more offended than others or think it's despicable, you know, the same way two females hold hands. But sometimes people, you know, we pray, we don't make a difference who it is over there. But I guess get them in a little romantic situation or something, I would, I mean, I see some guys and sometimes it doesn't bother me, sometimes it doesn't affect me, I mean, I just say, "What the hell, this is Seattle!" In a way, I'm getting used to it. I think it still bothers me in a way but again I understand that there are people around like that. I mean, I still don't accept that lifestyle but . . . (TL: You're getting used to seeing it?) Yeah. I'm getting used to seeing it.

At a national level, there is even less control over the movement of the culture in this downward direction. What can one person do against the media conglomerates? A Spokane father laments:

> I think it's more hostile now certainly than it was, I mean, there was all kinds of things you could never have come out of the closet with, you know, twenty years ago. (TL: What specific things do you look at, and say there's more hostility?) I mean, the abortion issue is one, certainly the whole gay rights thing is another thing that's changing, just sexuality in general. I mean, you watch TV now and there are things on prime-time TV that people would have been put in jail for when I was a kid. You know, it's the difference between "Married with Children" and "Leave It to Beaver." It's huge, really, when you start thinking of it from that perspective. So, to me those . . . (TL: So we've kind of become dulled as a culture as far as nothing fazes us anymore?) Yeah, well, I think our morality is defined by those in power in the entertainment industry much more than anything else, and that stuff, I mean, I don't know how spiritual you want to get here, but I view that as a big part of the spiritual battle, and that's a way for the enemy to get to our children, because no matter what you do to protect your children from it, they're going to see it, and they're going to experience it, and it's going to have an effect on them. It's going to program their minds, you know? It's just like you said, it's like if you are someone who thinks that you shouldn't have sex before you're married you're almost, well, you're some sort of nerd or geek or something that, you know, anyone who believes that now.

Even though society is inevitably moving in this direction and some Christians simply accept that fact, it still creates a great deal of angst for other Christians who feel more and more isolated from the general culture. In fact, General Social Survey data show that from 1988 to 1996, the gap between Christian conservative and mainstream opinion on homosexuality increased rapidly. I examined the proportion of the General Social Survey respondents who claimed that "homosexual relations are never wrong." In 1988, 2 percent of Christian conservatives claimed this, while 15.2 percent of other respondents did so, making for a 13.2 percent gap between the two groups.[1] In 1996, 8.2 percent of Christian conservative respondents claimed this, while 31.2 percent of other respondents did so, making for a 23 percent gap. Mainstream opinion on homosexuality is liberalizing more rapidly than Christian conservative opinion, perhaps making Christians feel more marginalized. This gap is especially meaningful for those who have children of an impressionable age. They are at risk of being tempted by various aspects of American culture, as the following theme explains.

Gay Men and Lesbians as Contagiously Diseased

The 1990s witnessed the creation and growth of numerous Christian ministries designed for the sole purpose of curing people of their homosexuality. Such ministries believe that, with the right types of therapy, a gay man or lesbian could either fully convert to heterosexuality, or at least refrain from engaging in homosexual acts. While the debate raged over whether or not homosexuality is something that can be "cured," the other implication of this disease rhetoric remained quietly in the background: homosexuality is something that can be "caught." If it *is* a disease and it can be caught, such a philosophy goes, then Christians must do everything in their power to make sure that their children are not exposed to any homosexuality, lest the children come down with it themselves.

Protecting children from vice has been a long-running theme in American society (Beisel 1997), and homosexuality is one of the most evident current vices in Christian conservative eyes. In previous chapters, we saw the concern Christians have over teaching about homosexuality in the schools. Some other Christians who mentioned this issue said something succinct, such as "homosexuality in schools," without describing it further, most likely because the idea of a curriculum that includes homosexuality is so patently offensive that it didn't warrant further explanation. One of the older Seattle respondents who works as a volunteer in numerous capacities tried to make the connection explicit. We were talking about what she called a "stridency" she perceived from the gay community:

(TL: The stridency of the homosexual community, what effect does that have? You kind of linked it to government in general, but what are the *effects*?) I think it has an effect on many things and because I work, or rather, am involved with high school students to a degree. (TL: You are in a tutoring program?) I tutor, I also am very active with the ministry in my own church. . . . And so I see how that tends to, it brings about a confusion a lot, in particularly the high school students. High school students are very idealistic many times and they want to give everybody a real fair shake. And I am not against giving everybody a fair shake. You know what

I am saying? But I think that that stridency kind of carries over into making students not want to listen to another side because they hear this so much and it is a popular thing.

An additional source of anxiety, then, may be the combination of the introduction of a gay-inclusive curriculum *and* the exclusion of a Christian conservative curriculum that would reiterate why homosexuality is wrong. Without equal airtime, Christians worry that kids will fall into the homosexual lifestyle without being fully aware of the risks to their souls.

Outside of the schools, children still may be at risk of catching homosexuality. One of the most common responses to the restaurant hand-holding scenario was to show concern that the children would see this homosexual display of affection. Most of these replies came from Spokane parents. Below are three examples of such a concern, the first from a Seattle pastor, the second from a Spokane evangelical leader, and the third from a Spokane nonactivist mother:

I wouldn't do anything but observe that. Whether I'd come back or not, well, I would expect that on Capitol Hill but if saw it here in Northgate, it wouldn't affect me one iota. But if I came back next week and I observed it again and again, probably I would not frequent the restaurant. (TL: So if it was one instance it wouldn't really affect you but if it kept happening . . .) I mean, you see that stuff all the time, two guys kissing on a bus, that's, but, you know, again, my wife and I both, there are restaurants that we go to where there are homosexual waiters. And we would not quit going to a restaurant because a waiter was homosexual. On the other hand, I probably wouldn't take my kids to a restaurant where there were males kissing on a regular basis. I wouldn't expose them to that.

I probably, if my kids were there, I would use it as a teaching opportunity. I don't think at this point in time I would go and say or do anything. I mean, I don't think it would profit anything. (TL: Would that affect how you feel about the environment?) I know if I was in an environment where that was constantly around me, I wouldn't feel good about it. I wouldn't be excited about having my kids or community exposed to that openly all the time. I wouldn't choose to go live in that environment.

I'd probably whisper about them [laughs]. Well, to be truly honest I think if I was sitting there with my husband, we would just sit there and giggle.

I don't think it would make me get up and leave, unless my kids were there, then I think just out of, to protect my kids from it, just because I'm kind of a sheltering mom that way, which I don't know that that's necessarily good, but they're so young. (TL: How old are they?) They're ten and eight. They are at that impressionable age. So, you know, I think that if my kids were there, it would make me want to just, "Well, let's just hurry up and go."

All three of these respondents use disease rhetoric. Just as a good parent should protect her children from exposure to deadly viruses, a good Christian conservative parent should protect her children from exposure to homosexuality. Because many Christians believe that homosexuality is a chosen lifestyle, they also believe that one will not choose this lifestyle if one doesn't know that such a lifestyle is an option. And if one does catch the disease? As one of the activist respondents from Seattle said: "I believe homosexuality is wrong. And if folks have it, they need to abstain."

Gay Men and Lesbians as an Unfortunate Target of Negative Christian Attention

Not all Christian conservatives think alike. In fact, a lot of Christians get quite upset at the actions and attitudes of other Christians and try to distance themselves from such actions. For example, some Christians believe that compassion is the only response to any social issue: those who have been led astray by evil forces must be shown the way, but only with the utmost care and understanding. Others believe in a tough-love approach: it is a battle over people's souls, and sometimes battle isn't pretty. The former vehemently believe that the latter are doing more harm than good. While both groups employ the phrase "Hate the sin; love the sinner," they disagree on what this love should look like: kind or tough.

One of the key social issues caught in the middle of these two groups is homosexuality. A number of Christian respondents thought that addressing homosexuality brought out the worst in this tougher brand of Christians. Because these tougher Christians also seem to have the louder voices, they give all Christians a bad name. The compassionate Christians aren't quite sure what to do about homosexuality (I will talk about this more in the final theme), but they certainly know what *not* to do. And when they see people responding to gay men and lesbians in these inappropriate ways, they can get very upset. In this theme, homosexuality is an issue that brings out the worst in some Christians and divides Christians into hostile camps. Such divisions, as I explained in chapter 5, are not desired by Christians because they would rather have a unified Christian community. Mainline churches have experienced great rifts over homosexuality (Hartman 1996). Christian conservatives, more diverse in their beliefs than many assume, are no exception.

Several responses that illustrate this division arose when I asked, "Are there any Christian elements that *are* represented in your city that you would prefer to *not* see represented?" Some Seattle respondents immediately looked at this as an opportunity to distance themselves from the other, tougher group:

> I don't like any groups that are anything that's sort of activist-oriented that is condemning of people. So anti-gay groups or anti-abortion groups that are activist and there's no love involved. I hate those groups. . . . I know there's probably some conservative churches that would say being gay is wrong and they'll say it with an edge to it. Even though they say they love the sinner and hate the sin, you kind of know there's a basic homophobia there.

> I am troubled by the persons that tend to label everything as destructive and reaching out, you know. I know there are a lot of Christians that will have absolutely nothing whatever to do with a homosexual, and would have nothing whatever to do with a Buddhist, you know, which to me is one of the areas where Christians are, we have settled into protectionism or something, you know?

> At times the people who are outspoken. I mean, I think at times, I've heard this from people I really respect. I haven't heard [a particularly conservative local pastor] on the radio but apparently he had a radio show, apparently he talked a lot about homosexuality as an issue. And I just think it's inappropriate to single out something like that and make it some sort of big issue. I think it's misrepresenting the message of the gospel. I think he's right in his conclusions probably, if I understand him correctly, but to dwell on that is not good.

These compassionate Christians seem almost embarrassed by these other Christians, for their reactions to homosexuality only serve to give all Christians a negative image. The tougher Christians also recognize this, though they do not feel that they are to blame. As an example, here is an interview excerpt from the Seattle pastor referenced in the previous quote:

> There's a lot of inflammatory words used to describe Christians who speak out: bigots, narrow-minded, homophobic, you know, all those terms that have come back to the vocal Christian community from the other side. Because we have strong views about certain things in the culture, like the word "hate" has been used to describe vocal Christians who speak on moral issues.

To this pastor, people who speak out are not doing anything wrong. To the more compassionate Christians, such behavior is not as acceptable.

Sometimes this struggle is an inner one: individual Christians do not like how they themselves react to gay men and lesbians. They know that they are supposed to respond with love. However, what they are feeling is not compassion but revulsion. This came up multiple times with the hand-holding scenario. Here are three examples of this reaction, two from Spokane, one from Seattle:

> It makes me nauseous. I, there are, I don't know what I'd do. I'd probably ask to be seated somewhere where I, well, I could tolerate them, we're supposed to love our, I could deal with it, but there are stores that I won't go into. There's a store in the mall that has all kinds of homosexual jewelry and stuff like that and I won't go in there. (TL: So you do choose where to go . . .) Yeah. And I don't want to be closed-minded about it, but, and it's only one store, and it gives me the willies to go in there.

> Probably not look over there. Except for one time. But it wouldn't enrage me. Honestly, it would probably disturb me as a person, only because I haven't seen much of that. (TL: You don't see that around?) No. It would surprise me to see that happen. (TL: Would that affect how you felt about that area, or that restaurant?) I sure hope it wouldn't. But if I want to be honest with you, it probably would. I am ashamed to admit that. But I hope it wouldn't.

> I have mixed feelings about that. In one sense I want people to be able to, with gay people specifically, I want them not to feel hated and judged and not valued as people. But I would have a negative reaction to seeing that, too. It's a tough one.

Homosexuality not only causes conflict within the Christian community, making it less cohesive. It also causes conflict within individual Christians who are ashamed of the way they react to it. If they are truly loving Christians, how could they be nauseous over seeing something like this? Hating the sin and loving the sinner sounds good in theory, but it can be difficult to carry out in practice. Gay men and lesbians don't make this strategy any easier, as one of the leading arguments in favor of gay rights firmly connects behavior with identity. When they claim that being gay is something you *are*, not something you *do*, it considerably complicates this Christian philosophy. If one's gayness is an integral and innate part of one's personhood, rather than simply a behavioral symptom or a bad choice that someone has made, how are Christians supposed to react to this? As more and more gays and lesbians openly make such claims about their identities, some Christians face considerable moral stress.

Gay Men and Lesbians as a Moral Quandary

Times were simpler when homosexuality was a deviant aberration that anonymous people would engage in behind closed doors. Christians could label the behavior a sin and leave it at that. Now, in ever increasing numbers, people are coming out from behind those doors. They are bearing gay identities and demanding the rights to do everything that heterosexuals do, demanding the right to be treated as if they were completely normal. Some even seek the holy grail of normalcy: the right to marry each other.

To most of the Christian respondents, the prospect of gay marriage was completely unacceptable. Most were fully in favor of forbidding gay marriages. For a small but significant number of respondents, though, things weren't quite so simple. Some had friends who are gay or lesbian. Some had serious reservations about the prospect of legislating against a group of people. Some just didn't see what all the fuss was about. Most of these people were on the younger side of the spectrum, and most were from Seattle. For them, homosexuality created not so much hostility as it did confusion. How do they resolve their faith with their personal realities?

Having a personal relationship with a gay or lesbian person has the potential to cause small cracks in one's conservative philosophy. While some Christians were in favor of banning gay marriages, they were troubled by the personal relationships they had with individual gay men or lesbians, as such relationships put a human face on the issue. Here are two examples from the Spokane interviews, the first from an activist, the second from a nonactivist. Both were responding to the gay marriage scenario:

So, you can't get married in Washington State if you're gay? To each other, I mean. I'd be thrilled, because I guess I really am struggling with the concept of the gay situation, because of the fact that I have a hard time believing that a man would love another man like he would a woman. I have a hard time with that. I mean, maybe if that would've happened, but it hasn't happened to me. I struggle with that. I struggle with the concept of what they represent. And I know some gays, and I love these people, because they are so talented. I've got a gay that works with me on the Special Olympics committee, and he's so good. But he's so evil inside.

I would be surprised. (TL: So you would be surprised that they would do something like that?) Yeah. Well, it's just kind of a special interest group and sometimes they can kind of side with the special interests. I would agree with that decision and not because of the personal people involved but just because of the moral statement it makes. That it's not acceptable. I don't know, it's such a touchy issue, just the whole thing, gays and lesbians. This is kind of off the subject, but just the perception is that Christians are so much against those people that it really kind of discredits us. (TL: Do you think that's a misperception?) Yeah. Because they don't. And a lot of Christians are very much against them, sadly. I mean, my [lesbian] friend that was here, I mean, some of the things that she'd tell me about, that people would say to her, that they would call, the mean things. And for us to be like Jesus Christ. (TL: Did she know that you were a Christian?) Yeah. So, for us to be Christians and to be that way, towards any person, it discredits your walk, and people say, "Well, how can you be a Christian?" or "I wouldn't want to be a Christian." And Jesus, those were the people Jesus hung out with, I mean, the people that were lost, as He would call them. So, I mean, I would be happy about the point that it makes. As far as personally with those people, it's not like I'm saying, "Ha ha, those people can't do that." But the point that would be made, I would be happy to hear that said.

It is sometimes hard to separate the personal from the political. While this latter respondent's political self sees the benefit of such legislation, his personal self (the part that has relationships with others) is troubled by it.

Others thought the antimarriage legislation was simply wrong. The philosophical reasons behind such a stance varied, as illustrated by the following young women from Seattle:

> I don't know if I could do anything about it but it would bother me. It would bother me, just because I feel like homosexuality is a sin and male and female sinners are allowed to get married, so I don't see any reason to prevent gay people from getting married. I don't feel like there needs to be a distinction made at all. So yeah, it would bother me, but I don't think I would get up and write a letter to the Senator. (TL: Would that affect how you felt about the state?) It might on some level impress me. Because while I don't necessarily agree with it, it seems like a rather conservative thing to do. I would say, wow, Washington.

> I don't think I would react, because I don't think it's something that should be done anyway. I don't know. I wouldn't react. Yeah, to me gay marriages is not biblically based. Because people think that way and they're hurt and probably I wouldn't, you know, be running around jumping for joy. I mean, you know, it's ugly, it's not showing them how Christians are supposed to . . . (TL: So that's not a very Christian action?) Yeah, to me it's not, I don't think so. (TL: Would that affect how you felt about the state if the state passed something like that?) No, but then if you really think about it if they did pass something like that, that's not separating church and state because what basis would they, they would use the Bible for whatever they feel that they want to use it for, take principles out of it to benefit them. (TL: So that's an example of breaking that church and state rule?) Exactly.

Given the nonrandom nature of the interview sample and the small number of interviews I conducted with younger people, I hesitate to claim that the younger generation of Christian conservatives is more conflicted over homosexuality than their elders. In his book *Evangelicalism: The Coming Generation,* Hunter (1987) claims that younger Christians are much closer to older evangelicals than they are to their similarly aged nonevangelical peers. But the data for this study are from the 1980s, when homosexuality had yet to fully enter the cultural mainstream. A national survey of high school seniors conducted in 2001 found that the Christian conservative students held significantly more anti-gay attitudes than other students (Gilbert 2001). Although this survey provides useful data, it did not let the students fully articulate their beliefs. When researchers do this, the nuances of young Christians' thinking on the issue become apparent. One gets a sense from these excerpts that younger Christians are still trying to fit the issue within the context of their faith, and such puzzle pieces may prove hard to fit together.

To bring this section to a close, homosexuality carries with it numerous meanings for Christian conservatives, most of which create even more hostility toward themselves. Many activists and pundits who take an anti-Christian stance claim that Christian conservatives simply are filled with a venomous homophobia and leave it at that. This does not give credence to the subtleties of Christian belief systems, nor does it offer much hope for resolution of the conflict. In varied and fascinating ways, Christian conservatives use homosexuality as a major marker of hostility in contemporary American culture.

Five Ways Gay Men and Lesbians Think about Christian Conservatives

At the beginning of this chapter, I remarked that gay and lesbian respondents spoke less about Christian conservatives relative to how much their Christian conservative counterparts spoke about them. Even more important are the much different *ways* they talk about them. Themes quite prominent in the Christian conservative interviews were virtually absent in the gay and lesbian interviews. For example, where many Christians use gays as a benchmark to judge how they are treated, gays do not use such a strategy. Where some Christians' reactions toward gays create even more hostility toward Christians, gays don't mention that they find themselves reacting to Christians all that often. Where gays symbolize and represent to Christians so much that is wrong with American culture, to gays Christian conservatives are simply *there*, on the political landscape, sometimes causing them trouble. In fact, that is the most common theme when gays and lesbians talk about Christian conservatives: a source of direct hostility. This theme is so pervasive that I felt it prudent to divide it up into three subthemes in order to adequately expose all of its subtleties. These themes, along with two additional themes, comprise the following list. To various gays and lesbians at various times, Christian conservatives are

- a source of direct hostility, by their mere presence
- a source of direct hostility, by the legislative harm they instigate

- a source of direct hostility, by the dubious information they purvey
- people that are hard to take seriously
- fellow Christians, albeit of a different type.

As I describe these themes below, I point out any similarities or contrasts to the Christian conservative responses.

Christian Conservatives Contributing Hostility through Their Mere Presence

A full one quarter of the references to Christian conservatives in the gay and lesbian interviews concerned the fact that they merely exist, sometimes in large numbers. This is similar to the Christian perceptions described above: the fact that they are there—regardless of whether or not they do anything—is the source of the hostility. Most of these mentions were very short: "Spokane seems like a big place for the Christian Right, not extremists, but it has that big Christian flair to it here," "I think over the east of the mountains is a problem. . . . You go over to the desert side of the state, there's a lot of hostilities, and I think a lot of that is the religious side of things. Eastern Washington is very Mormon. It's very Baptist. And very uptight."

I used the responses to the "family praying in the restaurant" scenario to attempt to assess to what extent gay men and lesbians are affected by the mere presence of Christians. The wording of the scenario was deliberately vague. Given that all it said was "a family says grace," it was up to the respondent to decide if this was a Christian conservative family or not. This vagueness led to some interesting results, the first of which is that a number of respondents *did* decide that they were Christian conservatives and were upset by their presence. Here are two examples of this, the first from a Spokane activist, the second from a Seattle activist:

> Oh [laughs], that's cool. It's just, I don't know, I have kind of a thing. (TL: Tell me about your thing.) Geez. I don't know. It's a different issue. It's kind of in my family. My dad's just become a born-again Christian in the last year or so, we were just discussing it. I don't have any problem with it. I think it's fine. I have a tendency to have an anti-Christian bent in my little mind. You know, I don't mean to, but so much of it just seems to breed bigotry and hatred instead of love and acceptance. I think that's the thing. Religions have not been particularly kind to people like me. So, I guess I

would think, "Are you raising them to be bigots, or are you raising them to be good Christians?" That would be my thought. Please don't fill them with hatred. I just hope. "Jesus taught love, remember that part. Be sure and share that. Judgment is mine, sayeth the Lord, remember that part?"

I guess I would observe it. My stereotypes, my stereotypes. I guess because of the stereotype of them being Christian, and then I would say, maybe they're extremists. I know my opinions would change regarding the environment because I would suddenly feel a little too close to what could potentially be, and I know that that's somewhat unfair but I do go there. . . . It would remind me that these folks exist in my area so it might make me think twice about where I lived.

These excerpts differ dramatically from the Christian conservative reactions to the same scenario. While some Christians were disturbed by the presence of gays, the gay response to the presence of Christians includes an element of threat: that these praying people and their compatriots potentially could do something that would create a more hostile climate for gays and lesbians. Similar to the findings in chapter 5, these findings show that gays and lesbians infuse these perceptions with personal risk while Christians do not.

Christian Conservatives Contributing Hostility through Legislative Harm

A second type of direct hostility that gay men and lesbians perceived regarded the legislation that Christian conservatives potentially could instigate. Gay men and lesbians consider Christian conservatives a formidable voting block, although a sometimes hidden one, as this Spokane activist suggests:

I think they're no different than the gay population as far as there are a lot of closeted ones. There's a lot of closeted people out there that are gay, there's probably a lot of closeted fundamentalists that when it comes to voting are really conservative and, you know, they don't see, it doesn't have to be just a gay issue, any issue that isn't "You're not just like me." (TL: So you don't really see it until they vote on it?) That's been my experience, and I say that because I've been pretty cautious and the people that I'm out to have always been real friendly and I have not had a problem, but I think so. I don't think the majority of them, just like the majority of gays aren't out there waving flags.

This respondent's thoughts are similar to economist Timur Kuran's (1995) concept of preference falsification: people keep their true thoughts to themselves, or even falsify them, until they get in a situation where they know they cannot be found out, such as the voting booth. While in some circles it has become unfashionable to openly express anti-gay attitudes, people still may hold such attitudes. Sometimes, though, the religious opposition is not as undercover as the above activist suggests. A lesbian in Spokane who had spoken at a hearing for the proposed human rights ordinance tells of her surprise at what she saw there:

I didn't realize there were so many people that were dead-set against it, and their reasons why. I went down to the human rights thing and spoke, and sat there and listened to what these people had to say, and I was really surprised by a lot of the pastors that came up and what they had to say. It just really set me back, as a person it was just kind of, "Hmm! For a pastor to say that!" (What did they say?) Oh, basically that we didn't have any more rights than a sex offender. I really have a hard time being put with people that I do not even see myself with.

Legislatively, Christian conservatives are viewed as a threat because they are often the ones who are most vehement about passing legislation that goes against gays or refusing legislation that goes in favor of gays. As illustrated above in several excerpts, even if Christian conservatives are personally on the less stringent side when it comes to homosexuality, they will often support anti-gay legislation because it signifies a pro-Christian value system. To gays and lesbians, Christian conservatives are legislatively dangerous.

Christian conservative politicians were also a source of hostility. The person gay men and lesbians talked about most was Ellen Craswell, the Christian conservative woman who was the Republican gubernatorial candidate in the 1996 Washington State election. Many respondents brought her up long before I mentioned her in one of the scenarios. Although Craswell lost by a significant margin, the 40 percent of the vote that she did get was cause for concern for some gay and lesbian respondents. Some rationalized the 40 percent away, claiming that there will always be people who will vote Republican, regardless of the candidate. But for many, this

40 percent was a sign that a larger proportion of the Washington State population was Christian conservative than they had originally thought. Two Seattlites (an activist and a nonactivist) express their concerns:

> You know, I was a little surprised too. I thought she wouldn't do that well. That 40 percent was high to me. It sort of helped me come to some of the beliefs that I probably had coming in here today which is that things are relatively conservative in this state. That's just one funny way to look at it, but yeah, OK, so Locke won, but you know, she's a lunatic as far as I'm concerned. She was the extreme of the extremes. She's *that* conservative. And she did that well.

> So that's 40 percent of the voters, which were—I don't remember how many voted that election—if you could take 40 percent of 100,000 people, 40,000 people actually put their little pins through that. And that's representative of 40 percent of the state. That's scary. (TL: So that 40 percent scares you?) Yeah, to me that shows, that again shows me that that opposition, that the Christian Right movement is huge, and that people, massive Jello-y people, are willing to be moved by it. (TL: So does that affect how you feel about Washington State?) Yeah, I didn't know that. It's affecting me just this moment.

Because of the substantial size of the Christian conservative community, some gay men and lesbians consider them a significant voting block that is blindly influenced by their leaders. In chapter 5, I provided evidence that such blindness may be infrequent: some Christian conservative respondents are quite critical of certain Christian politicians. However, even with such disagreements, Christian conservatives are politically prominent in their numbers. No Christian conservative respondents saw a threat from the gay community coming from their voting power. To them, gays are a small (yet vocal) special interest group who derive power not from their numbers, but from their ability to manipulate larger cultural elements into doing their bidding.

Christian Conservatives Contributing Hostility through Dubious Information

In chapter 3, one of the main themes about the public that arose in the gay and lesbian interviews concerned awareness. The fact that the general public now had gay and lesbian issues on their "radar screens" was taken as a very good sign. However, respondents wanted even more awareness, as they thought the public did not understand the details of their issues. Given the uninformed nature of the public, it makes sense that gay men and lesbians would be concerned about where the public was getting the limited amount of information they had. Even worse than an *un*informed public is a *mis*informed public. Some gay respondents claimed that Christian conservatives contribute hostility by misinforming a naive public about gay issues. Two activists—one from Seattle, one from Spokane—explain:

> (TL: How supportive is the U.S. in general of gay and lesbian causes?) I think that they are beginning, at one time, in general we are making advances, but it's really small right now. And the advances we are making are smaller because the religious right is confusing things. They're clouding the issues, they're saying things like that we're asking for special rights and stuff, and they're playing on people's fears. People aren't getting good information.

> (TL: How supportive is Washington State of gay and lesbian causes?) Probably more so than some other states, especially getting into the Midwest area, not as much as some others, like California or Oregon, but I think pretty well, if they really understand the issues and know, again, Spokane is more conservative than a lot of the rest of the state, but the state as a whole, it's fairly conservative. They'd have to really know what is going on. I think there's too many organizations like the Christian Coalition that give people the wrong information before HOW [Hands Off Washington, a gay-rights organization] or somebody like that can get out what's really going on.

Thus, for gays and lesbians who seek to educate the public on their issues, an uninformed public and Christian conservative organizations that are more than willing to provide inaccurate information are an unfortunate combination. Much of this culture war is over rhetoric: gays and lesbians must get their version of the rhetoric to the public before the public is affected by information coming from Christian conservatives.

Christian Conservatives as People Who Are Hard to Take Seriously

While there were plenty of examples of the real hostility associated with Christian conservatives, some gay men and lesbians found it difficult to take them seriously. In this theme, Christians are seen more as nuisance than as nemesis. The evidence for this theme comes from both scenarios. A common response to the family praying scenario was an amused rolling of the eyes. In contrast to those who saw actual hostility in the presence of such an act, these respondents saw something to mock contemptuously:

I would probably roll my eyes, but be quiet. (TL: Would it affect how you feel about the environment?) No, I would just think that they're a bunch of crazy people.

That's a good one [laughs]. I think they should keep their religious rituals out of public life. (TL: So that is something you would notice?) Yes, I think so. (TL: Would you do anything?) Yes, I think maybe I would like to set the center of the table on fire and perform a pagan ritual because I am a pagan and obviously religious rituals and actions can be portrayed and forced upon others in public, so that I should probably put on a black robe and cast a spell on them. That's what I will do.

I would think, well, depending on the family and the look of it, I would say, "Oh God, it's one of those Christian nutty families again, let's not eat here anymore," or if it was just a family saying grace, nothing about them, I'd think it was sweet that they, you know, encouraged their children to believe as they do and to actually practice. (TL: So you'd be looking for other elements?) You know, "Father grant us the right to get rid of those homosexuals."

This type of reaction was more common among the Seattle respondents. Remember that in Seattle, bigotry tended to be responded to with mockery rather than with fear. While a family praying is not bigotry, some Seattle gays and lesbians still opt for mockery because they see the family as having the potential to engage in bigoted behavior.

With the Craswell scenario, even though a number of people were scared by the 40 percent of the vote she received, another set of respondents just couldn't take her seriously: "Again, I'm conservative, and typically I probably would have voted along the lines of Ellen Craswell, had she not been a total complete kook, flake, nut, whatever you want to call her," "I'm glad that someone that far out was running. I almost voted for her in the primary because I thought that she would make a better candidate to defeat," "She's kind of a spooky little babe. . . . I think the Republicans were almost becoming embarrassed but, that was it, they had to vote for her." While Christian conservatives make up a sizable voting block, these gays and lesbians believed that their numbers are not significant enough to demand serious concern; the larger mainstream will always prevail. There were no Christian conservatives who made light of the influence of gays and lesbians, pointing to the relatively greater seriousness with which Christian conservatives approach the progress of their counterparts.

Christian Conservatives as Fellow Christians

I argued earlier in this chapter that Christian conservatives view gays and lesbians as their antithesis: gays are what Christians are not. Only a couple of Christian conservative respondents acknowledged the possibility that gay people themselves might be Christians. "We've got them in our churches," one Spokane pastor said. Another Spokane pastor acknowledged their presence in a Christian context, but he was upset at this presence:

> And I have sometimes just been really taken in public meetings, when we're talking about issues, and I find sitting next to me there is a gay minister, and I think they are imposing. I mean, I think everyone has their liberty to their own lifestyle, but if you're going to get over here and use that and say, "I'm going to do that in the name of Christianity," I can find no Christian concept to support this.

However, when I presented the family-praying scenario to the gay and lesbian respondents, the most common reaction was for the respondents to "come out" as Christians. Although some gay men and lesbians take issue with organized religion, many others are practicing Christians. Or, if they are not currently practicing, they *were* raised in a religious culture. Even though gays and lesbians may disagree with Christian conservative stances, they can understand a "Christian lifestyle" that would include saying grace before a meal. In contrast, to many Christian conservatives, the "gay lifestyle" is completely foreign and incomprehensible. As examples of this understanding of Christianity, take these gay nonactivists from Spokane:

> Doesn't bother me. I did that a lot. I think the only time it would bother me is if somehow they expected me to operate differently, but I'd never, no, actually I respect it, I respect anyone who follows their religion but

doesn't inflict it upon another person. And quietly praying before a meal certainly isn't a problem. And of course I have to put up with it whenever I go home [laughs].

That doesn't bother me. Cause we sit at home and we say grace every dinner. But I don't do it publicly. But when I was in South Carolina, I had dinner with a group of people, and we held hands and said grace so it doesn't bother me cause I've been raised in the church.

Many other gay respondents had very quick responses to this scenario, such as "That's fine. I do that," "Cool. Do it too," "That's great. I think there's not enough of that. And I do consider myself a Christian, so I always think that there's probably not enough of that." This type of response was more common in Spokane than in Seattle. Because they are surrounded by a Christian culture, Spokane gays and lesbians tended to have a greater potential for understanding the aspects of this culture. To some Seattle respondents, this behavior seemed foreign.

There were some gay respondents who, even though they had been raised in the church or consider themselves Christians, were bothered by this scenario. They wondered about the deeper meanings behind this display of identity, and about the type of Christianity that is being practiced. Here are two examples of this from nonactivists, the first from Spokane, the second from Seattle:

I think depending on what day it was I'd have a different reaction. (TL: Let's say it's a Tuesday.) Hmmm, OK, on Tuesday I'd probably say, well that's nice, family's doing something together, family's praying together. On a Wednesday I might say, just kind of roll my eyes and go, "Oh man!" But really, back to the live-and-let-live part, that's OK. I am a recovering Catholic myself, and I know that sometimes families that pray together like that have, it's great if that's all it is, but sometimes it's a symptom of things going on in the family and later on the kids in the family figure things out for themselves and have to go through a lot of growth about things. If it's simply a group of people giving thanks for what they have to eat, I think it's great. We all need to be grateful. It's the church-on-earth part that sometimes drives me wild.

Ohhhh, see, and that's the thing, as a Christian person, there's nothing wrong with that. But it gives me the heebie-jeebies. (TL: It does?) It really does. . . . It's funny because my mom and dad now know people who they feel very good about, who they think are beautiful kids, they are now missionaries, one's in India, one's in Mexico. When they get together and invite my mom and dad out to dinner, they all say grace. . . . I'm at the point where I have to take action and say, "Mom, do you realize that these people, if they knew about me, might not associate with you anymore? So you are at point of deciding, whether you know it or not, some time in the next year, it's them or me, not to pressure you, but they're going to say something, and you're going to have to decide." . . .(TL: So when you see it in a restaurant, it gives you the heebie-jeebies because it maybe . . .) Because, I don't know what I can do to show that, but, well, it's the same kind of thing, I mean think of it conversely then, it's the same conundrum. When I'm with a group of queer people, and we're at dinner, and someone says something about the Christians, well then I have to say, "Well, I consider myself a Christian." I mean, it's the same kind of witness, it goes both ways. It's one community or the other. The Christians who think they're Christians and people who have been shut out by the church, the traditional church, who think of Christians as "these people." And these people don't think Christians are being either. (TL: It's all very confusing.) Well, complicating. (TL: The fact that you are a Christian is complicating to your fellow queer friends?) Yeah, it might be, I'd have to ask them. It's like outing yourself, again, in a different way.

Even if gays and lesbians *are* Christian, they realize that there are conservative types of Christianity that may do themselves or others harm. One of the current flashpoints of gay and lesbian activism exists within churches, as gay Christians attempt to change their congregations from the inside. Unfortunately, I did not have the opportunity to delve into this interesting area in my interviews. The interview data do show that a large number of gays and lesbians do understand, at least partly, where Christians are coming from. The reverse—Christian conservatives understanding where gay men and lesbians are coming from—is much less likely.

Conclusion

Our understanding of the relationships between oppositional social movements is underdeveloped. Just as the civil rights movement of the '50s and '60s provided the model for much of the work on social movements in the

'70s and '80s, the pro-life/pro-choice drama has been the dominant example for studies of oppositional movements in recent years (Meyer and Staggenborg 1996). The pro-life and pro-choice movements attach drastically different sets of meanings to the fetus, making it difficult for the two groups to reach any kind of compromise (Luker 1984). Instead, each group tries to gain political power in order to make their cultural meanings the dominant ones, at least where legislation is concerned. The observations of social scientists primarily concern how one movement reacts to the tactics and rhetoric of the other movement. For example, the pro-life movement engages in a particular strategy, and the pro-choice movement is forced to react. Studies of oppositional movements have fallen into the dominant and seductive discourse of war (Best 1999): a recounting of how battles ensue, lines are drawn, and countermeasures are developed to react to opponents' strategies.

Some scholars are continuing in this vein with the battle over gay and lesbian rights, studying the gay movement versus the anti-gay movement. I find this limiting and depart from this model by focusing on the broader Christian conservative movement. This leads to questions that illustrate the limitations of this war analogy. For example, of all the battles that Christian conservatives could fight (abortion, school prayer, etc.), why have they been moving more troops toward the homosexual front? What is it about homosexuality that has caused such mobilization? In the interviews, Christians talked markedly more about homosexuality than abortion.[2] What explains why an issue becomes dominant to a movement with multiple issues? Focusing on just one part of the whole Christian conservative movement (its anti-gay aspects) detracts from addressing this question. It also detracts from studying Christian conservatives who disagree with anti-gay mobilization.

Furthermore, much Christian concern over homosexuality has nothing to do with the political mobilization of gays and lesbians. As we have seen many times, Christians are upset not only by what gays do politically, but what gays cause culturally by their mere presence. The typical fascination with political tactics distracts scholars from examining these cultural processes. The varied Christian responses to gay progress are indicative of a number of emotions: fear, fascination, sympathy, jealousy, self-anger. Just as researchers of social movements have begun to take emotions seriously (Goodwin, Jasper, and Polletta 2001), those who study countermovement interactions should pay attention to the emotions that mobilize each of these groups against one another. A fine example of research that does this is Arlene Stein's analysis of why a small Oregon town mobilized against gay rights when there was virtually no gay presence in the town (Stein 2001). She argues that an anti-gay group was so successful in stirring things up because it played upon preexisting, emotionally charged divisions such as class lines.

In my interviews, gay men and lesbians worry about what Christian conservatives could do to them politically. Christian conservatives worry about what homosexuality means symbolically and culturally for society as a whole. The implications of this asymmetry of concern are seldom considered by either movement activists or social movement scholars. While the tactical dance of social movements is interesting to watch, how each group perceives the other group—both within the contexts of social movements and outside of these contexts—is a topic worthy of greater attention.

7

Changing the Climates

So far, this book has been about perceptions of political climates, analyzing how Christian conservatives and gay men and lesbians perceive hostility from their environments. But people are active not only in the sense that they creatively interpret the climates around them. They may also consciously try to change those climates to make them more hospitable toward themselves and members of their group. Just as I have examined social change as a micro-level *receptive* activity, in this chapter I examine social change as a micro-level *productive* activity, looking at the ways people attempt to affect the climates around them.

I divide these efforts into two categories: conventional activism and everyday activism. When most people think of individual attempts to effect social change, they think of conventional activism: participating in social movement organizations, marches, protests, meetings, etc. With this type of activism, the individual achieves efficacy by becoming a part of something larger: a member of an organization or a loud voice in a march (Linneman 1999). If enough people participate in such activism, social institutions take notice, and the likelihood of macro-level social change rises: the media give coverage, the government changes its policies.

In addition to considering conventional activism, I explore an often overlooked kind of activism whose primary target is the general public, occurring within the context of people's everyday lives. People don't necessarily have to go to a meeting of a social movement organization in order to participate in social change. They can attempt to effect change at the micro level, on an individual-to-individual basis. For example, people may display stigmatized identities in attempts to normalize them or they may attempt to stigmatize behaviors that harm their group. While such individual actions may seem minuscule, especially in contrast to large-scale activity, I show in this chapter that people believe such everyday activism can have an effect on those around them. People consciously "do" social change in hope that others will notice. If members of the general public are faced with social change efforts from both the macro and micro levels, this one-two punch may be an effective combination that changes their attitudes. For example, a member of the public may be watching the evening news and see a march espousing the normalization of a group's identity. Then the next day at work he interacts with someone from this group, witnesses the enactment of this identity, and thus reinforces the mediated ideas he encountered the day before.

While both types of activism can feasibly change the political climates, this is not a one-way street. Political climates may affect individuals' propensities to engage in these activisms. If a climate is perceived as particularly hostile toward a group, individual members of the group may be extremely hesitant to engage in activism, as they expect negative repercussions if they do. This leads to a brutal Catch-22 for those who seek changes in political climates: the climates that are perceived as being most in need of change are precisely the climates where activism will be least likely. In climates perceived as hostile, people may be less likely to engage in activism. In climates perceived as hospitable, people may be more likely to engage in activism even though this activism is less needed in such environments. This climate/activism relationship tends to reproduce the status quo. However, this is not always the case. Social change in hostile environments *does* occur. Hostile climates may become less hostile due to the activism that occurs within them.

Before we delve into examples of activism among Christian conservatives and gay men and lesbians, we need to step back and briefly review the major aspects of political climates that upset each group the most, as discussed in previous chapters. What are the major climate-related goals of each movement? This is important because each group's goals affect the type of activism that it will employ.

Christian conservatives are most upset by the stereotypes that the media, the public, and the government hold of them. The dominant stereotype, described in previous chapters, is that of "Christian as fanatic." They feel that these stereotypes have two major negative effects. First, they deny Christians' efficacy in important public spheres, such as schools, government meetings, and the media. Christians are especially concerned about how their children are treated in the schools, especially if they feel they do not have a voice in school policies and programs. When Christians are denied access to the government, they cannot prevent liberal legislation, which they see as adding permanence and legitimacy to harmful social issues (including homosexuality). Denied access to the media, they feel that they do not have control over what types of information the public receives, thus perpetuating their negative stereotypes.

The second major effect of being stereotyped as fanatics is that it prevents Christians from pursuing one of their major goals: evangelism. If Christians are stereotyped as fanatics, then non-Christians will be more likely to keep their distance, making evangelistic conversions that much harder to achieve. This leads Christian conservatives to a precarious position: while activism often calls for rather bold gestures, such boldness may work in direct conflict with some of their most important goals. Therefore, what we will see below is an extremely cautious and tempered activism, especially in the context of their daily lives, concerned more for the well-being of individuals than for a political movement.

Gay men and lesbians are most upset by the lack of awareness of themselves and their issues. One of their primary goals, then, is to raise awareness. They see many of their group still subject to extreme stigmatization, not so much by the government and the media, but by individual members of the general public. The result of this stigmatization is twofold. First, it remains legitimate to harass gay men and lesbians, either verbally or physically. Second, it remains legitimate to discriminate against gay men and lesbians within the realm of employment. Therefore, gays and lesbians seek the normalization and destigmatization of gay and lesbian identities. Related to this is the simultaneous goal of stigmatizing anti-gay behavior. Gays and lesbians can accomplish this in two ways: they can use legal stigmatization, with social movement organizations creating or increasing sanctions against anti-gay behavior; or they can stigmatize such behavior in their everyday lives, showing individual members of the general public that it is no longer acceptable to engage in such activities. Therefore, what I illustrate below is an everyday activism that is sometimes merely expressive ("see, we're not that different from you"), sometimes highly contentious ("don't you *dare* engage in that anti-gay behavior again").

To examine both types of activism, I use various questions from the interviews. The questions regarding conventional activism come from the last section of the interview. I asked them what their political and activist activities were, and did they consider themselves a political person. I also asked them what they thought people's reasons were for being an activist and for *not* being an activist. Examples of everyday activism appeared throughout the interviews, and I have already offered some such examples in previous chapters (I will review these examples when appropriate). I did ask a specific interview question in the final section in order to illuminate this type of activism, the wording for which can be found in the appendix. In addition, I use the responses to two of the scenarios that involved the potential for everyday activism. One was the joke-telling scenario. The scenario for gay men and lesbians: You hear a coworker tell a joke about a lesbian; he uses a gruff, overly manly voice to tell the joke. The scenario for Christian conservatives: Your coworker's car sports a Darwin Fish, similar to the Christian fish on your car, only with feet. The other was the family scenario: One of your relatives says: "I wish (Christians, gays and lesbians) would just mind their own business." Contrasting the differing responses to these scenarios, both by group and by city, helps to elucidate the role that movement goals and risk play in people's decisions to engage in activism.

Gay and Lesbian Activisms

For your consideration: a Seattle nonactivist named Joe. I first heard about Joe from an activist I was interviewing. We were talking about the reasons people have for not being activists:

> Well, I think a good example would be my friend Joe. He's opinionated, like I am. He's got well thought-out viewpoints on topics and such, but it never goes any farther than that. He never joins any organization. We tried to get him to go. The classic time I remember, we tried to get him to go to a, this was about five years ago when there was one of those [anti-] gay initiatives they were working to put on the ballot, and there was a church up in the north end and . . . they were having a big meeting and pow-wow of the leaders, what was that guy's name, that conservative, he was showing up. So we went. We got Joe to go with us but he was really, he was uncomfortable being in that position. It was just out of his comfort zone to be out on the, to be there, to be out in public, maybe the possibility of being on television. I don't know what it is, but I couldn't really, he's a good friend, but I couldn't really dissect that, that he withdrew at a certain point and had to get out. He actually went back to the car, because he felt so uncomfortable.

Most people don't feel comfortable with the high-intensity confrontation or the high level of time commitment that some conventional activism entails. On the basis of this story, Joe seemed like a perfectly reasonable person for me to interview as one of the nonactivists in my sample, and I did so. Near the end of my interview with him, Joe responded to my question, "Do you consider yourself a political person?" this way:

> Yes and no. I'm very knowledgeable about politics. I have a lot of interest in politics. And yet I have very little patience for a lot of the process and the crap that you gotta go through. So therefore I am not really an activist, although I definitely have a lot of opinions about issues. I stay up on things, and I definitely have an idea about what is going on and how I feel about it. But am I going to go out and run for city council? No.

Joe, like many people (including most social scientists), seems to have a very limited view of what activism entails. Although he does not participate in activism in the conventional sense, there were several points during the interview at which he described attempts he makes in his daily life to effect social change. For example, he attempts to draw awareness to his gay identity and normalize it for the members of the general public with whom he spends the most time, his coworkers:

> I've got pictures of [my partner] on my desk, and his nephew, and my goddaughter, and my dogs and places we've been, quite a few of them. Just kind of a reminder that I have a family too. It may not be like yours, but it's my family, it's important to me, just like yours is important to you. I think that's the main reason I put them there, to tell you the truth.

Through a display of identity with which most people can identify, Joe tries to show the public (at least a very small portion of it) that gay people's lives are not so different. While this may be a tactic that relies too heavily on acceptance through conformity ("Accept me because I can be just like you"), and does not help people understand some of the more peripheral aspects of gay culture, Joe feels he is doing his part.

In addition to destigmatizing his gay identity, Joe tells of his attempts to stigmatize anti-gay behavior, another important form of everyday activism. He recounts a story about riding in a car with a coworker:

> Now, he's my supervisor, he wasn't then. I don't have any idea why he did this, and I don't think he thought this guy was gay, but some guy went by in a car and did something that pissed him off and he called him a fag and

I said, "I don't think that's necessary," and he just looked at me and said, "I didn't mean it that way," and I said, "I know, but I still don't think it was necessary," and I just left it at that. I haven't heard any more.

As far as the continuum of anti-gay behavior goes, this incident was fairly innocuous. Even though the coworker didn't seem to have malicious intentions, the unconscious use of the term "fag" or popular playground phrases such as "That's so *gay!*" contribute to the continued stigmatization of gay identity. They seep the message "gay equals bad" into the cultural subconscious. Moments like this are meant to bring this connection to light. Notice that Joe implies that his everyday activism was successful in achieving its goal: the anti-gay behavior has stopped.

In a typical assessment of activism, Joe would seem lethargic. However, once Joe starts talking about his everyday life, it is filled with small moments of effecting social change. He consciously tries to make the world a better place for gays and lesbians through interactions with his coworkers. Although we have no way of knowing whether or not Joe's coworkers are more pro-gay (or less anti-gay) because of his actions, Joe still feels that he is doing his part, and that his local microclimate is better because of his actions. Climates are lived experiences: they are perceived at the everyday level, and they can be changed at the everyday level, even though these changes may be very small ones.

Other gays and lesbians in Seattle spoke of the importance of identity display in changing people's attitudes. What is worthy of note in the following excerpts is the undeniably conscious nature of these displays. Gays and lesbians definitely connect these actions to social change:

On a real basic level, I want to see things change. I want to effect change. And there's a lot of ways that I do that. One way is coming out to someone or working at Lambert House [a gay youth organization] or walking down the street holding my girlfriend's hand. I think that there's a tendency to see political activism as very focused in the mainstream, but in actuality I think that anything can be a trigger for someone to broaden their awareness. And if someone who hasn't really thought about it sees me and my girlfriend holding hands, well, that could be just as much of a lightning bolt to have them change their perceptions as passing an initiative statewide. So there's all sorts of things coming from that perspective that I do that are political. But my focus is to broaden my awareness first of all, and to broaden other people's awareness that gays and lesbians don't have horns and we're not going to take your children away and corrupt them or whatever.

I guess the thing that we do is that Dave and I kiss goodbye and hello in public. And we do that lots of places. (TL: What are the motivations behind that?) I think any activity that gay people do in public is political whether they know it or not. Yes, it's a political activity. We do it because that's what we do. It's hard to remember why we did it initially, but that's what we do. The holding hands thing, I try and be supportive when I see people holding hands, I try and smile at them, whether they are two men or two women, and try and be supportive of them and smile and "Oh, isn't that nice" kind of a thing.

I do hold hands and hug and kiss and stuff and not just on Capitol Hill [the gay and lesbian section of Seattle], I just act naturally and so far I haven't been harassed. . . . And I am aware that it is a political thing. I do it intentionally and I think it is good for people to see and connect and say, "That's a lesbian," and I am very aware of that and that could be the first time they saw a real lesbian. (TL: A real live lesbian!) At Denny's!

Although these people do these things consciously and with intent, they imply that the intent is not necessary to make the behavior political. The act, due to its power to change perceptions, is political in its implications, even if others who engage in such behavior do so without political motivations. But do we really want to label such unintentional behavior activism? Or should the phrase "unintentional activism" be considered an oxymoron? If we define activism as any behavior that has the ability to change the political environment, then I think we must include these instances within the realm of activism, regardless of their intentionality.

There were also other examples of Seattle gays and lesbians seeking to change their environment by stigmatizing anti-gay behavior. As illustrated in one of the Joe examples above, the goal of such everyday activism is to establish new norms of behavior for the public, to tell the public: "You've been able to do these things in the past, but now the rules have changed." Sometimes, these incidents can get fairly heated, such as this example from a Seattle gay activist:

I go to a little gym downtown, a YMCA down over thataway, and went into the gym one day, and Rush Limbaugh was on the radio. I figured out pretty quickly, not that I had ever heard it before, but somebody had to be. . . . It used to be you could just turn the radio to whatever station you wanted to, and there were two people in there, a guy and a woman, and it was just the three of us so I said, well, is somebody listening to this garbage, I think I said [laughs], and nobody said anything so I went and turned it off, I didn't even turn it to another station, I just turned the whole thing off and then this guy comes up to me and said, "I was listening to that," and I said, "No, not in here." And he says, "Well, you know, I can listen to whatever I want," and I says, "I'll go to the front desk," and I did, and they said no you can't listen to talk radio in there, you can listen to music. So they went and told him, and he just went on and he says, "Well, why, whywhywhywhy," and I says, "Because I'm gay," I says, "and gay people don't listen to that crap."

As gays and lesbians more forcefully enter public space, those who are perceived as being against gays and lesbians—such as Rush Limbaugh and his followers—may be expected to leave, or at least to silence themselves. This activist does a lot to further the gay cause through conventional activism, but he also engages in everyday activism as he goes about his daily life.

The hypothetical scenarios offer more insight into the ways the Seattle respondents react to anti-gay behavior. Of the twenty-one Seattle gay respondents who heard the lesbian joke scenario, sixteen of them said they would react contentiously. By contentious, I mean that they would respond to the joke teller with a loud response that those present simply couldn't ignore. To these contentious reactors, such behavior was entirely reprehensible, unacceptable, and must be punished. The hypothetical joke teller had clearly broken a norm in Seattle culture, and needed to pay. The strength of some of the responses is notable:

It depends on who is around. Frequently I ignore it, frequently I confront them. Frequently I ask them if they're hiding their gay life. Which usually *really* stops them. I believe in confronting on their own level, ask them to tell a story just as bad about their straight life and things. If there's lesbians around, if there's women around, you know, then I'm more likely to say something. If they're saying it and there's a couple of men that are joking around about different things, I would probably say that it's not appropriate. But I wouldn't get as hostile as I would if there were lesbians around.

That would definitely rile me. I would probably be working in a company where there were harassment laws already laid down, and especially like when I worked for Starbucks that would not have been allowed, I could have reported that employee for sexual harassment or prejudice, or whatever, and he would have been reprimanded. (TL: You could have and you would have?) I would have, definitely. I don't allow it, I don't think it's funny. But then again I also live in a very safe world where I work for people where, the place where I work now is owned by a lesbian, so it definitely would have been okay to say, "This person said this." But if I worked somewhere else where it was not OK, I would probably be less likely to say, "This is what I heard and I don't agree with it."

If someone was daring enough to say something within my hearing. (TL: That would have to be daring for them to do that?) Yeah. I guess when you asked me about how people perceive me, I think then that that's telling. (TL: So what would you do?) I would say I'm sorry but you can't tell a joke like that. If you want to talk about it you can come inside my office.

Although this is only a hypothetical scenario, the Seattle respondents' willingness to retaliate against this anti-gay behavior was striking. Judging by the looks on their faces, some of them were flabbergasted by the mere possibility of such an occurrence in Seattle.

The family scenario produced similar results, with twelve of the twenty Seattle respondents reacting in a confrontational manner:[1] "That's my father [laughs]. Let's see, I usually get angry at him," "I would viciously argue," "They would no longer be a relative. I would disown them, they could disown me, whatever. But I would be in their face." In Seattle, it is appropriate to seek social change through in-your-face strategies.

In Spokane, this was the exception, not the rule. Whereas a majority of Seattle respondents said they would react contentiously toward the joke and family scenarios, only a minority of Spokane respondents would. Seven out of twenty-two Spokane respondents said they would be contentious in the joke scenario. Six out of twenty-one said they would take on their family members in an antagonistic way. These differences can be attributed to the climates in the two cities. In chapter 5, I discussed Spokane gays and lesbians' insistence that expressions of identity not involve "in-your-face" approaches. The same rule of thumb applies to their reactions to these scenarios and to everyday activism in general. In response to the family scenario, most Spokane respondents took a subtle approach: "I would probably ask them to clarify that question and find out what they mean by 'mind their own business' and sort of flesh that out a little bit," "I think I'd probably have a talk with them and say 'Well, you realize that there are gay people in our family,' and I'd let them know that I was," "Some of them there's not much point in saying a whole lot, and others where there maybe was some hope there, I'm sure that I would probably say something." One does not get a feeling from these responses that the family member had made a tremendous gaffe. This is in contrast to the Seattle responses, where the family member had obviously broken an unwritten norm.

The Spokane responses to the lesbian joke scenario were even more telling. Most of them would either do nothing, or they would do something that would not cause any sort of scene. Below are two examples of this type of reaction:

> Actually, I almost never say anything about that. I would probably never do anything other than not laugh, unless it was funny. That sort of thing makes me go, "God, I can't believe" . . . it makes me feel less safe because I remember that feeling of oh jeez, here I am just going about my day and doing my work and all of a sudden I didn't feel as safe. Sort of like, what would you all really think about a lesbian?

> I'd probably, depending on how it was presented, I probably wouldn't do anything there, either. I want the staff to feel comfortable with me and not have to worry about "Oops, I slipped up and called him a faggot," or something. Because I'll handle that, I'll deal with it.

The Spokane respondents were much more accommodating of such behavior. Several mentioned that they were so used to it that it wouldn't really faze them. A few said that they would be hesitant to react out of fear of losing their job. Even though the climate in Spokane toward gays and lesbians is improving, there is still a long way to go. The climate remains hostile enough that many gay men and lesbians do not feel comfortable confronting anti-gay behavior. Their reactions perpetuate the message that such behavior is acceptable, and the climate is likely to remain hostile in this respect.

The markedly more subtle nature of Spokane activism was also reflected in other parts of the interviews. Spokane gay men and lesbians do engage in everyday activism, but they do so in less brazen, less contentious ways. Some described the relationships they had developed with their neighbors, and the political implications of such mundane relationships. A Spokane lesbian activist describes such a relationship:

> I think the most significant thing that I do is to be out. And not an in-your-face kind of out, but just letting, the next time one of my neighbors goes to vote, and it's a gay issue, they're going to have to think, well, ____ is gay, this affects ____, and she's never done anything. She's kept a nice yard. She's been nice. She's checked our house during ice storms. You know, I mean, being a regular citizen, basically, and letting people know who we are. I think that's critical.

This is a very different type of identity-centered activism than that practiced by Seattle gay men and lesbians. Spokane gay men and lesbians want to make their identities known, but in much more subtle ways.

Sometimes the strategies they employ are meant to be noticeable only to one another. More common in Spokane than in Seattle was the use of gay symbols. One explanation for this involves the somewhat secret nature of such symbols: these respondents assumed a fair portion of the general public doesn't know what they mean. A gay activist in Spokane explained: "I have a little rainbow strip on the back of my car. I have a rainbow flag hanging from the *back* of the house that the people behind me can see. I'm not bold enough to put it up front yet, although I don't think a lot of people in Spokane have a clue what it is." Public ignorance, described in chapter 3 as an element of the climate that is hostile, does have its upside. It allows gay men and lesbians in Spokane to engage in this type of identity display with minimal risk. A Spokane lesbian activist described this strategy:

> The hats that I wear when I'm out are not an in-your-face kind of thing. The hat just says "OUT." Some grandma walking down the street isn't going to look at it and say, "Oooooh." People who are gay will know, or people who are gay-friendly will know. I have my pride shirts. I don't wear those that often. I tend to wear the ones that don't have the big old triangle on them, that are less noticeable.

This subtle type of identity display is limited in its potential effects, for it may be preaching to the choir, as the above excerpt suggests. If members of the public are unlikely even to notice such displays, this is not a reliable strategy for raising their awareness or achieving attitude change. One lesbian was more optimistic about this. In response to the everyday activism question, she replied:

> Those are things that I believe help just as much if not more. I have a flag on my car, a rainbow flag, and I wear a rainbow necklace sometimes out, not just gay bars, but out. (TL: Regarding the rainbow necklace or the rainbow flag, of the general population, what percentage understands that?) I think the extremes: the ones who are gay and the ones who really hate gays know about it. But I also like to wear the necklace because people ask me what it is. (TL: Oh, OK, so it's a way to start conversation.) Well, I feel proud wearing it, and they're like, "Oh, nice necklace," "Oh, thanks." You know, yeah, I do it, not just for myself, I *do* do it for other reasons that are more important. I mean, obviously *I* already know [laughs], so I want to wear it and I want people to know about it, so yeah. Most people don't know what the flag is, that's why people shouldn't be embarrassed to put it on their cars or wear it as a necklace because people don't even know, but they *do* ask.

While this is a possibility, this technique is more likely a useful intramovement strategy among gay men and lesbians in Spokane as a way to show one another that they are moving about, albeit somewhat secretly, in public space.

While everyday activism is prevalent among the respondents in both cities, and the respondents feel that they are impacting their climates through their daily lives, the differing climates affect the nature of the everyday activism. In Seattle, where gays and lesbians face a hospitable climate, the activism is contentious and therefore noticeable. It is hard to deny that gays and lesbians exist in Seattle. In Spokane, where most gays and lesbians believe they face a relatively more hostile climate, the activism is subtle and sometimes invisible, making the chances of achieving social change more slim. In the words of one Spokane activist, "We're like pieces of the paneling: you can't really see us that well, but we're everywhere." Organizational analyst Debra Meyerson, in her research on social change within a business context, speaks of "tempered radicals": those who seek change through small increments without rocking the boat (Meyerson 2001). Spokane activists fit this description.

The effect of the perceived climates also appeared when I discussed conventional activism with the respondents. In response to the question regarding why people *don't* become involved in activism, some people offered typical answers, such as "people are too busy" or "people are cynical about politics." But the most common response in both cities—seven people in Seattle, twelve in Spokane—was fear. I mentioned some of these responses in chapter 5 when I discussed Spokane activists' thoughts about the consequences of a closeted community. They believed that much of this fear that nonactivists have is unfounded. These claims of fear as a reason not to be an activist were evenly divided among the activist and nonactivist respondents. Among the nonactivists, the rhetoric of the closet was combined with limited ideas of what it means to be an activist:

> I'm sure that has to do a lot with their comfort level, in terms of do they really want to be out on a large-scale basis, if we're talking gay and lesbian causes. Certainly everybody has their different comfort levels. I don't think, I mean, it's a lot easier to write a check out a couple times a year and put it in the mailbox, as opposed to stump from door to door and get signatures, or go to a meeting at city council and speak to the community.

The fact that this was also the most common response in Seattle is surprising. Most of these claims were from activists, who, just like the activists in Spokane, thought that this fear was unfounded:

> So many people are so closeted and once you get involved and you interact with the gay community, you tend to get involved with more things and it kind of snowballs. A lot of people are just too scared of the ramifications, too scared of coming out and being visible and gay, because of their jobs or families or whatever reason. Because once you're out, you really can't go back in. And I think that that's frightening for people. (TL: So even around here you see that a lot?) Oh yeah, I mean I know people, even in the social organization [of lesbians] we certainly don't give out membership names and addresses to anyone. They will only register as their first name. And these are women in their thirties and forties. And while we're just social, we put on dances and cruises and we do retreats, the women have such a fear of coming out for a variety of reasons that they will not give their full names, will not give out phone numbers and that was surprising to me because I was so out. And because even

though you reassure people, "We're not going to give out your names or addresses," people are still very frightened. Some people are very very closeted.

I think they're afraid they're going to be put down. I think a lot of them are ashamed of who they are. I think they're still semicloseted, trying to hide within themselves. Activism is hard. I mean, it's hard to get out of your, you know, it's like marching in the gay rights parade takes guts. Cause everybody's going to see you. And everybody's going to think you're gay. And it's, "What will horrible people think of me?"

In Seattle, they couldn't really comprehend why someone would have fears in such a liberal climate. One explanation was offered by a nonactivist who had been an activist earlier in life. Even in a completely hospitable climate, she suggests, there may be hostile microclimates, such as the person's family, that can affect her propensity toward activism:

One thing that always struck me about Queer Nation [an activist group in the eighties] was almost everybody in Queer Nation at the time I was there either had come from a very strong family background, either they were actively supportive, quietly supportive, or at least they were just families of the sort "We don't care who you are, you're our family, we still support you through whatever you decide to do." And I think that most people don't have that to begin with, and most queer people don't have that at all. So obviously that's going to make someone less likely to stick their neck out. To ever want to try and stick their necks out.

Even in hospitable Seattle, individuals may still have long-standing hangups that prevent them from participating in social change. In Spokane, rather than raising such individualized problems, respondents spoke of a climate of fear that needed to be dispelled before people would be willing to participate in activism.

Christian Conservative Activisms

Christian conservative activism looks much different from gay and lesbian activism. To begin to understand such activism, it is critical to understand a common Christian conservative worldview and the evangelistic impulse it fosters. This is captured best by a Spokane nonactivist's response to one of the hypothetical scenarios:

> Say my cousin Glenn was saying, "I wish you would mind your own business about your Christianity." I would say to him, "Look, Glenn, we're all going to spend eternity somewhere, I want you to be in heaven with me. Or would you rather be in total pain and agony for eternity? Do you understand there's a big difference between that? And the freedom and the beautiful wonderful place it is to be? Forget this level, where do you want to be for eternity?"

Christian conservatives feel they are foot soldiers in a war between God and the devil, a spiritual war for people's souls. Given the choice to allow someone to burn in hell or attempt to save him from this, many Christians feel an obligation to the latter.

Partly because of this worldview, the most common form of everyday activism among Christian conservatives is evangelism. Most of the references to evangelism were not restricted to one specific part of the Christian interviews. The respondents brought up the topic at a variety of points. These references appeared in similar numbers in both cities (eleven in Seattle, sixteen in Spokane) and among both activists (thirteen references) and nonactivists (fourteen references). Most respondents believed that evangelism should be carried out on a one-on-one basis. A common theme among Christian conservatives is their mission to win over one soul at a time (Smith 1998). This strategy not only fits other elements of Christian philosophy, it also helps to prevent any sort of backlash. A Christian nonactivist from Spokane uses such a strategy:

> (TL: You don't feel any hostility?) No. And probably not too many of them do, because most Christians don't do anything to be hostile about, or have anybody say hostile things about them. You know, they're secret service agents. I mean, people don't know that they're Christians. And again, I believe the way Christians should act is try to change the hearts of other people, one-on-one, through friendships.

Christian conservatives are quite cognizant of others' sensitivity to religious issues. Because they see religion as a very personal part of people's lives, many do not brashly enter into evangelistic opportunities, such as this activist from Spokane:

And that's what I stress to Christians: you should prove yourself. There's nothing wrong with proving yourself first. . . . That's why sometimes I don't do that. Because you haven't earned the right to say anything to them about your spiritual life, which is very personal. That's like trying to right out ask them, "Well, how's your sex life with your wife?" I mean, *what*!? I mean, it's a very personal thing and you have to earn the right to be able to talk to people.

Among the passages about evangelism, a recurrent theme concerned the need to be selective about evangelistic opportunities. In their stories of evangelism, Christians recounted moments when the timing just felt right. And they took this as a sign from God that they were being called to witness at that moment. An activist from Seattle recalled such an occurrence:

Another time I was on a flight to New York, and I was sitting next to this girl, and she just started asking me questions about my being in the army, and one thing led to another, and the next thing I knew she was confessing to me that she was an adulteress and needed to get her life right with God, after I began witnessing to her and everything. I prayed with her, and never saw her again. But I know that God put me in a situation at that time for a specific reason. And there are other things, too. On cross-country trips, picking up a hitchhiker, after praying with him, his wanting to go back home to get his life in order, it's just God knowing when to use you and where to use you at given times. And you're not trying to force it.

While they are selective about these opportunities, many Christian conservatives definitely feel an obligation to evangelize at least once in a while, especially when an opportunity is obviously presenting itself. A nonactivist from Seattle and I were talking about his discomfort when people read their horoscopes out loud at the market research firm where he works. He finds horoscopes offensive because of their connections with the occult, but this is not what really bothers him about such moments:

I'm not uncomfortable because I think it's going to screw with my head. I'm uncomfortable because it puts me in an awkward position. As an evangelical Christian, you have a responsibility to evangelize others. And they're evangelizing you. So it points to the fact that, one of my own shortcomings, I haven't been doing the same thing. So, if I'm going to walk away from that, and not deal with it, then it's my problem. Like a failure, that I haven't dealt with it. So it creates a problem. And that's actually happened. And I was irritated, but I didn't say anything. I didn't really know what to do, so I just said, "Great," and I left.

Besides evangelism, many of the other responses involving everyday activism occurred when I asked Christian conservatives the pointed question about such activism. The three behaviors I suggested were similar to those I suggested to the gay and lesbian respondents in that they were all examples of public displays of identity. In response to these suggestions, Christian conservatives often stated immediately that they did engage in such behaviors, but they did not claim that this had political ramifications or that they were doing this to increase the public's awareness of the presence of Christians. For example, while twenty-four of the Christian respondents (roughly equal numbers in both cities) said that they prayed in public, mostly before meals, often this was all they said. They made few claims about the reasons they prayed in public, or of the consequences this behavior might have. This contrasts with many of the gay and lesbian responses in which the respondents spoke specifically about the political effects of such identity-related behavior. The following excerpt from a Seattle nonactivist is about as close as Christian conservatives came to linking behavior with consequences:

> My grandfather was famous for praying out loud in restaurants. It drove my dad crazy, so my dad never did it. When I was growing up and we went to restaurants, we never prayed. But we always did it at home, so my dad would try to play it both ways. I've kind of gone back to, not necessarily praying out loud, just the bowing your head thing. That's definitely noticeable. It's not necessarily distracting or rude, but it lets people know where you stand. And that's important.

Christian conservatives simply did not voice such connections that often. With regard to the intentionality of everyday activism, gays and lesbians seem to make these political connections more often than Christian conservatives. However, remember that many gays and lesbians were affected by the presence of praying Christians in one of the hypothetical scenarios. Behavior that lacks political motivations may still have climate-related ramifications.

A number of Christian conservatives in both cities said that they have worn clothing or jewelry that identifies them as a Christian. The Christian retailing industry has grown tremendously, with sales of Christian products in bookstores exceeding 3 billion dollars annually by the early 1990s (McDannell 1995). This was reflected in my interviews, as twenty-six of the Christian respondents, both Seattlites and Spokanites, both activists and nonactivists, spoke of wearing such things. But as with praying in public, the respondents weren't very introspective about why they engaged in such behavior. Here is a typical example of this behavior from a nonactivist mother in Spokane:

> I pray in public. Every time we go out to dinner, we pray as a family. I pray with my husband. I pray with whoever I'm with. I wear a cross all the time [taking it out from under her shirt]. I attend outdoor activities, like Saturday Night in the Park. I have a "God Moves" sticker in the back of my car. I have a fish on my Jeep. I wear T-shirts. I love my Christian T-shirts.

Now, there may be political implications in such examples, but the Christian conservative respondents did not make explicit political connections like the gay and lesbian respondents did.

There were a couple of respondents who mentioned the strategic use of subtle symbols, a theme that appeared in the gay and lesbian interviews: some of these symbols could be understood only by those in the know. Below are two examples of using symbols, the first from a Christian student, the second from a Christian bookstore owner, both from Seattle:

> And I have shirts from events that I've attended that can be conversation starters that don't even say anything about being a Christian. For instance, my DCLA97 just says "Youth Evangelism SuperConference." It could be evangelism for Buddhism for all they know. It's just that it might be a conversation starter.

> (TL: Can you characterize your feelings towards those people who come in to your store and want the fish for the back of their cars, or . . .) We sell thousands of those. And speaking of thousands, the little "W.W.J.D." [What Would Jesus Do?], you've seen those around . . . that's *huge* right now. I've never seen anything in the stores fly out of here like those do. (TL: When did that all start?) I don't know, last year at some time, maybe it was as much as a year ago. But it really didn't take off until last summer, or fall. So it's only been six months. (TL: And most of it just says

W.W.J.D.?) Yes. (TL: Now, if you're an average Seattlite walking down the street, and you see a shirt or a hat which says W.W.J.D., you're probably not going . . .) Yeah, the average Seattlite is probably not going to pay any attention to it. I mean, you see all kinds of stuff on hats and shirts. So, you know, I suppose if you and I had just met and I had no idea whether or not you were a Christian, but we were chatting over lunch or something and you noticed that I had a W.W.J.D. bracelet on, you may feel free to ask what in the world that means. I mean, you know those are not my initials. And I think that kind of stuff happens a lot. I think a lot of it serves to remind the wearer.

Implied in these excerpts is the hope that the symbol may help to open up an evangelistic opportunity. While this theme of subtle symbols was more prevalent in Seattle than Spokane, the relationship was not as clear as the contrast among the gay and lesbian respondents (among whom Spokane respondents engaged in subtle activism more often than Seattle respondents). In general, those who wore Christian-related clothing or put the Christian fish on their cars were not concerned about the risk of doing so. One Christian nonactivist in Spokane did express concern about wearing his shirts in the public school where he is a teacher, and the Christian mother quoted above also said that she might refrain from wearing a Christian-themed shirt when visiting her children's principal. Other than that, though, there were few references to risk.

Some Christian respondents did not like this "bumper sticker theology," as one respondent called it. Four respondents in each city expressed dismay at the displays on shirts or bumper stickers, arguing that this went against God's wishes. Two activists in Seattle laid out their philosophies this way:

Well, first of all the Lord says that when you pray, go into your closet, and your father who knows your secret will hear you. To make a show of the faith to me is gauche, for lack of a better term. And as far as putting bumper stickers and so forth, I've often said that when persecution comes, a lot of those bumper stickers are going to come off. It's very easy and convenient to be a wide-open Christian in an environment that's not ready to put your neck in a guillotine. But when the persecution comes as prophesied, then I think a lot more people will be a lot more secretive about their faith. But I would also say, too, just like anything else, wealthy people very seldom flash their wealth if they've earned it, if they have a real appreciation of what their wealth means. It's people who can't handle wealth who try to look wealthy, and a lot of times they're broke, or end up broke. It's like the old saying: those who can *do*, those who can't *talk* about it. I'm always leery of people who parade their Christianity. My personal experience is that people who are out there blustering about it, I'm not saying they need to be secretive about it, they should be bold when it's time to be bold. But people who are flashing it all over the place with the T-shirts and the other stuff, I have found to be, generally, not the strongest believers, they're the type who are more judgmental and more prideful.

As a matter of fact, I bought two cars this past year, and got them from people who had fishes on them and I scraped them off. Cause I just think there's no winning with that. Because if I drive bad, people have an excuse to say, "Oh, those fish people." There's no winning with it. There's no good. It's preaching to the choir, in one sense.

These references are illustrative of the more general theme regarding the fear Christians have that the public will stereotype them, with the result that they will not take Christianity's role in the culture seriously. Expressing one's Christian identity must be done carefully, and some Christians think that fish on cars is not careful enough.

Themes about evangelism and identity came up again and again when I presented the Christian respondents with the Darwin fish scenario. I was a little concerned when I started the interviews that some Christians may not be familiar with the Darwin fish. Fortunately, I was wrong, as only three of the Christian respondents (two in Spokane, one in Seattle) were unfamiliar with it. Most respondents immediately reacted with a knowing nod of the head or a perturbed smile. While a lot of Christians took it as a joke, some of these same people were offended by the Darwin fish and took it as a sign of anti-Christian hostility. Here are three examples of this view, the first two from Seattle and the last from Spokane:

(TL: How would you characterize Seattle in terms of issues pertaining to Christians: hostile, hospitable, or both? Why do you feel this way?) Now that I'm thinking about it, there's more Darwin kind of fish on cars than I've ever seen before. And I kind of attribute that to people going out, it's really funny because if you're a Christian and you really strongly believe in it, you're going to go out and get something for your car. So where is this coming from that people come and go to stores and look for Darwin? Because it's not like they have Darwin churches or institutions and they're rallying up with other Darwin people to feel like this. I really feel like a lot of times the society here really wants to cling onto "this is liberal, I can do whatever I want" feelings, kind of back to the sixties/seventies kind of free love and we don't want your Christian influence and stuff.

My reaction would be, that this is very typical of the culture that I live in. If I lived in Montgomery, Alabama, I wouldn't see very many of those on the back of the car. But you see them here, because people think it's cool to be anti-Christian, and this is one of the ways they can express it. (TL: So it's a fad?) Yes, it's a very trendy thing. And I'm not sure that they even understand who Darwin was or what it means. They don't even understand the theory of evolution. But, because it is a symbol of anti-Christianity, they're going to put it on their car. (TL: So they may not even understand . . .) Most of them don't. (TL: Do you see a lot of those around?) I see a lot of those around. I sure do. (TL: So, does that affect how you feel about the environment?) Yes, it does. It just reconfirms that I am living as a minority in a very liberal environment. They're lost, they're lost, the culture is lost.

It makes me mad because it's turning, it's like a blasphemy. I just hate it because they're taking a Christian symbol, and whether or not the symbol is even biblical, I don't know. But it is a symbol that stands for Christianity and for them to turn it around to make it look like that really irks me. It's like hanging an upside-down cross or something, it's not necessarily religion itself, but you know what I'm saying. I think it's just one more ploy to take something away from the Christians.

Not only do many Christians recognize the Darwin fish, but they also interpret it as a sign of anti-Christian hostility. One would think, then, that they would take steps to stigmatize this obvious source of hostility if given the chance. On the contrary, few respondents said they would engage in vitriolic confrontation with their coworkers. In fact, only two respondents (one in each city) said that their response would be at all confrontational.[2] Much more common was the theme of "bridge building" (the term comes from the respondents themselves). Christian respondents saw the Darwin fish as yet another opportunity to evangelize others. Below are two such examples, the first from a pastor in Spokane, the second from a nonactivist in Seattle:

> I don't know if you've seen the reply to that one, the one where the bigger fish is eating up the Darwin fish, that makes me laugh. I wouldn't be surprised, and as a co-worker I would probably look for an opportunity to dialogue with that person and just kind of talk with them about it and get their opinion and find out where they stand and an opportunity to build a bridge so they don't think that Christians are just a bunch of unthinking people who checked their brain at the door when they entered science class. So, it wouldn't bother me, I'd look forward to the opportunity to have a little dialogue.

> I wouldn't, like, confront that person and say you should get rid of your fish. And I wouldn't sort of come up and say you really need to get rid of that. If they're not a Christian, I would ask them what they think of that, and I would really try and model Christianity in a way that probably would be satirical towards the fish and "Christianese," and I would try and develop the relationship to show that Christians are not that way. That they're relevant to culture. And I would try to work overall in that relationship to show them who Jesus is.

In reaction to the Darwin fish, the respondent has essentially two choices: he can use the interaction as an opportunity to dispel stereotypes of Christians as relentless "my way or the highway" eccentrics, or he can react contentiously and reaffirm these stereotypes.

Another common response was quiet pity. In his recent book, Christian Smith characterizes some of his Christian conservative interviewees as having a sense of moral superiority (Smith 1998). I also find this in my study, as many Christian conservatives responded to the Darwin fish with feelings of pity and remorse for the owner of the car. I illustrate this theme with three short excerpts, from a Seattle activist, a Spokane activist, and a Spokane nonactivist:

> It makes me feel a little sad. It doesn't surprise me. It almost amuses me, since Darwin died a Christian, that they just don't understand. I think they're just kind of deceived.

I think those poor people don't have a concept of the person who loves them enough to create them. And I don't feel angry about it, I think they haven't heard. And they have been sold a bill of goods by an academic community that keeps changing the rules because they keep finding things that don't fit.

Guy must not be too smart. . . . Mainly it says that a person is going to hell because they don't know Christ. That was mainly my reaction. I may not be too smart, but I can't understand how anybody can swallow evolution.

In a way, references that fit this theme also speak of evangelism. Souls who are lost to such an extent that they actively profess anti-Christianity probably cannot be saved through evangelism, so the only thing that can be done is to pity them, and perhaps pray for them.

The family scenario also had the potential to elicit everyday activism. Again, as with the joke scenario, Christian conservatives were less likely than gays to say they would engage in confrontation. Eight respondents (four in each city) said they would engage in angry confrontation with their family member. This is in contrast to eighteen gay and lesbian respondents who said they would respond with confrontation. Those who would confront would do so rather strongly, such as the nonactivist at the beginning of this section who would ask her relative, "Do you want to be in pain and agony for eternity?" or this Seattle activist: "I would challenge that. I've had relatives that say that. I would challenge them as to what made them feel that being a Christian caused you to lose your rights to your opinion," or this Spokane nonactivist: "Well, I'd probably have to ask them 'Are you afraid of Christians? What's the problem here? Why don't you want Christians to talk?' Obviously, that would upset me." Most respondents, though, would not confront like this. They may instead simply ask what they meant by that statement, or try to build more bridges.

A surprising response was for the respondent to agree with the relative. Seven Christian conservative respondents (four in Seattle, three in Spokane) addressed the scenario in this way, reflecting a discomfort among some Christian conservatives with some types of activism. Responses to this scenario helped them to further distance themselves from the type of Christian with whom they would prefer to not be associated. While some types of minding-other-people's-business is acceptable, other types are not. Below are two examples of this view from two nonactivists, the first from Seattle, the second from Spokane:

206 | *Changing the Climates*

Actually, they do need to mind their own business. That is so funny that you said that because in Second Thessalonians, Chapter Three, and I'm not smart like that, I just happen to know that because I just taught that to the children last night. We are supposed to mind our own business in some ways and we're supposed to work hard and we're not supposed to get involved in people's lives as far as pushing ourselves into people's lives. But we are supposed to say what we believe but not force somebody to do it one way or the other. So if it was a relative saying that because an Aunt Gertrude was saying, "You need to do this and you need to do that," then that person would have the right to say that, I think. If he was saying that because these people are expressing how they believe in a nonconfrontational way, then I think the person would need a little talking to.

Well I, see, it kind of depends. If the person is saying they're Christian and they go and put a bomb in an abortion clinic, well I don't agree with them. But if it's a Christian going around door-to-door inviting them to church, which they could say that for that, then I could say, "Well, it's just Christians caring about you." Because there are people who call themselves Christians who I wish they would quit doing what they're doing.

What explains this lack of confrontation on the part of Christian conservatives, especially in contrast to the higher likelihood of confrontation on the part of gay men and lesbians? One explanation is methodological: the joke scenarios were not as parallel as they should have been, and the gay version implied a moment of confrontation more so than the Christian version did. However, the family scenarios were identical, yet there still was less confrontation from Christian conservatives. Another explanation is that anti-Christian sentiment is more acceptable in society than is anti-gay sentiment, especially anti-gay sentiment in Seattle. If this were true, it would explain why more Christians are not willing to stigmatize such sentiment. However, I believe the most convincing explanation involves the major movement goals. For gay men and lesbians, the goal is to legitimize gay identities. Because anti-gay sentiment delegitimizes such identities, it is to the benefit of gay men and lesbians, if the climate permits, to quash such sentiment whenever possible. For Christian conservatives, the goal is to win souls for Jesus Christ. To confront coworkers and family members may not be the wisest of moves if your ultimate goal is to evangelize them. As many of the excerpts suggest, some Christian conservatives believe that reacting angrily can only fuel the stereotypes some people hold of them. Christian conservatives, then, are rather limited in their possible responses to such attacks. Although survey research has shown that Christian conservatives are more willing to accept the use of contentious protest tactics than those from mainline denominations (McVeigh and Sikkink 2001), my data show that they are quite wary of contention in their daily interactions.

When I asked the Christian respondents why people don't get involved in conventional activism, the most common response regarded fear. Six respondents in each city included fear as a reason people aren't involved. This may seem odd, since in reports earlier in the book risk and fear played small roles in Christians' perceptions of climates. But when gay talk about the fear of activism is linked to one of their main sources of hostility, the fear of identity revelation, Christian conservatives talk about the fear of activism itself. Here are two examples of such fear, the first from an activist in Spokane, the second from a Seattle pastor:

Fear I think is the number one. Always fear. (TL: What kind of fear?) Fear that they won't be successful at it. Fear that they might not be on the right side. Fear they might lose. Fear that they don't have enough talent, enough resource to do when they get in the middle of something. Fear is always the biggest motivator to keep people from doing things.

I'm willing to risk my life to go into underprivileged areas with the hope of the gospel and hopefully with some practical solutions to economic situations, because when you live in tough areas of town as a believer, you're putting yourself at risk. When you work there. Even when you reach out to people. If I'm running a ministry for alcoholics, I'm putting myself at risk cause you're going to come into contact with all kinds of people . . . people who run the Union Gospel Mission are putting themselves in harm's way. Every night there's some little fracas in the foyer of the mission, some drunk guy who has been denied entrance and is unhappy about it. So I guess it takes an element of courage to be involved, and some people are not involved because they're preoccupied, they lack courage, they're not willing to take risks, they don't believe what they really believe. They don't believe it enough anyway to leave their comfort zone to expose themselves to danger. It's the same with evangelism. I mean, there are people who don't evangelize because it's too big a risk. The weight of the convictions is not heavier than the weight of the personal risks involved, like losing my job or something like that.

A number of Christians claimed that the source of the risk would be the activism, not the fact that it would reveal their Christian identities. To them, activists take strong stands, and this is inherently dangerous. Also, charity-oriented Christian activists, as this second excerpt explains, risk physical harm from being in the less savory parts of the city. Unlike gay men and lesbians, Christians do not seem to fear being exposed as Christian. Rather, as throughout the rest of the interviews, they are afraid of taking contentious stances that might make any activist seem unapproachable or dangerous. Such fears do not seem to be at all linked to local climates, but rather to a national distaste for activists of all sorts, as this Seattle activist suggests:

> You get shot at, you get trouble, you get bad mail, you lose money. You lose sleep, people hold you hostage. They want to discredit you on national television or radio, they threaten you. Happens all the time. You can't sign anything anywhere without getting into the culture wars.

Conclusion

Though the cliché "one person can make a difference" may sound trite to those ensconced in social movement activism, many of my respondents believe it to be true. Through the course of their daily lives, many Christian conservatives and gays and lesbians attempt to effect change. However, the two groups have different approaches to such everyday activism. Christian conservatives see the most good coming from carefully evangelizing others by building relationships with them and by modeling Christianity in a positive light. Gay men and lesbians seek a world where they can exist openly, and therefore try to normalize gay and lesbian identities and stigmatize anti-gay behavior. The likelihood that individuals will participate in gay activism is more dependent on climate differences than Christian activism is. This is partially due to the nature of each group's activism and the extent to which gay men and lesbians think about risk. Seattle gays are more brazen than Spokane gays partially because they can afford to be.

At its beginnings, social movement research concentrated on the individual, characterizing him as an irrational and fanatical follower susceptible to the emotion of crowd behavior (Hoffer 1951; Le Bon 1895). In reaction to this view, later movement researchers swung the pendulum to the other side, characterizing individuals in movements as purely rational actors who immersed themselves in social movement organizations to gain material benefits (McCarthy and Zald 1977; Olson 1965). The resource mobilization and political process approaches have made much progress in understanding how movements use organizations to achieve their goals. Yet in doing so, they lost sight of the individual. Recently, scholars have moved beyond this organizational emphasis and have begun to pay attention to culture and emotion in social movements (Goodwin, Jasper, and Polletta 2001; Johnston and Klandermans 1995). Because climates have a cultural component to them, this chapter has spoken to this new wave of social movement research by illustrating how individuals seek to change cultural definitions and social norms. Those who study norm emergence tend to concentrate on how norms develop within close-knit groups (Fine 2001) or within certain professions (Schudson 2001). I show that people try to effect changes in norms through interactions with people in their everyday lives, thus changing the climates they experience on a daily basis. Everyday activism is an important part of many people's social-change repertoires, even if these people do not consider themselves to be activists in the stereotypical sense. As small and ineffectual as such behaviors may be to the larger picture, many respondents in my study took such moments very seriously.

8

Concluding Thoughts

Through this project's planning stages, the weeks working with data sets, the months in the microform room looking at editorial pieces, the many trips back and forth across the state of Washington in my trusty '81 Honda Civic, the hours of interviewing, and the tedium of transcription and coding, I continually tried to remind myself of the big picture. This project addresses two central sociological questions: How do people perceive the worlds around them, and how do they try to change these worlds? I believe I have contributed to our understanding of these issues, though I'm aware that my findings may only lead to more questions.

In this final chapter, I discuss the book's implications for the various areas to which it speaks. Some of these implications are substantive, regarding how my findings affect our understanding of political climates, social movements, activism, and the two groups at the center of the study. Other implications are methodological, concerning how to study these processes in future research.

The Potential of Political Climates

Taking a phrase from popular political discourse and making it a subject of academic inquiry is no easy task. Rather than just being a pet phrase that politicians regularly invoke to defend their decisions, "political climates" have meaning for real people at the grassroots. People have interesting ways of assessing the levels of hostility around them. And they are indeed affected by these climates. In the introductory chapter, I claimed that political climates exist only through people's perceptions. Yet the strength of these perceptions makes these climates real in their consequences. One need only witness the caution of Spokane gay men and lesbians or Christian conservatives' virulent loathing of major social institutions in order to understand that these perceptions are powerful enough to shape behavior. In some cases these perceptions of hostility can impair activism, while in others they can incite it.

When planning the project, I was concerned that if I asked the respondents to talk about hostile and hospitable aspects of their climates, I would commit a grave mistake: asking people to do something that they are unable or unwilling to do. This fear quickly abated as I began conducting the interviews. The respondents were more than willing to tackle these difficult questions, and the immediacy with which they often responded signaled that these were issues about which they often thought. Many have written about the political ignorance of Americans (Converse 1975; Page and Shapiro 1992). While this may be true of a good number of Americans, I sensed from the interviews that people from these two groups may have, on average, a greater stake in remaining aware of the political and cultural trends around them. True, half of the people I interviewed were activists who were more likely to be politically alert, but even the nonactivists had little trouble assessing the various climate elements we discussed. This may be because climates are cultural as well as political in nature. It wasn't only their ability to answer these questions, but also the passion with which they answered them. A contribution of this work is showing that climates are important: people try to understand them in order to assess where their group stands in society.

But why should this be considered a vital contribution? In other words, is this realization able to withstand the ever important "so what?" question that often plagues social science? I believe that it does, for this insight provides a critical connection between the macro and the micro levels of analysis. Faced with a vast array of information about their surroundings, people develop mental shortcuts for understanding their environments well enough to live in them effectively. What information do they draw together to form coherent stories about the hostility they face on numerous fronts? Unable to hire polling agencies to assess how their neighbors, politicians, and media feel about them on a daily basis, people strike out on their own to accomplish these tasks. Based on how they perceive what's going on, they decide how to interact with their surroundings. It is these perceptions, then, that provide a key link between an individual's behavior and his or her environment.

While this much became clear to me by the end of the project, what remained elusive was an assessment of the factors that *most* contribute to the overall perceptions of a hostile or hospitable climate. I know these factors to a certain extent because of the topics that the respondents brought up on their own with the greatest frequency. For example, it was evident that hate crimes were of great concern to gay men and lesbians, and it doesn't take many such occurrences to send a paralyzing chill through an entire community. Christian conservatives brought up school issues again and again, making them a clear marker on their cognitive maps. I fear, though, that some of the interview questions may have led them to place greater importance on some issues than they would have if I had not prompted them.

This problem of what factors most determine a climate, combined with the somewhat limited sample of this project, leads me to conclude that the next step in studying climates might involve a component of survey research. With an elaborate survey, one would be able to determine, for a much larger group of people, what aspects of their climate factor most significantly into their overall perceptions of their environment. The sample for such a survey could involve a wider range of general political climates, ranging from the extremely liberal to the extremely conservative. Also, a larger sample would allow one to study the effects of intersecting identities on climate perceptions. While my sample had a fair amount of variation in gender, race, social class, and age, the sample was not large enough to make contrasts based on these identities. For example, do the higher levels of fear of violence experienced by women (Hollander 2000) affect how much lesbians fear hate crimes? Does one's higher social class color one's climate perceptions, or give one more leverage to change the climate? A significant methodological problem remains because sampling individuals from the two groups remains problematic. However, some social scientists have recently developed ingenious ways of studying representative samples of both Christian conservatives (Smith 1998) and gay men and lesbians (Barrett, Pollack, and Tilden 2002; Klawitter and Flatt 1998).

In addition, one could survey groups beyond the two studied in this project. Political climates are probably just as important for a number of other social movements. For example, support for the tenets of environmentalism varies considerably across the country, as does support for the civil rights movement, the women's movement, and the pro-life movement. Studying other issues is especially important because the two groups in this study employ significantly different tactics in perceiving climates. For example, it is important to determine whether gay men and lesbians are unique in their focus on identity, or whether this theme would arise in conversations with adherents of other movements as well. What other groups besides Christian conservatives revile the media?

Political climates are nonstatic: they can change, and often do so rather quickly. To assess this assertion, I asked the respondents: "Has this [political climate] changed over the past five years? How, specifically, has it changed? Can you give some examples?" This allowed the respondents to speculate on the effects of recent changes. To better assess how people formulate these perceptions of change, it would be wise to conduct a longitudinal study in which one could track changes in people's perceptions of political climates over time. In doing so, one could observe the effects of specific events. For example, since the completion of my interviews, significant change has occurred in Spokane. On January 26, 1999, the Spokane City Council passed an ordinance "banning most discrimination against homosexuals" (Hansen 1999). This led to significant mobilization on the part of some Christian conservatives, who organized an unsuccessful voter referendum to repeal the ordinance. Conducting a long-term study could further enlighten our understanding of political climates and the role that such events play in changing them. One could track the occurrence of events in various locales and then study their effects: a school board decision in one city, a hate crime in another city, and a first annual political march in yet another. However, it would also be useful to pick one site and study it over a long period of time, anticipating that the appropriate climate-changing events will occur. One could employ the use of respondent diaries, in which those taking part in the study keep track of occurrences that affect their climate perceptions. Though such a method would elicit interesting results, it could also compel the respondents to be more cognizant of their surroundings than usual, thus limiting the generalizability of these results.

The Context of Social Movements

I consider this work to be a contribution to the growing body of social movement research that takes context to be of utmost importance. From Bernstein's work on how various manifestations of lesbian and gay movements deploy identity politics in different political environments (Bernstein 1997) to Miller's work on the development of antinuclear activism in three geographic areas near Boston (Miller 2000), more researchers are moving beyond the assumption that movement activity is constant throughout vast geographic areas. There are factors unique to certain areas that strongly affect the type of activism that arises, or whether it arises at all.

My contribution to this area concerns the perceptual component of context. While other researchers focus on the objective differences between various locales, my project took two differing environments and sought to understand how people perceived these climates. In doing so, I expose a good number of differences between "objective" climates and their subjective interpretations. For example, while the analysis of editorial pieces showed that the Seattle paper was more hospitable toward gay and lesbian issues than the Spokane paper, Spokane gays and lesbians perceived their paper to be quite hospitable. Gay activists and nonactivists in Spokane had different perceptions regarding the level of hostility among the general public of their city. Rather than focusing on objective measures of public opinion, Christian conservatives often used more subjective strategies to assess these elements—strategies that were quite demanding of the public.

Although studying objective differences in the political opportunity structures of various environments is important, we must keep in mind that these structures are subject to interpretation. These interpretations have implications: if you don't think the government will hear your case, you may not even try. In his model of political process, McAdam (1982) included this factor, calling it "cognitive liberation," but subsequent work on political process has given short shrift to these subjective processes (Jasper 1997). Although the social movement scholar's task is made much more difficult by giving subjective interpretations their due, this acceptance will lead to more in-depth understandings of social movement processes such as mobilization and tactical choices. For example, understanding the perceptual differences between activists and other members of the community for whom they speak could shed insight into why it is difficult to create new activists in these communities. Taking such insights into account could help activists frame their appeals for action (Snow et al. 1986).

Most researchers see movements as such large creatures that most of their attempts to study them are limited in their scale. In-depth studies of single movement organizations are common, and most large-scale surveys of movement participants concentrate on people involved in a single movement campaign (Jasper 1997; McAdam 1988). It is necessary to move beyond these tendencies and design broader studies that will allow us to compare oppositional movements as well as various local incarnations of national movements. For example, using an umbrella organization such as the National Association of Evangelicals as a starting point would be a useful way to conduct a large-scale study of Christian organizations and activists. One could similarly study gay and lesbian rights groups by tapping into national networks of organizations and digging down into the grassroots from there, being careful not to favor local groups because of their national connections. By comparing all contexts within which movements exist, we will have a better understanding of the role that this context plays in movement activity and movement outcomes.

Activism: Different Risks, Different Forms

Renowned social movement scholar Doug McAdam is one of few researchers who have analyzed the role of risk in people's decisions to engage in activism. Most of the activism he studies is what he labels "high risk": participating in the Mississippi Freedom Summer project in the 1960s (McAdam 1988) or the sanctuary movement in the 1980s (Wiltfang and McAdam 1991). These examples of activism are not only high risk, but also high intensity: traveling hundreds of miles into the hostile territory of segregationists, hiding political refugees in one's own home. It is obvious that some people are not going to be willing to participate in these activities given the extent to which they vary from ordinary daily life. These activities and the types of risk associated with them are very different from the behaviors and risks that the respondents in my project discuss. Some people found risk in ordinary, everyday behaviors. For example, the gay and lesbian respondents concentrated on risk as it related to identity issues. For gays and lesbians in some environments, displaying their gay identities within the course of their daily lives was perceived to be a great risk. While some have studied the risk of engaging in such identity politics, even considering it "high-risk" activism (Taylor and Raeburn 1995), my findings suggest that there is more work to be done in the area of risk and activism.

For example, one type of risk that arose many times in the interviews was the risk of being considered an activist. What is it about our culture that labels activism as deviant behavior? Many of the nonactivists, both in the Christian and in the gay interviews, characterized the "activist lifestyle" as being too unusual for them. Many activists also gave this reason for others' nonparticipation. Respondents commonly said they are not activists because they fear being labeled an activist and, by extension, a deviant individual. These fears have connections to processes found most often in the literature on social deviance. Associating with particular types of deviant people makes one more likely to become deviant too. A person may get involved by stuffing envelopes for an organization, but before she knows it she may be engaging in civil disobedience in the streets. Labeling processes carried out by dominant institutions in society make it hard for the labeled person to function in the mainstream. Few researchers have attempted to wed the literature on social movements with the literature on deviance. Such a combination could provide a useful explanation for why so few people become involved in social activism. One could conduct a content analysis that addresses the ways in which activism and activists are portrayed in a variety of mainstream media: film, television, newspapers, magazines. The next step might be to interview both activists and nonactivists, assessing their ideas about activism and activist lifestyles, perhaps presenting them with some of the media images from the content analysis and measuring their reactions. As a final component of such a project, one could perform a longitudinal participant observation of those in the midst of developing "activist lifestyles," assessing changes in their relationships with nonactivist friends and family members.

A second aspect of risk that needs to be further explored is its subjective nature. Just as some perceive hostile climates where others do not, some see risk where others do not. In reference to McAdam's work, most would agree that housing illegal refugees is risky behavior. As my findings show, the risk involved in other forms of activism is not so clear-cut. To study the differences in these perceptions, one could use a series of hypothetical scenarios designed with different types of activism in mind, assessing where people draw the line in terms of risk. If this study were combined with a survey assessing people's perceptions of the more general climate, one could causally link these assessments to see how one set of perceptions affects the other. This is especially important, given that qualitative research, such as that used in this book, is not the best method for making causal arguments (Lofland and Lofland 1995). However, using a qualitative method, one could attend movement events—from gay pride marches to pro-life rallies—in a variety of political environments and interview the participants about the levels of risk they perceive as they participate in such activities.

In addition to studying the risks associated with this conventional activism, we must also consider other types of activism. Studying activism outside of conventional social movement locations is becoming more prevalent. For example, Raeburn (1999) completed a study of gay and les-

bian organizing in the workplace, and Schmitt and Martin (1999) characterize a type of activism they call "unobtrusive activism" inside institutions, in which activists try to change social institutions from the inside
rather than protesting outside. Meyerson (2001) writes of "tempered radicals" who attempt incremental changes in their work environments. While
my study helps to identify various forms of everyday activism, each of
these forms is worthy of its own study. Identity politics has been the subject of much theorizing (Phelan 1997), but little empirical research has
been conducted on the strategies that people employ and the types of situations in which they employ them. The presence of symbols in social
movements is well documented (Jasper 1997; Woliver 1996), but there are
few studies of the processes through which symbols are employed. A separate analysis of the extent to which ideology affects people's consumer decisions would also be welcome. Another type of identity-based everyday
activism, too infrequent to have reported in earlier chapters, may be uti-
lized more often in the future: database activism. A form of identity politics used by some gay men and lesbians, it involves allowing oneself to be
represented as a gay man or lesbian in various census, survey, or market-
ing databases. Only a couple of gay men and lesbians mentioned it in my
interviews, but the rise of information politics suggests that this type of
activism may increase.

Other movements' causes also lend themselves to everyday activism.
Pichardo-Almanzar and colleagues have recently studied everyday environmental behaviors (Pichardo-Almanzar, Sullivan-Catlin, and Deane 1998).
"The personal is political" has been a rallying cry of the women's movement
for decades now (Evans 1979). Everyday confrontation is a common tactic
in the animal rights and the antismoking movements (Jasper and Nelkin
1992; Wolfson 1995). A comparative study of a number of social movements would help discern whether everyday activism is indeed a common
type of activism among those who seek social change.

Even less research has been conducted on the effectiveness of everyday
activism. Just because people consciously engage in such activism does not
mean that it is an effective tactic in the pursuit of social change. Unfortunately, studying the effects of activism has been problematic (Cress and
Snow 2000; McAdam and Snow 1997; Gamson 1990). Given the subtle
nature of some of these everyday tactics, such actions may be completely
ineffectual. For example, remember that several Christian conservatives,
when faced with the hypothetical scenario of two gay men holding hands
in a restaurant, assumed that the men were either praying or were from

Europe. How conscious of everyday activism are its targets? Developing a study to answer such a question would be a challenge. One could possibly perform participant observation. For example, one could position two same-sex hand holders in strategic locations and have a third person observe people's reactions from afar. Or, one could interview people about their reactions to someone wearing a Christian-themed shirt in various settings. Just as studying the effects of conventional activism is problematic, studying this aspect of everyday activism is equally difficult, if not more so.

Christian Conservatives, Gay Men, and Lesbians: A Necessary Comparison

In the introductory chapter, I said that some people may have problems with a study that compares gays to Christian conservatives. In terms of sheer numbers, the comparison appears flawed: one group makes up almost a third of the American population, while the other comprises less than 5 percent. One has many members in the highest echelons of power, while the other has many members who hide in plain sight. By this point in the book, though, it should be clear why a rigorous contrast of these two groups is appropriate. In the interviews, it was common for Christian conservatives to compare themselves with gays and lesbians, to take on the role of a besieged minority. In fact, the dominant trend was for Christian conservatives to perceive *much* greater hostility than gay men and lesbians, from every major institution I examined: the media, the public, and the government. With regard to social change, Christian conservatives very seldom perceived an increasingly hospitable climate (unlike gays and lesbians, where this was common). Christian conservatives were much more likely to perceive an increasing hostility on a number of fronts. Using the objective measures I collected, it is more difficult to make this case. There is little evidence of increasing hostility in public opinion, and limited evidence of increasing hostility in the editorial pages (granted, only a part of the entire media system). Why are Christian conservatives so eager to appear beleaguered, while gays and lesbians seem equally keen to perceive decreasing hostility?

To address this question, I suggest that we must examine the role hostility plays in each of these movements. In the Christian conservative

movement, hostility is a motivational tool that fits nicely within its dominant worldview. Christians are told that they should *expect* increasing hostility as the endtimes scenario approaches. Feeling embattled solidifies
their sense of collective identity and increases the likelihood that Christians will mobilize. The interviews hold numerous examples of Christians
responding to increased hostility by getting more involved. As such increased involvement could bring about further hostility (as they are likely
to be stereotyped as contentious Christians), a feedback loop could be put
in motion: a more hostile climate spurs activism, and more activism creates a more hostile climate.

Hostility toward gay men and lesbians has a different effect because it is
wrapped up in issues of risk and identity. Gays were much more likely
than Christian conservatives to talk about risk-related issues. This propensity has consequences: the presence of hostility is more likely to have a
dampening effect on gay mobilization. Remember that Spokane gay activists yearned for ways to show their constituents that they were misper-
ceiving hostility and should not be afraid to engage in activism, both the
conventional and everyday varieties. Therefore, in the interest of pro-
pelling social change, gays and lesbians try to find evidence of decreasing
hostility. This has the potential to create a different kind of feedback loop:
a more hospitable climate brings about activism, and more activism creates a more hospitable climate.

While I believe this perception-based theory explains at least part of
what I observed, it is important to emphasize that Christian conservatives
do face high levels of hostility in certain contexts. In speaking about
Christian conservatives at conferences around the country, I myself have
encountered some of the stigma that my respondents said they faced. I
am asked questions such as, "How can you study those people?" or "How
creepy was it to talk to people like that?" Normally staid intellectuals can
suddenly get very fervent about Christians, and not in a good way. My
research complements other current studies of Christian conservatives
(Stein 2001; Smith 2000) in that it demystifies them and makes their
voices real. While the respondents were ardent Christians with conservative views, they made coherent arguments, lived "normal" lives, and were
good citizens. Their conservative religious beliefs did lead them to some
interesting ways of looking at the world, but according to their world-
views, it all made perfect sense. I cannot say that I was not shocked at
times by some of the things they said. But for the most part, I view

Christian conservatives with a greater level of appreciation than I did before I began this project. Some may question whether the respondents simply told me what they thought I wanted to hear. While this is a possibility, I think anyone who has read all of the excerpts in this book would agree that these people gave me their real, unadulterated views.

Because of the size of the Christian conservative population, more and more social scientists are paying attention to them. Social science conferences regularly hold sessions on Christian conservatives, but some of this work remains in the "Christian as oddity" category. I think a fruitful question would be: What is the source of this caustic disdain for Christian conservatives? A common theme among the Christian conservative respondents was that American society was becoming more and more accepting of all groups *but* Christians. Could this common perception be supported by data? It is difficult to examine such questions objectively, but we must try if we are to understand how this large proportion of the American population fits in with the rest of society.

Another area in need of research is the occasionally thorny relationship among various types of Christian conservatives. A number of respondents expressed their disapproval of the tactics used by some of the national Christian conservative organizations or spokespeople. While they may have agreed with the underlying philosophy that was invoked, they sometimes thought that these national leaders were acting in un-Christian ways. Rather than assuming that Christian conservatives are all part of a unified front, it would be prudent to examine this state of affairs more closely. For example, how much does an everyday Christian conservative have to disagree with the conservative establishment before she will make a significant ideological break? Are Christian conservatives satisfied with their usually dichotomous policy options (conservative option, nonconservative option), or do they find this limiting? By continuing to interview grassroots Christians, we will gain further insight that goes beyond the rhetoric of the national Christian conservative organizations.

We also must continue to explore Christians' intriguing ways of responding to the increasingly public face of homosexuality. As I have illustrated throughout the book and especially in chapter 6, Christian conservatives think about homosexuality quite a lot, and too often researchers overlook the complexity of these thoughts. An expanded study of the topic would most likely involve further in-depth interviewing of Christian conservatives, using an interview that concentrates on their views about homosexuality. Topics within the interview might include their views on the origins of homosexuality, their response to national campaigns against homosexuality (such as the recent ex-gay movement), their feelings about the tactics and accomplishments of the movement for gay and lesbian rights, and their direct experience with gay men or lesbians. More creative methodologies could also be employed. For example, one could conduct interviews with Christian conservatives while on a walking tour through a gay and lesbian neighborhood or during a gay pride parade. This short excerpt from a Christian conservative woman in Spokane hints at the type of data such interviews might elicit:

> We were just out in New York for the Fourth of July and the gay pride parade happened. It was a *six-hour* parade. (TL: That's a long parade.) It was *incredible.* I have never seen so many different, strange people in my life. And there was a lot of hand holding and hugging and kissing of the males. Some of them are dressed up like women, *gorgeous* women.

The methodological possibilities for studying Christians' attitudes toward gays and lesbians are endless and should go far beyond survey approaches, which seldom glean the nuances of these beliefs.

While gay men and lesbians did not talk about Christian conservatives quite as much as the reverse, this topic is still worthy of study. What interests me here is the intersection of gay social-change goals with Christian conservative lives. The school system provides the clearest example of this intersection. Many gays and lesbians feel that school issues are at the forefront of the gay agenda: establishing gay-straight alliances, prohibiting anti-gay harassment, getting students to stop saying, "That's so *gay!*" As we saw repeatedly in earlier chapters, many Christian conservative children attend the public schools. Is the tenuous "let both groups have their space" strategy viable in the long run, or does one group's progress necessarily become the other group's setback? Christian conservatives definitely seem to think the latter, especially where gay progress involves open attacks on Christians. A nationwide study of how gay-straight alliances (student groups, of which there are hundreds) confront these issues within the schools would be enlightening. Another point of intersection is the growing movement within churches (mainly mainline denominations) toward inclusion of gays and lesbians. How do gays and lesbians convince others that they take their Christianity just as seriously as everyone else does? The fact that many Christian conservatives did not acknowledge that gays can be Christians is a sign that this battle is a difficult one indeed.

The process whereby gay men and lesbians assess the climate in new environments is a potential object of study. While most of the gay respondents in my study had lived in their city for quite a while, a couple respondents had moved there only a year or two ago. Hearing how these respondents had initially assessed their new cities, both before and after they arrived, was quite enlightening. The strategies that gay men and lesbians use to map out their new environments—figuring out what behavior is acceptable where—would add further insight to the study of climate perceptions. Do they rely on information provided by newfound acquaintances in the community, or do they figure such things out on their own? Keeping in mind the lesbian in Seattle who had moved from the conservative South and was amazed that people remained closeted in a liberal city, to what extent does one's previous climate experiences color one's present perceptions and actions?

Gay men and lesbians, many of whom use everyday forms of activism, also provide a fruitful way to study the various routes to social change. Though most gays and lesbians would like to see anti-gay behavior fully stigmatized, there are several ways to accomplish this. For example, with reference to the joke scenario, some respondents said they would use the power of informal sanctions in order to isolate the coworker, while others made reference to official workplace policies that prohibit such behavior. The question then becomes: How much of the fight for social change is political (involving legislation) and how much is cultural (involving informal norms)? Some of the Christian conservative respondents definitely felt pressured by these informal norms, as everything they said against homosexuality was perceived as hateful, bigoted speech. The recent movement toward stigmatizing anti-gay speech is one of the most logical targets of future research. Recently, a controversy raged over the fate of Dr. Laura Schlessinger's television talk show. Gay rights groups mobilized to end the show because of Dr. Laura's repeated references to gays and lesbians as "biological errors." My content analysis of editorials shows that anti-gay pieces have become increasingly stigmatized over time (measured by the number of hostile pieces written in response). A broader analysis of media would help us understand what aspects of anti-gay speech are seen as the most offensive, and what utterances have become more offensive over time. Such cultural changes are important signifiers of the progress gays and lesbians have made.

Conclusion

While writing this book, one phrase from the interviews kept entering my mind. It comes from a lesbian schoolteacher in Spokane. Describing how she decides whether or not to engage in certain behaviors, such as holding her partner's hand in the park or reading her schoolchildren gay-positive books, she said it all depends on "the feel of the air around you." The hostility she perceives is a lot like the air: she can't really see it or touch it, but she definitely knows it's there. Political climates, through our perceptions, are all around us. We may not notice that they are there, or that we think about them at all. We may not realize the perceptual processes we use to measure (and thus create) these winds of change. It has been my goal to make these winds more tangible. We must be more cognizant of these winds if we hope to harness their potential to effect social change in the world around us.

Appendix
Methods

I am a firm believer in approaching a research question from numerous angles, using multiple social research methods. This strategy is essential for studying political climates, as objective and subjective measures of climates can differ substantially. Three goals guided my research:

1. To objectively measure the political climates and changes in the political climates of the United States, Washington State, Seattle, and Spokane as they relate to Christian conservatives and gay men and lesbians.
2. To assess how members of Christian conservative populations and members of gay and lesbian populations, in both Seattle and Spokane, perceive the political climates and changes in the political climates of their city (and, secondarily, their state and nation).
3. To assess how members of Christian conservative populations and members of gay and lesbian populations attempt to change the climates they face.

To address the first goal, I used secondary analysis of numerous public opinion data sets and a content analysis of area newspapers. To address the second and third questions, I conducted and analyzed in-depth interviews. Below, I explain how I carried out each component of the research.

Secondary Analysis

I used three sources of data for the secondary analyses: the General Social Survey, the American National Election Studies, and the Front Porch Forum Poll.

I used the General Social Survey (GSS) in order to assess changes in national opinion on issues pertinent to Christian conservatives and gay men and lesbians. The GSS is an almost annual personal interview survey conducted by the National Opinion Research Center (NORC). The NORC began conducting the GSS in 1972, and has since interviewed over 35,000 people. The population from which GSS samples are drawn is all noninstitutionalized Americans aged eighteen and above. The multistage probability sampling procedures used for the survey have varied slightly over the years, but the NORC has consistently produced response rates between 73 percent and 82 percent. Because many of the GSS questions are replicated each year, this survey is very useful for analyzing changes in American attitudes. For these analyses, I used the four questions regarding homosexuality, four questions regarding abortion that represent a continuum of situations in which an abortion might be sought, and several questions regarding religious beliefs and behaviors.

Questions about Homosexuality

What about sexual relations between two adults of the same sex—do you think it is always wrong, almost always wrong, wrong only sometimes, or not wrong at all?

Set of three questions that began with the following:

And what about a man who admits that he is a homosexual?
1. Suppose this admitted homosexual wanted to make a speech in your community. Should he be allowed to speak, or not?
2. Should such a person be allowed to teach in a college or university, or not?
3. If someone in your community suggested that a book he wrote in favor of homosexuality should be taken out of your public library, would you favor removing this book, or not?

Questions about Abortion

Set of four questions that started with the following:

Please tell me whether or not you think it should be possible for a pregnant woman to obtain a legal abortion if:
1. The woman wants it for any reason?

2. If the woman's own health is seriously endangered by the pregnancy?
3. If she is married and does not want any more children?
4. If the family has a very low income and cannot afford any more children?

Question about School Prayer

The United States Supreme Court has ruled that no state or local government may require the reading of the Lord's Prayer or Bible verses in public schools. What are your views on this—do you approve or disapprove of the court ruling?

Questions about Religious Views

Which of these statements comes closest to describing your feelings about the Bible?
1. The Bible is the actual word of God and is to be taken literally, word for word.
2. The Bible is the inspired word of God but not everything in it should be taken literally, word for word.
3. The Bible is an ancient book of fables, legends, history, and moral precepts recorded by men.

Fundamentalism/liberalism of religion: Fundamentalist, moderate, liberal

I used the American National Election Studies (NES) for the same reasons I used the GSS: to assess changes in national opinion on issues pertinent to Christian conservatives and gay men and lesbians. In addition, because the NES contains a variable that allowed me to identify the state of residence of the survey respondent, I used the NES to contrast Washington State with the rest of the country. The NES is a series of surveys conducted during national election years, starting in 1952. While the overall sampling procedure involves national multistage area probability sampling of voting-age Americans, each NES study includes some respondents who were part of previous NES surveys. Also, most of the NES respondents are interviewed for both a preelection study and a postelection study. The NES has achieved response rates of between 71 percent and 74 percent, with 87 percent to 89 percent of those interviewed for the preelection survey agreeing to be reinterviewed for the postelection survey.

The NES contains a large number of questions regarding various social issues, such as homosexuality, abortion, and morality, as well as questions assessing religious behaviors and attitudes. For these NES analyses, I used three questions about gays and lesbians, two questions about abortion, numerous "feeling thermometer" questions about various political and religious groups, and several questions about morality and religious behaviors. Below is the wording for each of these questions.

Questions about Homosexuality

I'd like to get your feelings toward some of our political leaders and other people who are in the news these days. I'll read you the name of a person and I'd like you to rate that person using something we call the feeling thermometer. Ratings between 50 degrees and 100 degrees mean that you feel favorable and warm toward the person. Ratings between 0 and 50 degrees mean that you don't feel favorable toward the person and that you don't care too much for that person. You would rate the person at the 50 degree mark if you don't feel particularly warm or cold toward the person. . . . Gay men and lesbians, that is, homosexuals.

Do you favor or oppose laws to protect homosexuals against job discrimination?

Do you think homosexuals should be allowed to serve in the United States Armed Forces, or don't you think so?

Do you think gay or lesbian couples, in other words, homosexual couples, should be legally permitted to adopt children?

Questions about Abortion

There has been some discussion about abortion during recent years. Which one of the opinions on this page best agrees with your view? You can just tell me the number of the opinion you choose.
1. By law, abortion should never be permitted.
2. The law should permit abortion only in case of rape, incest or when the woman's life is in danger.
3. The law should permit abortion for reasons other than rape, incest or danger to the woman's life, but only after the need for the abortion has been clearly established.

4. By law, a woman should always be able to obtain an abortion as a matter of personal choice.

Would you favor or oppose a law in your state that would require parental consent before a teenager under 18 can have an abortion?

Would you favor or oppose a law in your state that would allow the use of government funds to help pay for the costs of abortion for women who cannot afford them?

Would you favor or oppose a law in your state that would require a married woman to notify her husband before she can have an abortion?

Question about School Prayer

Which of the following views comes closest to your opinion on the issue of school prayer?
1. By law, prayers should not be allowed in public schools.
2. The law should allow public schools to schedule time when children can pray silently if they want to.
3. The law should allow public schools to schedule time when children, as a group, can say a general prayer not tied to a particular religious faith.
4. By law, public schools should schedule a time when all children would say a chosen Christian prayer.

Questions about Religious Views

Four questions using feeling thermometer described above:
1. Evangelical groups active in politics, such as the Moral Majority.
2. Evangelical groups active in politics.
3. Christian Fundamentalists.
4. Christian Coalition.

Would you call yourself a born-again Christian, that is, have you personally had a conversion experience related to Jesus Christ?

Which one of these words best describes your kind of Christianity: Fundamentalist, Evangelical, charismatic or spirit filled, moderate to liberal, or something else?

Which of these statements comes closest to describing your feelings about the Bible?
1. The Bible is the actual word of God and is to be taken literally, word for word.
2. The Bible is the word of God but not everything in it should be taken literally, word for word.
3. The Bible was written by men and is not the word of God.

I used the Front Porch Forum Poll in order to assess the difference in the opinion climates of Seattle and Spokane. Elway Research of Seattle conducted the Front Porch Forum Poll in April 1996. The sponsors of the poll were the *Seattle Times* (the largest circulation newspaper in Seattle), KCTS-TV (the public television station in Seattle), KPLU-FM, and KUOW-FM (two public radio stations in Seattle). The poll involved telephone interviews with a random sample of six hundred residents of Washington State. The pertinent questions were:

Do you think families in this country are threatened more today by an economic climate? Or are they threatened more by a moral climate? Or are neither of these an important threat to this country?

America is getting too far away from God. (Agree strongly, agree mildly, disagree mildly, or disagree strongly.)

When it comes to social and political matters, do you more often agree or disagree with stands taken by Christian conservatives?

How often do you attend religious services? (Once a week or more, 2–3 times a month, once a month, several times a year, holidays, never.)

Content Analysis

To provide a better picture of the changing political climates as they concern Christian conservatives and gay men and lesbians in Seattle and Spokane, I conducted a content analysis of editorials, editorial cartoons, and letters to the editor in the largest circulation general newspapers (the *Seattle Times* and the *Spokane Spokesman-Review*) in each city from 1982 through 1997.

I began by performing a preliminary analysis of the *Seattle Times*. For this analysis, I used the *Seattle Times* CD-ROM version to locate articles and editorial pieces that were catalogued under certain headings (homosexuality or religion, for example). While this analysis was preliminary, it did provide information that helped me plan the subsequent content analysis and parts of the interview schedule used for the in-depth interviews. While performing this preliminary analysis, I decided that, if expanded, it could serve as a useful objective measure of the cities' climates. I began planning the new analysis in late 1997. Bearing in mind that (a) I wanted to expand the analysis to examine a significant time period; (b) I wanted to expand the depth of the analysis in terms of what was coded from each editorial piece; and (c) the *Spokane Spokesman-Review* is not available on CD-ROM, and therefore both papers needed to be analyzed by hand using microfilm, I offered a course at the University of Washington during the Winter Quarter of 1998, titled "Sociology 499: Undergraduate Research in Political Sociology." Given the nature of the course, and the fact that students had to meet with me before I would allow them to register, the class attracted high-quality students who wanted to gain research experience. For the fifteen students who took the course, their mean cumulative grade point average was 3.50 (out of 4), with a median cumulative grade point average of 3.63.

Based on my preliminary analysis of the *Seattle Times*, I developed a draft of a coding mechanism. Presented with the coding scheme and fifteen editorial pieces that I had chosen, the assistants used the coding mechanism, asked questions about it, and critiqued it. Taking some of their questions and criticisms into consideration, I revised the mechanism. The vast majority of the pieces were quite easy to code.

Figure A.1 represents the final version of the coding mechanism. One sheet was filled out for each editorial piece. I assigned my assistants and myself four three-month time periods to analyze the editorial pieces. The coding process took one month, with my assistants turning in code sheets for one three-month period every week. At the end of this month of coding, I handed all the sheets back to my assistants, and we developed a set of codes for the subjects of the pieces. After the assistants had completed the data input procedure, I compiled a master data set, which had a total of 6,930 cases.

This data collection procedure was rather rushed, given that this part of the project had to be conducted within the confines of a ten-week academic quarter. While I spent a significant amount of time discussing the coding mechanism with my assistants, I would have preferred to allot more time for this process. However, the vast majority of the pieces were very straightforward to code. Editorial writing is, by its very nature, highly

Coder's Initials:_____

Date of piece:_____

Piece found in which newspaper: ☐ The Seattle Times
☐ The Spokane Spokesman-Review

Type of piece: ☐ Letter to the Editor
☐ Paper's Editorial
☐ Editorial Cartoon

TO FILL OUT FOR ALL PIECES:
Piece is: ☐ <u>Mainly</u> about conservative Christians, or a CC issue
☐ <u>Mainly</u> about gays and lesbians, or a GL issue
☐ <u>Equally</u> about both groups

Piece is: ☐ Hostile towards conservative Christians, or a CC issue
☐ Neutral or mixed towards conservative Christians, or a CC issue
☐ Hospitable towards conservative Christians, or a CC issue
☐ No opinion expressed

Piece is: ☐ Hostile towards gays and lesbians, or a GL issue
☐ Neutral or mixed towards gays and lesbians, or a GL issue
☐ Hospitable towards gays and lesbians, or a GL issue
☐ No opinion expressed

Number of references to this piece: Hostile:_____ Hospitable:_____ Neutral:_____

Short description of topic of piece:_____

How sure are you about the coding of this piece? ☐ Very sure
☐ Somewhat sure
☐ Not sure

TO FILL OUT ONLY FOR LETTERS TO EDITOR:
Author of letter:_____

Location of writer (Seattle, Burien, etc):_____

Letter writer identifies him/herself as: ☐ A Christian
☐ A member of a conservative Christian organization
☐ Friend or family of Christians
☐ A gay man / lesbian
☐ A member of a gay/lesbian organization
☐ Friend or family of gays and lesbians
☐ None of these identifications

Letter makes reference to previous piece: ☐ No
☐ Another letter to the editor from (author and date): _____
☐ Paper's editorial from (date):_____
☐ Editorial cartoon from (date):_____
☐ Reference is hostile towards previous piece
☐ Reference is neutral towards previous piece
☐ Reference is hospitable towards previous piece

Figure A.1. Coding Mechanism Used for Content Analysis

opinionated, and these opinions are seldom masked. Using the students' coding of the fifteen pieces from the training session, I calculated the intercoder reliability by taking the number of agreements in coding and dividing it by the sum of agreements plus disagreements for several key categories regarding content and hostility of the pieces (Miles and Huberman 1994). The reliability was .84. After this, there were several more discussions of coding procedures. If I had tested the reliability again, it would most likely have been higher than this. Unfortunately, due to time constraints, I was unable to test the reliability again.

The In-Depth Interviews

Based on my theoretical concerns, I constructed several drafts of an interview schedule. I pretested the schedule by using it to interview two Christians, a gay man, and a lesbian, all from Seattle. While these interviews caused me to make some slight modifications in the schedule, they went smoothly and generated the kinds of information required. Below are the questions. Key to the project was developing an interview schedule that worked for both Christian conservatives and gay men and lesbians. However, for obvious reasons, there are some differences between the schedules used for the two groups. I note such differences below.

Section One: About the City

How long have you lived in _____?
Why did you move here?
Do you like the city? What do you like about it?
What don't you like about it?
Let's say you are visiting an acquaintance in another part of the U.S., whom you haven't seen in years. If this person knew nothing about the city, and wanted to know a few things about it, what would you tell them?
How, if at all, has the city changed since you've lived here? (If longtime resident: last five to ten years.)

Section Two: About the Person

What terms or phrases would you use to describe yourself? What are the most important aspects of your identity?

Has this changed over time? If so, how?

If your friends were to describe you to a stranger, what terms or phrases do you think they would use? That is, who do people think of you as?

Tell me a little bit about your development as a (Christian, gay man/lesbian). That is, has your sense of yourself as a (Christian, gay man/lesbian) changed over time?

When you first meet people, do they usually find out that you are a (Christian, gay man/lesbian)? If yes, how do they find out?

If they do not find out when you meet them, do they *ever* find out? If yes, how do they find out?

Section Three: The Person in Relation to the City

What is it like to live in _____ as a (Christian, gay man or lesbian)? Can you illustrate this with any stories or incidents?

Would you recommend this city to another (Christian, gay man or lesbian) who is thinking of moving here?

How would you characterize _____ in terms of issues pertaining to (Christians, gay men and lesbians): hostile, hospitable, or both? Why do you feel this way?

Has this changed over the past five years? How, specifically, has it changed? Can you give some examples?

Are there some areas of the city which are more hostile/hospitable than others? What makes you feel this way?

How supportive of (Christian, gay and lesbian) causes is the general population of _____, do you think?

TWO QUESTIONS FOR CHRISTIAN CONSERVATIVES

What about conservative Christian politicians, how supportive is the general population of _____?

What about prayer in schools, how supportive is the general population of _____?

TWO QUESTIONS FOR GAY MEN AND LESBIANS

What about gay marriage? How supportive is the general population of _____?

What about gay/lesbian issues in school? How supportive is the general population of _____?

Are there any (Christian, gay and lesbian) elements that are not represented
in _____ that you would like to see represented?

Are there any (Christian, gay and lesbian) elements that ARE represented in
_____ that you would prefer to NOT see represented?

Do you think the (*Seattle Times* [or *P.I.*]/*Spokesman-Review*) treats
(Christian, gay and lesbian) issues fairly? Why do you think this way?
Can you offer any specific examples?

What about other local media—such as TV news programs?

Section Four: The Person in Relation to the State

While I have you thinking along these lines, let me ask you about Washington State. What is it like to live in Washington State as a (Christian, gay
man or lesbian)?

Can you illustrate this with any stories or incidents?

Would you recommend this state to another (Christian, gay man or lesbian)
who is thinking of moving here?

How would you characterize Washington State in terms of issues pertaining
to (Christians, gay men and lesbians): hostile, hospitable, or both? Why
do you feel this way?

Has this changed over the past five years? How, specifically, has it changed?
Can you give some examples?

How supportive, do you think, is the general population of WA State of
(Christian, gay and lesbian) causes?

TWO QUESTIONS FOR CHRISTIAN CONSERVATIVES

And conservative Christian politicians? How supportive is WA State?
And prayer in schools? How supportive is WA State?

TWO QUESTIONS FOR GAY MEN AND LESBIANS

And gay marriage? How supportive is WA State?
And teaching about gay and lesbian issues in schools? How supportive is
WA State?

Section Five: The Person in Relation to the U.S.

Let me ask you about the U.S. in general, how would you characterize the
U.S. in terms of issues pertaining to (Christians, gay men and lesbians):
hostile or hospitable? Why do you feel this way?

Has this changed over the past five years? How, specifically, has it changed?
Can you give some examples?
How supportive is the U.S. in general of (Christian, gay and lesbian) causes?

TWO QUESTIONS FOR CHRISTIAN CONSERVATIVES

What about conservative Christian politicians on a national level?
What about prayer in schools?

TWO QUESTIONS FOR GAY MEN AND LESBIANS

What about gay marriage on a national level?
What about teaching about gay and lesbian issues in schools?

Section Six: Scenarios

I handed the respondent a sheet at the beginning of this section that contained the two questions I wanted him or her to answer for each scenario:

What would you do, if anything, in reaction to such an event?
Would your opinions change regarding the environment in which you are living?

THE SCHOOL BOARD SCENARIO

For Christian conservatives: Your local school board denies the formation of a student prayer group that would meet before school.
For gays and lesbians: Your local public school board denies the formation of a H.S. gay/lesbian/bisexual student group.

THE JOKE SCENARIO

For Christian conservatives: Your co-worker's car sports a "Darwin Fish," similar to the Christian fish on your car, only with feet.
For gays and lesbians: You hear a co-worker tell a joke about a lesbian. He uses a gruff, overly manly voice to tell the joke.

THE GAY MARRIAGE SCENARIO

For Christian conservatives: The Washington State legislature passes a bill forbidding gay marriages.
For gays and lesbians: The new governor of Washington comes out in favor of gay marriage.

THE CARTOON SCENARIO

For Christian conservatives: Your local newspaper features an editorial
cartoon which makes Christians out to be small-minded.

For gays and lesbians: Your local newspaper features an editorial cartoon
which pokes fun at gay men as being promiscuous.

THE COMMUNITY GROWTH SCENARIO

For Christian conservatives: A local evangelical church in your town moves
into a larger space due to its overwhelming success.

For gays and lesbians: A gay/lesbian community center in your town moves
into a larger space due to its overwhelming success.

THE SUPREME COURT SCENARIO

For Christian conservatives: The U.S Supreme Court rules that the Christian
Coalition cannot distribute voters' guides in churches.

For gays and lesbians: The U.S. Supreme Court, having a chance to
decriminalize sodomy, refuses to do so.

THE CRASWELL SCENARIO

For Christian conservatives and for gays and lesbians: Ellen Craswell,
outspoken Christian conservative, loses the gubernatorial race by a
60%/40% margin.

THE RELATIVE SCENARIO

For Christian conservatives and for gays and lesbians: One of your relatives
says "I wish (Christians, gays and lesbians) would just mind their own
business."

THE RESTAURANT SCENARIO

For Christian conservatives: At a local restaurant, you see a male couple
holding hands across the table.

For gays and lesbians: At a local restaurant, you see a family saying grace
before they start to eat.

THE CHOOSE-YOUR-OWN-SCENARIO SCENARIO

For Christian conservatives and for gays and lesbians: Is there anything else
you can think of which would affect your perceptions of how hospitable
your environment is towards (Christians, gays and lesbians)?

Section Seven: Gauging the Respondent's Activism

Do you consider yourself a political person? How so?

Do you participate in any groups or organizations? These can be activist-oriented or otherwise, part of the (Christian, gay and lesbian) community or otherwise. Tell me about them and what you have done for them.

There are many reasons people have for being an activist. What do you think some of these reasons are?

There are many reasons people have for not being an activist. What do you think some of these reasons are?

Question for Christian conservatives: People do a wide variety of things in order to "further the cause" of Christians, and I am wondering if you engage in any of these activities. These may be seemingly insignificant actions or even unintentional actions. Please think about this carefully. For example, some actions that other people have mentioned are: praying in public, letting people know that you are a Christian, wearing something that identifies you as a Christian.

Question for gay men and lesbians: People do a wide variety of things in order to "further the cause" of gays and lesbians, and I am wondering if you engage in any of these activities. These may be seemingly insignificant actions or even unintentional actions. Please think about this carefully. For example, some actions that other people have mentioned are: holding hands in public, wearing identifying buttons, using same gender pronouns in conversations.

With regard to the answers from the previous question: how risky do you feel these actions are? That is, in doing these actions, do you ever feel that there could be negative consequences?

Do you ever refrain from such actions because they are too risky?

Earlier we talked about how different areas of the city might be thought of as more hostile or hospitable. Do such characteristics of an area determine where you go (such as restaurants or shopping) in the city?

Do such characteristics of an area determine how you act when you venture out into that area?

Section Eight: Demographics

Age:
Occupation:

Your Income: please choose the appropriate category:

_____ $0–$9999

_____ $10,000–$19,999

. . .

_____ $80,000 and up

Your Household's Income: please choose the appropriate category:

(Same categories as above)

Religious affiliation/denomination:

Name of church you attend:

How often do you attend church services?

Besides church services, how often do you participate in other church-related activities?

Highest year of education completed:

Marital/Partnership Status:

Race/Ethnicity:

Number of children (ever, if any):

Do you own your home, or do you rent?

Name of neighborhood where you live:

I planned to conduct a total of eighty in-depth interviews, ten interviews from eight different groups of people:

Gay/lesbian activist Spokane residents

Gay/lesbian nonactivist Spokane residents

Gay/lesbian activist Seattle residents

Gay/lesbian nonactivist Seattle residents

Christian conservative activist Spokane residents

Christian conservative nonactivist Spokane residents

Christian conservative activist Seattle residents

Christian conservative nonactivist Seattle residents.

While the variation in city and group was obviously necessary, this list shows another variable as well: activists versus nonactivists. I decided to include this variable for two reasons. First, level of activism is used in some of the arguments as a variable to be explained. Second, in terms of how people amass information about the political climates around them, I hypothesized in the introduction that people may have differing levels of information regarding the political climates due to their involvement in their communities. I define this difference quite simply: activists are key people within their respective communities. They are either leaders of key organizations within their communities or have organized important events in their communities. Nonactivists are people who may have been peripherally involved at one time or another, but who hold no key posts and do not consider activism to be a defining characteristic of their identities.

The sampling technique can best be described as heterogeneous representative purposive sampling (Hunter 1987). While a random sample of these two populations is virtually impossible to obtain, I attempted to represent as many different facets of the communities as I could, when possible matching people with similar organizational positions in each city. I began this process in Spokane. Given that Spokane has a smaller population than Seattle, it had a more limited selection of organizations.

I obtained a copy of the directory of gay and lesbian organizations in Spokane and from it drew up a list of organizations that represented a wide array of interests within the community. I then attended the Spokane Gay and Lesbian Pride Day festival, at which most of these organizations and their leaders were present. I presented them with a cover letter and set up many of these interviews on the spot. Setting up the Spokane gay and lesbian interviews proved quite straightforward.

To obtain entrée into the Christian conservative community in Spokane, I solicited advice from two university colleagues who were active in the evangelical community. One of them arranged for me to meet with two of the leading evangelical pastors in Spokane. The first of these pastors with whom I met was extremely helpful in that he had the directory of the Greater Spokane Association of Evangelicals and made this available to me. From this list, I drew a large number of pastors and leaders of Christian conservative organizations in the Spokane area.

I asked the activist respondents to help me in locating the nonactivist respondents. At the end of each interview with an activist, I would tell them that I was interviewing both active people like themselves and people who were significantly less active. I would then ask them for the names of two or three people who might fit this latter description. Most of the activist respondents knew exactly the type of person to whom I referred. While this technique of locating nonactivists worked well, it is potentially vulnerable to criticism. These nonactivists in the study could very well differ from other nonactivists, given that they had some sort of tie to key members of the community. Due to these ties, they may have more information than people who are completely cut off from the community. However, they do satisfy my requirements for nonactivists: they perform little, if any, activist work for their communities, and they do not view themselves as activists.

After I had conducted a good number of interviews in Spokane, I started to develop the Seattle samples, using a matching technique that involved finding activists in Seattle who were similar to the activists I had already interviewed in Spokane. For example, having interviewed the director of a gay youth group in Spokane, I located a director of a gay youth group in Seattle. Having interviewed a pro-life ministry director in Spokane, I located a pro-life ministry director in Seattle. Although I could not find identical matches for some respondents, in most cases I was successful.

To entice potential interview respondents to complete an interview, I offered monetary compensation. Respondents could either be compensated themselves or designate an organization that I would then compensate. The rate of compensation was ten dollars per hour. Respondents could also deem compensation unnecessary. In summary: I compensated ten respondents themselves at an average rate of $13.18; I compensated thirty-three respondents' organization of choice at an average rate of $14.09; I compensated one respondent with an old microwave; and forty respondents deemed compensation unnecessary.

I conducted eighty-four interviews. To summarize the sample, I list the interview subjects below. In addition to these lists, table A.1 provides a demographic summary profile of the respondents, both overall and within each of the eight groups studied.

Spokane Gay Men and Lesbians

Activists

Member of Human Rights Association, Male, Age 40
Pride Day Coordinator, Female, Age 33
AIDS Network Worker, Male, Age 33
Empress of Sovereign Court (drag queen org.), Male, Age 31
President of PFLAG Chapter, Male, Age 43
Treasurer of PFLAG Chapter, Male, Age 48
Activist Democrat, Male, Age 29
Director of Youth Group, Female, Age 29
Director of Community Center, Male, Age 49
Board Member of EMCC (G&L church), Female, Age 31
President of Business Association, Female, Age 31

TABLE A.1
Demographic Summary of Interview Subjects

Group	Number of Subjects	Average Age	Average Household Income (in 1000s)	% Who Attend Church Regularly	% With College Degrees or Higher	% Who Own Their Homes	% Non-White	% Female
Overall	84	41	50	57% (n=48)	63% (n=48)	67% (n=56)	19% (n=16)	44% (n=37)
Spokane gay and lesbian activists	11	36	32	27 (n=3)	73 (n=8)	55 (n=6)	0 (n=11)	36 (n=4)
Spokane gay and lesbian nonactivists	11	36	40	9 (n=1)	64 (n=7)	55 (n=6)	27 (n=3)	55 (n=6)
Spokane Christian conservative activists	10	48	51	100 (n=10)	60 (n=6)	100 (n=10)	30 (n=3)	20 (n=2)
Spokane Christian conservative nonactivists	10	49	53	100 (n=10)	50 (n=5)	80 (n=8)	10 (n=1)	60 (n=6)
Seattle gay and lesbian activists	11	38	60	18 (n=2)	82 (n=9)	55 (n=6)	18 (n=2)	36 (n=4)
Seattle gay and lesbian nonactivists	10	34	48	20 (n=2)	60 (n=6)	40 (n=4)	30 (n=3)	60 (n=6)
Seattle Christian conservative activists	11	52	64	91 (n=10)	64 (n=7)	91 (n=10)	18 (n=2)	27 (n=3)
Seattle Christian conservative nonactivists	10	33	59	100 (n=10)	50 (n=5)	60 (n=6)	20 (n=2)	60 (n=6)

Nonactivists

Young Person, Male, Age 20
Animal Shelter Agent, Female, Age 30
Broadcast Technician, Female, Age 23
Retired Professor, Male, Age 66
Professor, Male, Age 52
Mother/Student, Female, Age 35
Driver/Courier, Female, Age 31
Unemployed Salesperson, Male, Age 33
Elementary School Teacher, Female, Age 38
Park Ranger, Female, Age 38
Veterinary Technician, Male, Age 30

Spokane Christian Conservatives

Activists

Pastor of Nondenominational Church, Male, Age 40
Pastor of African American Church, Male, Age 59
Director of Salvation Army, Male, Age 57
Director of Pro-Life Ministry, Female, Age 47
Administrator at Nondenominational Church, Male, Age 32
Director of Shelter, Male, Age 43
Pastor of Assembly of God Church, Male, Age 52
Republican Activist, Female, Age 54
Owner of Christian Bookstores, Male, Age 40
Director of Charity Organization, Male, Age 43

Nonactivists

Attorney, Male, Age 53
Mother, Female, Age 36
Personnel Supervisor, Female, Age 56
Salesperson, Male, Age 63
Manager, Male, Age 44
Homemaker, Female, Age 71
Retired Nurse, Female, Age 55
Student/Mother, Female, Age 28

Hospital Chaplain, Female, Age 56
Teacher, Male, Age 26

Seattle Gay Men and Lesbians

Activists

Member of Gay/Lesbian Human Rights Commission, Male, Age 37
AIDS Walk Coordinator, Female, Age 40
Speaker for PFLAG, Male, Age 35
Empress of Sovereign Court, Male, Age 39
Student Activist, Male, Age 28
Associate Pastor of EMCC, Male, Age 59
President of Business Association, Male, Age 48
Director of Youth Group, Female, Age 30('s)
Pride Day Coordinator, Female, Age 32
Worker at Community Center, Female, Age 30
Foundation Coordinator, Female, Age 30

Nonactivists

Homemaker/Writer, Female, Age 37
Office Administrator, Female, Age 32
Student, Male, Age 19
Writer, Female, Age 40
Baker, Female, Age 27
Administrator, Female, Age 31
Salesperson, Male, Age 29
Physician, Male, Age 34
Nurse/Mother, Female, Age 46
Storage Analyst, Male, Age 40

Seattle Christian Conservatives

Activists

Pastor of Non-Denominational Church, Male, Age 61
Pastor of Assembly of God Church, Male, Age 51

Director of Charity Organization, Female, Age 38
Director of Shelter, Male, Age 55
Owner of Bookstore, Male, Age 57
Editor of Biblical Newsletter, Male, Age 59
CEO of Charity Organization, Male, Age 54
Pastor of African American Church, Male, Age 48
School Board Candidate, Female, Age 61
Director of Pro-Life Ministry, Female, Age 48
Youth Pastor of Nondenominational Church, Male, Age 37

Nonactivists

Market Analyst, Male, Age 28
Office Administrator, Female, Age 29
Mortgage Banker, Male, Age 28
Government Worker, Female, Age 33
Consultant, Male, Age 51
Campus Intern, Male, Age 26
Student, Female, Age 20
Student, Female, Age 23
Housewife, Female, Age 68
Student, Female, Age 23

I conducted the first interview in May 1997, the last in June 1998. The bulk of the interviews took place during the summer and fall of 1997. I conducted most interviews in respondents' homes or offices. However, I went anywhere the respondent requested: some interviews were in coffeehouses, some in bars, some in public parks. I tape-recorded each interview.

I first had the respondent carefully read over the consent form. It is paramount to note that in the consent form, and at other points before and during the interview, the respondents were not told *which* groups were involved in the study. That is, the gay and lesbian respondents did not know that I was also interviewing Christian conservatives. The Christian conservative respondents did not know that I was also interviewing gay men and lesbians. If the respondents asked, either about the project or about me (which they did surprisingly infrequently) before or during the interview, I told them that I would be happy to speak with them about such matters only after the interview was completed.

For each interview, I wore casual dress clothes, often wearing a tie if the location of the interview was more formal, such as a business or church office. I would classify my personal demeanor and appearance during the interviews as conservative and nonthreatening. Most of the respondents were eager participants, and most enjoyed the interview experience. The interviews ranged in lengths from forty-five minutes to two hours, with an average length of around seventy-five minutes.

Once all the interviews were transcribed, I analyzed them using a text analysis program called FolioViews. I created a coding mechanism made up of over 350 codes. The program allowed me to analyze the frequency of and connections among various types of information in the interviews.

Notes

NOTES TO CHAPTER 1

1. Because the terms "gay men and lesbians" and "the gay and lesbian rights movement" are somewhat unwieldy, especially in complex sentences, I sometimes use the shorthand such as "gays" and "the gay movement," as the term "gay" has sometimes been used as an all-encompassing term.

2. With the advent of queer theory, the stability of sexual identity has been called into question. One of the major goals of queer theory is to problematize categories relating to gender and sexuality.

3. Since the other group I am studying is gay men and lesbians, I want to comment on the Christian conservative argument against homosexuality. Christian conservatives use passages in the Old Testament of the Bible, such as a list of proscriptions in the Book of Leviticus or the story of Sodom and Gomorrah, as evidence that God believes that homosexual behavior is wrong. While many have made forceful arguments that such interpretations are incorrect (Bawer 1997; Boswell 1995), Christian conservatives remain steadfast in their condemnation of homosexual behavior. There is some evidence that some Christian conservatives have moved to a more therapeutic model of "hating the sin, loving the sinner" with the goal of removing the individual from the "homosexual lifestyle" (Herman 1997; Hunter 1987). I expand on this theme in later chapters.

4. Spokane's gay newspaper—*Stonewall News Northwest*—folded in 1997, a troubling sign for the community.

NOTES TO CHAPTER 2

1. We coded 334 pieces as being about both groups, meaning that, in the course of the editorial piece, equal amounts of treatment were given to both Christian conservatives and gays.

2. The ownership of some of these issues may be contested. Take abortion, for example. Although it is clear that some lesbians and gay men may be extremely involved in the abortion debate, on a group level it is Christian conservatives who have played a major role in this issue. We therefore coded it as a Christian conservative issue.

247

3. I examine these data by dividing the sixteen years in the analysis into four four-year periods: 1982–1985, 1986–1989, 1990–1993, 1994–1997.

4. Before I do that, I need briefly to explain how I organize and discuss climate claims: the claims that individuals make about the social and political climates around them. The claims have several basic characteristics: content, level, and direction. The content of the claim is simply what the claim is about: the media, the public, the government, etc. The level of the claim concerns the size of the environment the interview respondent is referencing: a very localized climate (a neighborhood, a part of town), the city's climate, the state, the country, even the world. Given that the bulk of the interviews concerned the respondents' cities, the majority of the claims I will discuss are at the city level. When appropriate, though, I occasionally will discuss the other levels, such as state governmental climates or national opinion climates. The direction of the claim refers to whether the claim is about hostility or hospitableness.

Most of the climate claims fit into one of the following four categories: hospitable, hostile, increasingly hospitable, or increasingly hostile. Given the complicated nature of political climates, though, I characterized a small proportion of claims as mixed (in talking about a subject, the person perceives both hospitableness and hostility), neutral (neither hospitable nor hostile, but somewhere in the middle), or uncertain (instances where the person claims that the climate is difficult to characterize). Mostly, though, I talk about claims that had an obvious direction to them.

5. Seattle has two mainstream newspapers: the *Seattle Times* and the *Post-Intelligencer* (the "*P.I.*"). The *P.I.* has a smaller subscriber base than the *Seattle Times*.

6. Christian-produced media, on the other hand, is quite strong, with the presence of Dr. James Dobson's radio program and *The 700 Club*, just to name two of the most popular shows. However, such programs do not help Christians on a more local level.

NOTES TO CHAPTER 3

1. The latest data I analyze are from 1996. The GSS and NES have conducted studies since then (the GSS in 1998 and 2000, and the NES in 2000). However, I write about these results in connection to my interviews, which I conducted in 1997–1998.

2. As explained in the methodological appendix, the four choices for this question were "always wrong," "almost always wrong," "wrong only sometimes," and "never wrong."

3. Some might argue that the wording of this question is inherently biased: the word "admits" carries with it a negative connotation: one admits guilt, wrongdo-

ing, etc. Therefore, the question might imply that homosexuality is wrong. However, this question was used in the earliest GSS surveys, and in order to observe trends in opinion, the wording has remained the same.

4. Although "Christian Fundamentalists" may be slightly different from Christian conservatives, this is the most similar group in the ANES.

5. Evidence shows that there has been some polarization of opinion on abortion over the years (DiMaggio, Evans, and Bryson 1996), possibly creating a more hostile climate toward Christian conservatives.

6. Because this question was asked only in 1992, this statistic is based on a sample size of only forty-one Washingtonians.

7. I investigated these relationships further by using regression techniques, which allowed me to examine the city effect while controlling for education, age, and church attendance. Does this difference between the cities remain once these other variables' effects are taken into consideration? The results show that the city of residence has a strong and significant effect. For illustrative purposes, I calculated a predicted likelihood of agreeing with Christian conservatives for a hypothetical respondent by using the modal responses for the other variables: a high school graduate, aged 35–49, who goes to church weekly. A Seattle resident with these characteristics has a 27 percent chance of agreeing with Christian conservatives. A Spokane resident with the same characteristics has a 58 percent chance of agreeing. For a second regression model, I used the "getting away from God" question as the dependent variable. The results show that the city of the survey respondent has the largest effect of all the variables in the regression model.

8. The Spokane pride parade was one of my first exposures to the gay and lesbian community there, and it was an interesting experience: a parade without an audience. This is in marked contrast to the Seattle pride parade, which completely shuts down part of the city and attracts many non-gay supporters.

Note to Chapter 5

1. These hate crimes related to religion could be crimes against those from any religion: Christians, Jews, Muslims, and others.

Notes to Chapter 6

1. I divided the respondents into two groups: Christian conservatives (those who took the Bible literally *and* identified themselves as fundamentalist in their religion) and everyone else.

2. In the interviews, in contrast to ninety unsolicited references to homosexuality, there were fifty-two unsolicited references to abortion.

NOTES TO CHAPTER 7

1. Occasionally, due to time constraints, I was forced to skip a scenario here or there with certain respondents. Thus, rather than the twenty-one respondents to the joke scenario, there were only twenty respondents to the family scenario.

2. If one counts the Spokane man who said, half jokingly, that he tries to drive in front of Darwin fish cars so that they can see the Christian fish on his car, it makes three instances.

Bibliography

Adam, Barry D. 1995. *The rise of a gay and lesbian movement*. New York: Twayne.

Aho, James A. 1994. *This thing of darkness: a sociology of the enemy*. Seattle: University of Washington Press.

Almeida, Paul, and Linda Brewster Stearns 1998. Political opportunities and local grassroots environmental movements: the case of Minamata. *Social Problems* 45:37–60.

Ammerman, Nancy Tatom 1987. *Bible believers: fundamentalists in the modern world*. New Brunswick, NJ: Rutgers University Press.

Barrett, Donald C., Lance M. Pollack, and Mary L. Tilden 2002. Teenage sexual orientation, adult openness, and status attainment in gay males. *Sociological Perspectives* 45:163–182.

Bawer, Bruce 1997. *Stealing Jesus: how fundamentalism betrays Christianity*. New York: Crown.

Bawn, Kathleen 1999. Constructing "us": ideology, coalition politics, and false consciousness. *American Journal of Political Science* 43:303–334.

Bayer, Ronald 1991. *Private acts, social consequences: AIDS and the politics of public health*. New York: Free Press.

Bayer, Ronald 1987. *Homosexuality and American psychiatry: the politics of diagnosis*. Princeton, NJ: Princeton University Press.

Becker, Howard S. 1963. *Outsiders: studies in the sociology of deviance*. Glencoe, IL: Free Press.

Beisel, Nicola K. 1997. *Imperiled innocents: Anthony Comstock and family reproduction in Victorian America*. Princeton, NJ: Princeton University Press.

Benedetto, Richard 1998. Republicans aim for goal of Senate control; Political climate favors GOP. *USA Today*, 9 September, 12A.

Beniger, James R., and Susan Herbst 1990. Mass media and public opinion: emergence of an institution. In *Change in societal institutions*, edited by Maureen T. Hallinan, David M. Klein, and Jennifer Glass. New York: Plenum Press.

Bernstein, Mary 1997. Celebration and suppression: the strategic uses of identity by the lesbian and gay movement. *American Journal of Sociology* 103:531–565.

Berube, Allan 1990. *Coming out under fire: the history of gay men and women in World War Two*. New York: Free Press.

Best, Joel 1999. *Random violence: how we talk about new crimes and new victims.* Berkeley: University of California Press.

Boswell, John 1995. *Same-sex unions in premodern Europe.* New York: Vintage.

Bull, Chris 2002. Frank and outspoken. *The Advocate,* 5 February, 27–31.

Bull, Chris, and John Gallagher 1996. *Perfect enemies: the religious right, the gay movement, and the politics of the 1990s.* New York: Crown.

Burstein, Paul 1985. *Discrimination, jobs, and politics.* Chicago: University of Chicago Press.

Button, James W., Barbara A. Rienzo, and Kenneth D. Wald 1997. *Private lives, public conflicts: battles over gay rights in American communities.* Washington, DC: Congressional Quarterly Press.

Campbell, Colton C., and Roger H. Davidson 2000. Gay and lesbian issues in the congressional arena. In *The politics of gay rights,* edited by Craig A. Rimmerman, Kenneth D. Wald, and Clyde Wilcox. Chicago: University of Chicago Press.

Chauncey, George 1994. *Gay New York: gender, urban culture, and the making of the gay male world, 1890–1940.* New York: Basic Books.

Converse, Philip 1975. Public opinion and voting behavior. In *Handbook of political science,* vol. 4, edited by Fred Greenstein and Nelson Polsby. Reading, MA: Addison-Wesley.

Cox, Harvey 1995. The warring visions of the religious right. *Atlantic Monthly,* November, 59–69.

Crapanzano, Vincent 2000. *Serving the word: literalism in America from the pulpit to the bench.* New York: New Press.

Cress, Daniel M., and David A. Snow 2000. The outcomes of homeless mobilization: the influence of organization, disruption, political mediation, and framing. *American Journal of Sociology* 105:1063–1104.

Danielian, Lucig H., and Benjamin I. Page 1994. The heavenly chorus: interest group voices on TV news. *American Journal of Political Science* 38:1056–1078.

D'Emilio, John 1998. *Sexual politics, sexual communities: the making of a homosexual minority in the United States, 1940–1970.* Chicago: University of Chicago Press.

Diamond, Sara 1998. *Not by politics alone: the enduring influence of the Christian right.* New York: Guilford Press.

DiMaggio, Paul, John Evans, and Bethany Bryson 1996. Have Americans' social attitudes become more polarized? *American Journal of Sociology* 102:690–755.

Duberman, Martin 1993. *Stonewall.* New York: Dutton.

Einwohner, Rachel L. 1997. The efficacy of protest: meaning and social movement outcomes. Ph.D. diss., University of Washington.

Eisinger, Peter K. 1973. The conditions of protest behavior in American cities. *American Political Science Review* 67:11–28.

Epstein, Steven 1996. *Impure science: AIDS, activism, and the politics of knowledge.* Berkeley: University of California Press.

Evans, Sara 1979. *Personal politics: the roots of women's liberation in the civil rights movement and the new left.* New York: Vintage.

Everett, Kevin D. 1992. Professionalization and protest: changes in the social movement sector, 1961–1983. *Social Forces* 70:957–975.

Falk, Steven 1999. All sprawled out; political climate warms to initiatives on quality of life. *San Francisco Chronicle,* 22 January, A23.

Fields, James M., and Howard Schuman 1976. Public beliefs about the beliefs of the public. *Public Opinion Quarterly* 40:427–448.

Fine, Gary Alan 2001. Enacting norms: mushrooming and the culture of expectations and explanations. In *Social norms,* edited by Michael Hechter and Karl-Dieter Opp. New York: Russell Sage Foundation.

Fine, Gary Alan 1995. Public narration and group culture: discerning discourse in social movements. In *Social movements and culture,* edited by Hank Johnston and Bert Klandermans. Minneapolis: University of Minnesota Press.

Gamble, Barbara S. 1997. Putting civil rights to a popular vote. *American Journal of Political Science* 41:241–269.

Gamson, Joshua 1998. *Freaks talk back: tabloid talk shows and sexual nonconformity.* Chicago: University of Chicago Press.

Gamson, Josh 1989. Silence, death, and the invisible enemy: AIDS activism and social movement "newness." *Social Problems* 36:251–367.

Gamson, William A. 1992a. *Talking politics.* New York: Cambridge University Press.

Gamson, William A. 1992b. The social psychology of collective action. In *Frontiers in social movement theory,* edited by Aldon D. Morris and Carol McClurg Mueller. New Haven: Yale University Press.

Gamson, William A. 1990. *The strategy of social protest.* Belmont, CA: Wadsworth.

Gamson, William A., David Croteau, William Hoynes, and Theodore Sasson 1992. Media images and the social construction of reality. *Annual Review of Sociology* 18:373–393.

Gamson, William A., and David S. Meyer 1996. Framing political opportunity. In *Comparative perspectives on social movements: political opportunities, mobilizing structures, and cultural framings,* edited by Doug McAdam, John D. McCarthy, and Mayer N. Zald. Cambridge, UK: Cambridge University Press.

Gamson, William A., and Gadi Wolfsheld 1992. Movements and media as interacting systems. In *Citizens, protest, and democracy,* edited by Russell Dalton. Annals of the American Academy of Political and Social Science 528.

Gardner, Carol Brooks 1995. *Passing by: gender and public harassment.* Berkeley: University of California Press.

Garner, Roberta 1996. *Contemporary movement and ideologies.* New York: McGraw-Hill.

Giddens, Anthony 1984. *The constitution of society.* Berkeley: University of California Press.

Gilbert, Dennis 2001. Hamilton College gay issues poll. Research report, Hamilton College.

Gitlin, Todd 1980. *The whole world is watching: mass media in the making and unmaking of the new left.* Berkeley: University of California Press.

Glynn, Carroll J. 1989. Perceptions of others' opinions as a component of public opinion. *Social Science Research* 18:53–69.

Goodwin, Jeff, James M. Jasper, and Francesca Polletta 2001. Why emotions matter. In *Passionate politics: emotions and social movements,* edited by Jeff Goodwin, James M. Jasper, and Francesca Polletta. Chicago: University of Chicago Press.

Gould, Deborah 2001. Rock the boat, don't rock the boat, baby: ambivalence and the emergence of militant AIDS activism. In *Passionate politics: emotions and social movements,* edited by Jeff Goodwin, James M. Jasper, and Francesca Polletta. Chicago: University of Chicago Press.

Gross, Larry 2001. *Up from invisibility: lesbians, gay men, and the media in America.* New York: Columbia University Press.

Hansen, Dan 1999. City bans discrimination against homosexuals. *Spokane Spokesman-Review,* 26 January, A1.

Harding, Susan Friend 2000. *The book of Jerry Falwell: fundamentalist language and politics.* Princeton, NJ: Princeton University Press.

Hardisty, Jean 1999. *Mobilizing resentment: conservative resurgence from the John Birch Society to the Promise Keepers.* Boston: Beacon Press.

Hartman, Keith 1996. *Congregations in conflict: the battle over homosexuality.* New Brunswick, NJ: Rutgers University Press.

Herbst, Susan 1998. *Reading public opinion: how political actors view the democratic process.* Chicago: University of Chicago Press.

Herman, Didi 1997. *The antigay agenda: orthodox vision and the Christian right.* Chicago: University of Chicago Press.

Hilgartner, Stephen, and Charles L. Bosk 1988. The rise and fall of social problems. *American Journal of Sociology* 94:53–78.

Hoffer, Eric 1951. *The true believer: thoughts on the nature of mass movements.* New York: Harper and Row.

Hollander, Jocelyn A. 2000. Vulnerability and dangerousness: the construction of gender through conversation about violence. *Gender and Society* 15:83–109.

Honig, Douglas, and Laura Brenner 1987. *On freedom's frontier: the first fifty years of the American Civil Liberties Union in Washington.* Seattle: American Civil Liberties Union of Washington, 1987.

Howard, Judith A. 2000. Social psychology of identities. *Annual Review of Sociology* 26:367–393.

Hunter, James Davison 1987. *Evangelicalism: the coming generation.* Chicago: University of Chicago Press.

Jasper, James M. 1997. *The art of moral protest: culture, biography, and creativity in social movements.* Chicago: University of Chicago Press.

Jasper, James M., and Dorothy Nelkin 1992. *The animal rights crusade: the growth of a moral protest.* New York: Free Press.

Jelen, Ted G. 1992. Political Christianity: a contextual analysis. *American Journal of Political Science* 36:692–714.

Jenkins, J. Craig, and Charles Perrow 1977. Insurgency of the powerless: farm worker movements (1946–1972). *American Sociological Review* 42:249–268.

Jenson, Jane 1987. Changing discourse, changing agendas: political rights and reproductive policies in France. In *The women's movements of the United States and Western Europe: consciousness, political opportunity, and public opinion,* edited by Mary Fainsod Katzenstein and Carol McClurg Mueller. Philadelphia: Temple University Press.

Johnston, Hank, and Bert Klandermans, eds. 1995. *Social movements and culture.* Minneapolis: University of Minnesota Press.

Johnston, Hank, Enrique Larana, and Joseph R. Gusfield 1994. Identities, grievances, and new social movements. In *New social movements: from ideology to identity,* edited by Enrique Larana, Hank Johnston, and Joseph R. Gusfield. Philadelphia: Temple University Press.

Katz, Jonathan Ned 2001. *Love stories: sex between men before homosexuality.* Chicago: University of Chicago Press.

Katz, Jonathan Ned 1995. *The invention of heterosexuality.* New York: Dutton.

Kitschelt, Herbert P. 1986. Political opportunity structures and political protest: anti-nuclear movements in four democracies. *British Journal of Political Science* 16:57–85.

Klandermans, Bert 1992. The social construction of protest and multiorganizational fields. In *Frontiers of social movement theory,* edited by Aldon D. Morris and Carol McClurg Mueller. New Haven: Yale University Press.

Klandermans, Bert 1984. Mobilization and participation: social-psychological expansions of resource mobilization theory. *American Sociological Review* 49:583–600.

Klawitter, Marieka, and Victor Flatt 1998. The effects of state and local antidiscrimination policies for sexual orientation. *Journal of Policy Analysis and Management* 17:658–686.

Kuran, Timur 1995. *Private truths, public lies: the social consequences of preference falsification.* Cambridge, MA: Harvard University Press.

Kurzman, Charles 1996. Structural opportunity and perceived opportunity in social-movement theory: the Iranian revolution of 1979. *American Sociological Review* 61:153–170.

Lang, Kurt, and Gladys Engel Lang 1993. Off the bandwagon: some reflections on the influence of perceived public opinion. Paper presented at the Annual Meeting of the American Association for Public Opinion Research, St. Charles, IL.

Laumann, Edward O., John H. Gagnon, Robert T. Michael, and Stuart Michaels 1994. *The social organization of sexuality: sexual practices in the United States.* Chicago: University of Chicago Press.

Le Bon, Gustave 1895. *The crowd: a study of the popular-mind.* New York: Viking Press.

Lee, Matthew T., and M. David Ermann 1999. Pinto "madness" as a flawed landmark narrative: an organizational and network analysis. *Social Problems* 46: 30–47.

Lehring, Gary 1997. Essentialism and the political articulation of identity. In *Playing with fire: queer politics, queer theories,* edited by Shane Phelan. New York: Routledge.

Leung, Rebecca 1998. "Attacking Hate" (Online), 6 July 1998, retrieved on 22 May 1999, Available: http://abcnews.go.com/sections/us/DailyNews/hatecrimes law980706.html.

Linneman, Thomas J. 1999. Representing social movements: advocacy and activism in northwest bookstores. *Sociological Perspectives* 42:459–480.

Lipset, Seymour Martin 1996. *American exceptionalism: a double-edged sword.* New York: Norton.

Lofland, John, and Lyn H. Lofland 1995. *Analyzing social settings: a guide to qualitative observation and analysis.* Belmont, CA: Wadsworth.

Loftus, Jeni 2001. America's liberalization in attitudes toward homosexuality, 1973 to 1998. *American Sociological Review* 66:762–782.

Lowney, Kathleen S., and Joel Best 1995. Stalking strangers and lovers. In *Images of issues,* edited by Joel Best. New York: Aldine de Gruyter.

Luker, Kristin 1984. *Abortion and the politics of motherhood.* Berkeley: University of California Press.

McAdam, Doug 1988. *Freedom summer.* New York: Oxford University Press.

McAdam, Doug 1982. *Political process and the development of black insurgency: 1930–1970.* Chicago: University of Chicago Press.

McAdam, Doug, and David A. Snow 1997. *Social movements: readings on their emergence, mobilization, and dynamics.* Los Angeles: Roxbury.

McCarthy, John D., and Mayer N. Zald 1977. Resource mobilization and social movements: a partial theory. *American Journal of Sociology* 82:1212–1241.

McDannell, Colleen 1995. *Material Christianity: religion and popular culture in America.* New Haven, CT: Yale University Press.

McVeigh, Rory, and David Sikkink 2001. God, politics, and protest: religious beliefs and the legitimation of contentious tactics. *Social Forces* 79:1425–1458.

Mapes, Lynda V., Paul Turner, and Grayden Jones 1997. The great divide. *Spokane Spokesman-Review,* 27 July, sec. H.

Martin, William 1996. *With God on our side: the rise of the religious right in America.* New York: Broadway Books.

Mead, George Herbert 1934. *Mind, self, and society from the standpoint of a social behaviorist.* Chicago: University of Chicago Press.

Melucci, Alberto 1985. The symbolic challenge of contemporary movements. *Social Research* 52:789–816.

Messner, Michael A. 1997. *Politics of masculinities: men in movements*. Thousand Oaks, CA: Sage.

Meyer, David S., and Suzanne Staggenborg 1996. Movements, countermovements, and the structure of political opportunity. *American Journal of Sociology* 101: 1628–1660.

Meyerson, Debra E. 2001. *Tempered radicals: how people use difference to inspire change at work*. Boston: Harvard Business School Press.

Miles, Matthew B., and A. Michael Huberman 1994. *Qualitative data analysis: an expanded sourcebook*. Thousand Oaks, CA: Sage.

Miller, Byron A. 2000. *Geography and social movements: comparing antinuclear activism in the Boston area*. Minneapolis: University of Minnesota Press.

Mottl, Tahi L. 1980. The analysis of countermovements. *Social Problems* 27:620–635.

Mutz, Diana C. 1998. *Impersonal influence: how perceptions of mass collectives affect political attitudes*. New York: Cambridge University Press.

Mutz, Diana C. 1994. Contextualizing personal experience: the role of mass media. *Journal of Politics* 56:689–714.

Nichols, Bill 1999. '99 political climate threatens proposals. *USA Today*, 20 January, 4A.

Nichols, Lawrence T. 1997. Social problems as landmark narratives: Bank of Boston, mass media and "money laundering." *Social Problems* 44:324–341.

Noelle-Neumann, Elisabeth 1993. *The spiral of silence: public opinion, our social skin*. Chicago: University of Chicago Press.

Oegema, Dirk, and Bert Klandermans 1994. Why social movement sympathizers don't participate: erosion and nonconversion of support. *American Sociological Review* 59:703–722.

Oliver, Pamela E., and Daniel J. Myers 1999. How events enter the public sphere: conflict, location, and sponsorship in local newspaper coverage of public events. *American Journal of Sociology* 105:38–87.

Olson, Mancur 1965. *The logic of collective action: public goods and the theory of groups*. Cambridge, MA: Harvard University Press.

Page, Benjamin I., and Robert Y. Shapiro 1992. *The rational public: fifty years of trends in Americans' policy preferences*. Chicago: University of Chicago Press.

Paulson, Don, with Roger Simpson 1996. *An evening at the Garden of Allah: A gay cabaret in Seattle*. New York: Columbia University Press.

Perrin, Andrew 2002. National threat and political culture: authoritarianism, anti-authoritarianism, and the September 11 attacks. Paper Presented at the Annual Meeting of the American Sociological Association, Chicago.

Perrin, Robin, and Armand Mauss 1993. Strictly speaking . . . : Kelly's quandary and the Vinyard Christian Fellowship. *Journal for the Scientific Study of Religion* 32:125–36.

Peshkin, Alan 1986. *God's choice: the total world of a fundamentalist Christian school*. Chicago: University of Chicago Press.

Phelan, Shane, ed. 1997. *Playing with fire: queer politics, queer theories.* New York: Routledge.

Pichardo-Almanzar, Nelson A., Heather Sullivan-Catlin, and Glenn Deane 1998. Is the political personal? Everyday behaviors as forms of environmental movement participation. *Mobilization* 3:185–205.

Piven, Frances Fox, and Richard A. Cloward 1977. *Poor people's movements: why they succeed, how they fail.* New York: Vintage.

Plummer, Ken 1995. *Telling sexual stories: power, change, and social worlds.* New York: Routledge.

Priest, Susanna Hornig 2001. *A grain of truth: the media, the public, and biotechnology.* Lanham, MD: Rowman and Littlefield.

Putnam, Robert D. 2000. *Bowling alone: the collapse and revival of American community.* New York: Simon and Schuster.

Raeburn, Nicole 1999. The rise of lesbian, gay, and bisexual rights in the workplace. Ph.D. diss., Ohio State University.

Renfro, Paula C. 1979. Bias in selection of letters to the editor. *Journalism Quarterly* 56:822–826.

Rozell, Mark J., and Clyde Wilcox 1995. *God at the grassroots: the Christian right in the 1994 elections.* Lanham, MD: Rowman and Littlefield.

Salzman, Jason 1998. *Making the news: a guide for nonprofits and activists.* Boulder, CO: Westview Press.

Schmitt, Frederika E., and Patricia Yancey Martin 1999. Unobtrusive mobilization by an institutionalized rape crisis center: "all we do comes from victims." *Gender and Society* 13:364–384.

Schudson, Michael 2001. The emergence of the objectivity norm in American journalism. In *Social norms,* edited by Michael Hechter and Karl-Dieter Opp. New York: Russell Sage Foundation.

Schuman, Howard 1972. Two sources of antiwar sentiment in America. *American Journal of Sociology* 78:513–536.

Scott, Alan 1990. *Ideology and the new social movements.* London: Unwin Hyman.

Seelye, Katharine Q. 1998. Packwood, sensing change of climate, weighs a race. *New York Times,* 9 April, A21.

Seidman, Steven 2002. *Beyond the closet: the transformation of gay and lesbian life.* New York: Routledge.

Sharp, Elaine B. 1999. Introduction. In *Culture wars and local politics,* edited by Elaine B. Sharp. Lawrence: University Press of Kansas.

Sigelman, Lee, and Barbara J. Walkosz 1992. Letters to the editor as a public opinion thermometer: the Martin Luther King holiday vote in Arizona. *Social Science Quarterly* 73:938–946.

Singer, Bennett L., and David Deschamps 1994. *Gay and lesbian stats: a pocket guide of facts and figures.* New York: New Press.

Smith, Christian 2000. *Christian America? What evangelicals really want.* Berkeley: University of California Press.

Smith, Christian 1998. *American evangelism: embattled and thriving.* Chicago: University of Chicago Press.

Smith, Jackie, John D. McCarthy, Clark McPhail, and Boguslaw Augustyn 2001. From protest to agenda building: description bias in media coverage of protest events in Washington, D.C. *Social Forces* 79:1397–1423.

Snow, David A., E. Bruke Rochford, Jr., Steven K. Worden, and Robert D. Benford 1986. Frame alignment processes, micromobilization, and movement participation. *American Sociology Review* 51:464–481.

Stein, Arlene 2001. *The stranger next door: the story of a small community's battle over sex, faith, and civil rights.* Boston: Beacon Press.

Stevens, Mitchell L. 2001. *Kingdom of children: culture and controversy in the homeschooling movement.* Princeton, NJ: Princeton University Press.

Tarrow, Sidney G. 1994. *Power in movement: social movements, collective action and politics.* New York: Cambridge University Press.

Taylor, D. Garth 1982. Pluralistic ignorance and the spiral of silence: a formal analysis. *Public Opinion Quarterly* 46:311–335.

Taylor, Verta, and Nicole C. Raeburn 1995. Identity politics as high-risk activism: career consequences for lesbian, gay, and bisexual sociologists. *Social Problems* 42:252–273.

Taylor, Verta, and Nancy E. Whittier 1992. Collective identity in social movement communities: lesbian feminist mobilization. In *Frontiers in social movement theory,* edited by Aldon D. Morris and Carol McClurg Mueller. New Haven: Yale University Press.

Vaid, Urvashi 1995. *Virtual equality: the mainstreaming of gay and lesbian liberation.* New York: Anchor Books.

Walters, Suzanna D. 2001. *All the rage: the story of gay visibility in America.* Chicago: University of Chicago Press.

Watson, Justin 1999. *The Christian Coalition: dreams of restoration, demands for recognition.* New York: St. Martin's Griffin.

Wiltfang, Greg, and Doug McAdam 1991. Distinguishing cost and risk in sanctuary activism. *Social Forces* 69:987–1010.

Wolfe, Alan 1998. *One nation, after all: what middle-class Americans really think about God, country, family, racism, welfare, immigration, homosexuality, work, the right, the left, and each other.* New York: Viking.

Wolfson, Mark 1995. Organizational mediation of social movement participation: tobacco control in Minnesota. Paper Presented at the Annual Meeting of the American Sociological Association, Washington, D.C.

Woliver, Laura 1996. Rhetoric and symbols in American abortion politics. In *Abortion politics: public policy in cross-cultural perspective,* edited by Marianne Githens and Dorothy McBride Stetson. New York: Routledge.

Woodberry, Robert D., and Christian S. Smith 1998. Fundamentalism et al.: conservative protestants in America. *Annual Review of Sociology* 24:25–56.

Yang, Alan S. 1997. Attitudes towards homosexuality. *Public Opinion Quarterly* 61:477–507.

Index

261

About the Author

Thomas J. Linneman was raised in Kankakee, Illinois, and studied at Rice University and the University of Washington. Currently, he is Assistant Professor of Sociology at the College of William and Mary in Williamsburg, Virginia, where he teaches courses on American society, social change, statistics, and the media.